THE CONSTRUCTION OF ORTHODOXY AND HERESY

THE CONSTRUCTION OF ORTHODOXY AND HERESY

NEO-CONFUCIAN, ISLAMIC, JEWISH, AND EARLY CHRISTIAN PATTERNS

JOHN B. HENDERSON

STATE UNIVERSITY OF NEW YORK PRESS

Published by
State University of New York Press, Albany

For information, address State University of New York Press,
State University Plaza, Albany, N.Y. 12246

Production by M. R. Mulholland
Marketing by Nancy Farrell

Library of Congress Cataloging-in-Publication Data

Henderson, John B., 1948–
    The construction of orthodoxy and heresy : Neo-Confucian, Islamic, Jew-
ish, and early Christian patterns / John B. Henderson.
        p.   cm.
    Includes bibliographical references and index.
    ISBN 0-7914-3759-0 (alk. paper). — ISBN 0-7914-3760-4 (pbk. : alk. paper)
    1. Heresy—Comparative studies. I. Title.
BL85.H39 1998
291.6'5—dc21   97-26847
                                                                         CIP

10 9 8 7 6 5 4 3 2 1

CONTENTS

CONTENTS

ACKNOWLEDGMENTS

Many people have contributed to the writing of this book. First, I would like to thank my colleagues, students, and the secretarial staff in the Department of History at Louisiana State University for their cheerful support and helpful advice on matters related to this book. My good friend and former LSU colleague, Stephen Farmer, also deserves much credit for having widened my world-historical perspective and shared with me over the years his insights on comparative intellectual history. My home institution, LSU, greatly contributed to the composition of this book by presenting me with a new 1994 sabbatical in which I wrote the first draft.

I had the opportunity to give papers related to parts of this book in several venues, including SUNY Binghamton, Stanford University, Louisiana State University, Rutgers University, and the annual meeting of the Association for Asian Studies, for which I would like to thank the following organizers and commentators: John W. Chaffee, Naoki Sakai, P. J. Ivanhoe, Yin Lujun, Meredith Veldman, Ching-I Tu, Thomas H. C. Lee, Kai-wing Chow, On-cho Ng, and Benjamin Elman. José Cabezón's invitation to write an article on Neo-Confucian scholasticism for a volume he is editing on comparative scholasticisms also helped to clarify and stimulate my thinking on matters discussed in this book. And Carol Bargeron, Irene Bloom, Khalid al-Dajani, David Halivni, Jeffrey T. Kenney, Randall Rogers, Jeanette A. Wakin, and John Whittaker offered valuable bibliographical guidance. I would also like to express my gratitude to librarians at the following institutions for their help: Columbia University, New York University, Jewish Theological Seminary, Union Theological Seminary, Yivo Research Institute, Stanford University, and particularly the LSU interlibrary loan department.

Lionel Jensen and Gregory Smits read all or parts of earlier drafts, providing many constructive criticisms and valuable suggestions for improvement, as did three anonymous readers for SUNY Press. Nancy Ellegate, acquisitions editor at SUNY, also deserves much credit for her sympathetic and patient handling of the review process and for her helpful and courteous answers to my inquiries.

Finally, I would like to thank members of my family for their love and support over the years.

INTRODUCTION

For most of the past two thousand years in the history of Western, Middle Eastern, and even Chinese civilizations, the primary form of deviance and expression of dissent was religious heresy. All but unknown in the era before the rise of the great religions, the heretic attained the status of the ultimate "other" in these postclassical civilizations. He was all the more dangerous because the threat he posed came from within the culture, though he might be imaginatively associated with dark forces from beyond the pale. To control this threat required the strenuous and disciplined efforts of the greatest philosophers and theologians in several religious traditions, such as Augustine (354–430), al-Ghazali (1058–1111), Maimonides (1135–1204), and Chu Hsi (1130–1200), all of whom were celebrated for their identification, description, and refutation of heresy, that is, for their *heresiography*. Although this term is sometimes used to refer to a literary genre, it may be more generally characterized as "the science of the errors of others."[1] By this definition, much of what today passes as philosophy and theology in several religious traditions is hidden heresiography. In the opinion of al-Ghazali, perhaps the greatest of all Muslim theologians, "the aim of the theologians was to defend dogma against heretical aberrations and innovations."[2]

Most modern students of heresies have used the antiheretical writings of the orthodox primarily as sources for the investigation of the heresies themselves, often lamenting the unreliability of such sources and the distortions they contain.[3] It can hardly be denied that many heresiographical writings fail to treat their subjects in a very accurate or empathetic way, or that they often portray what might have been the very rich spiritual and social life of an heretical sect by the invocation of a few standard polemical formulas. In view of the limitations of our (mostly orthodox) sources, it would be quite an achievement to see many ancient heresies, Christian or otherwise, through a glass darkly, let alone face to face.

The approach followed in this book, however, does not aim primarily to reconstruct lost heresies, either their beliefs and practices or their social and cultural contexts, but rather to present the orthodox perception and interpretation of heresy, *heresiography* (the term mainly used by Islamicists), or *heresiology* (used by scholars in Patristics). I began this study with a search for "antiheretical commonplaces" or "patterns of refutation"[4] in several heresiographical traditions, but then widened my focus when it became apparent that orthodox interpretations of heresy could not be adequately understood without some notion of orthodox constructions of orthodoxy itself. The propaganda of the victorious, it seems, must include an account of both self and other, of orthodox as well as heretical; for the former positions and defines itself by reference to the latter, even arises and develops historically by constructing an inversion of the heretical other. This heretical other was as essential to the creation and preservation of orthodoxy in some traditions as the category of crime is to the institutionalization of punishment. André Suarès has argued that "Heresy is the lifeblood of religion. It is faith that made heretics."[5] But it might be equally true to say that heretics have made faith, or at least the faith.

Although he was referring primarily to Christian heresies, Suarès's statement recognizes, at least implicitly, the generality of the phenomenon of religious heresy, that it is not confined to any one religious tradition. This brings up the possibility of a comparative approach to the study of heresiography, if not of heresy. While the particular heresies that have arisen in various religious traditions seem to be so multifarious in form and content as to defy any attempt to construct a comparative order, the perception and interpretation of heresy does betray common and convergent features in these traditions. One might apply the neo-Darwinian idea of convergent evolution to illustrate the existence of these common points. Just as different biological lineages sometimes evolve similar adaptations to deal with common problems, such as the hexagonal patterns in the cells of honeycombs and in the interlocking plates of some turtles,[6] so heresiographers in traditions as diverse as the early Christian and the Neo-Confucian developed similar antiheretical strategies to deal with common challenges that had only a few optimal solutions. Some of these solutions, these "antiheretical commonplaces," are so universal that they have been applied in modern ideological polemics as well as in modern studies of social deviance and psychological aberrations, in fact on almost any occasion when the representatives of order and orthodoxy must deal with a threatening internal other. It may even be possible to discover a universal grammar for constructing this otherness, one as applicable to the interpretation of ancient heretics as of modern ideological, social, and even psychological deviants.

Despite the recent vogue for mulitculturalism in our land, the comparative method that this approach to heresiography entails seems to be an idea whose time has gone, at least in religious studies. As a prominent scholar in the field has written recently, "religious studies as a whole . . . have for the large part abandoned comparative questions in favor of local interpretations and thick description."[7] Yet he also suggests that "magic might also spring from comparisons between religions or cultures geographically remote."[8] In hopes of evoking such magic, I have included in this study one heresiographical tradition, the Neo-Confucian, having little if any contact with the other three, those of early Christianity, Sunni Islam, and rabbinic Judaism. Further, in order to accentuate the comparisons, I have organized this book topically instead of allotting a chapter to each of the four main heresiographical traditions considered. Chapter One gives a preliminary overview of heresy and heresiography in these four traditions, and Chapter Two discusses the formation of orthodoxy in each tradition, giving an historical context for the more analytical chapters that follow. The final two chapters, "The Construction of Orthodoxy" and "The Construction of Heresy," treat the more comparative or comparable aspects of the topic. They show how similar strategies were evolved for dealing with the problem of heresy, despite the wide variations in the historical processes by which orthodoxy was formed in each tradition. I hope that this approach will contribute to the development of a general grammar of heresiography, and even of interpretations of deviance and dissent in general, that may help to explain how order and orthodoxy in any field, not just the religious, establishes and perpetuates itself.

In view of the universalist ambitions of this project, it might well be wondered why I have generally restricted myself to only four major heresiographical traditions, those of early Christianity, Sunni Islam, rabbinic Judaism, and the Ch'eng-Chu school of Neo-Confucianism. Since "It is rare for a religion to achieve the evenness of belief and practice required by an orthodoxy,"[9] one would expect conceptions of heresy to have arisen in most if not all major religions. So why have I for the most part left out the other great Eastern religions, particularly Hinduism, Buddhism, and Taoism? Inasmuch as writers in at least two of these traditions, Hinduism and Buddhism, present heresiographical strategies similar to those in the three Western traditions and Neo-Confucianism, they might well be included in the scope of this study. But I have not done so for two reasons: (1) limitations of space; and (2) the greater difficulties entailed in establishing a Hindu or Buddhist center or standard of orthodoxy in either institutional or intellectual terms. Moreover, the very idea of doctrinal (or religious) error was suspect in some Hindu and Buddhist circles (or mandalas). What might appear to be such was supposedly only fixation on a lower or preliminary version of truth.[10]

The four major religious traditions that remain have not developed equally extensive ideologies of orthodoxy and heresy; some are more heresiographical than others. The existence and importance of Christian heresies is so well known, if not very widely understood, that many Westerners associate heresy exclusively with Christianity. Even such a revered authority in twentieth-century theology as Karl Rahner has asserted that "heresy is only really found here [in Christianity]."[11] More well-informed observers have fallen back on a quantitative argument, asserting that "The Christian religion has produced more heresies than any other religion."[12] Islam, however, has incubated quite a fair number of heresies as well, canonically as many as seventy-two, though it might still fall short of Christianity in an actual head count. This may seem remarkable for a religion lacking a clergy in the Western sense, a pope, and church councils, and is particularly surprising in view of the widespread tendency to regard Islam as a monolith "imbued with a spirit of conformity."[13] Not only heresy but also heresiography flourished in Islam, to the extent that "heresiography" is a well-established branch of Islamic studies.

Unlike Christianity and Islam, the third great monotheistic religion of the Western (and Middle Eastern) world, Judaism, lacked a continuous heresiographical tradition and established literary genre. Although the early rabbis were generally more latitudinarian and lenient in their treatment of heresy than were their Christian counterparts, conceptions of orthodoxy and heresy in rabbinic (or protorabbinic) Judaism may be traced back to the first century A.D., a time of a great proliferation of Jewish sects. "The challenge of these splinter organizations was faced by the rabbis of the Talmud, who were more deeply concerned with the fate of Judaism from corrosion within than from the danger of attack from without."[14] Rabbis of ancient and medieval times, however, may well have hesitated to engage openly in heresiographical controversies for fear of thereby advertising false beliefs.[15] Even so, modern students of Judaism, perhaps too anxious to present this faith as one of tolerance and accommodation in pleasing contrast to medieval Christian polemics and persecutions, have sometimes "glided over contradictions and conflicts in Jewish history."[16] As Elisheva Carlebach has pointed out recently in her book, *The Pursuit of Heresy*, "Great internal Jewish polemical wars occupy a distinguished place in Jewish history. The premises and goals differ substantially from Jewish polemics directed at other faiths."[17]

Like their Judaic counterparts, some sinologists have also presented Chinese religion in general as a closer approximation to the enlightenment values of toleration and accommodation than were the medieval Western monotheistic religions,[18] adducing explanations for this benign state of affairs ranging from the cosmological to the political. Yet, there are some remarkable parallels, drawn out particularly in Chapter Four of this book, between Western heresiographies and those of the orthodox Ch'eng-Chu school of Neo-Confucianism that flourished in late imperial China.[19] These parallels indicate that heresy and heresiography were not monopolized by the monotheistic, revealed religions of West Asia and Europe, but existed in Chinese religion as well. One of the principal aims of the present study is to illuminate a relatively little-known Chinese heresiographical tradition, that of Ch'eng-Chu Neo-Confucianism, by comparison with its more well-known and thoroughly investigated analogues in the West (and Middle East).

In pursuing this aim, I do not propose to force fit the Chinese case into a Western mold. Instead, I hope to use the "magic" of comparison to clarify both the Chinese and Western cases, as well as to illuminate the more universal historical problem of how order and orthodoxy relate (and create) themselves by reference to heresy. Such a comparative enterprise may not be pleasing to modern adherents of the *Volkgeist* approach to Chinese history, a field in which espousing "heretical" views on the issue of cultural relativism is particularly risky. But as Benjamin Schwartz has written, "one is more often more impressed by the degree to which Chinese ideas and orientations are involved in transcultural, universal human problems rather than by the degree to which they are frozen within the matrix of a changeless 'Chinese mind.'"[20]

1

PRELIMINARY OVERVIEW OF HERESY AND HERESIOGRAPHY

Error, of which heresy might be considered as a special case, is probably at least as old as mankind. The capacity for error may even be stipulated in our genetic instructions. It is, in any case, one of the main ways by which we are distinguished from the lower animals, most of whom, like the Pope speaking ex cathedra, are condemned to "absolute infallibility."[1] With respect to religious phenomena, error perhaps first came to be recognized in the performance of ritual, particularly when a ritual action was not followed by the anticipated results. The importance of avoiding ritual error is attested in the earliest work of Chinese literature, the *Songs Classic*, which exclaims, "Very hard have we striven, that the rites might be without mistake!"[2]

In Western traditions, a form of religious error, perhaps even a sort of protoheretic, appears in the persons of some of the "false prophets" who grace the pages of the Old Testament. But it is rather unlikely that full-blown heresy, or at least heresiography, could have appeared before the establishment of literacy, which seems to have greatly encouraged "the definition of a boundary between systems of belief."[3] But literacy, though arguably necessary for the constitution of heresy and heresiography, was certainly not sufficient, as evidenced by the fact that the "pagan religions" of classical antiquity did not emphasize the importance of right belief.[4] On the other hand, heresy is not such a fragile hothouse plant that it requires the services of a monotheistic doctrine, a central ecclesiastical authority, an inquisition, or even a creed. Neo-Confucianism in China lacked all of the above and yet developed notions of orthodoxy and heresy.

Heresy and heresiography, then, seem to have risen, and in some cases declined, with the universalistic religions of the world. But in no case did conceptions of orthodoxy and heresy spring forth full blown from the brow of the founders of the major heresiographical religions—Christianity, Islam, rabbinic Judaism, and Neo-Confucianism.

Nor, having emerged, did these conceptions always manifest themselves in obvious ways. Hence the need to establish in a preliminary way the significance, and in some cases even the existence, of heresy in the four traditions considered. We will begin with the most well-known and thoroughly documented heresiographical tradition, that associated with early Christianity.

Significance of Heresy and Heresiography

To many moderns, the early Christian battles over heresy appear to be little more than "splitting hairs" or "useless bickerings over microscopic distinctions."[5] But to Christians of late antiquity, orthodoxy and heresy were more like matters of life and death, even eternal life or death. With respect to this world, religious differences, particularly the distinction between orthodoxy and heresy, were the most significant divisions in human society, even (or especially) in the multicultural, multiethnic, and multilinguistic Byzantine empire. In the words of Samuel Lieu, "Racial or cultural differences did not form the same barrier as did heresy" in Byzantium.[6] In fact, the Byzantine government feared heresy even more than armed rebellion. So, apparently, did the Western ecclesiastic Vincent of Lérins (fl. c. 434), who remarked that as a result of the rise of the Arian heresy, "Not only relationships by marriage and by blood, friendships, families, but cities, provinces, nations—even the whole Roman Empire—were shaken and uprooted from their foundations."[7] Since heresy was a matter of such grave import, the "knowledge of the individual heresies and of definitions which condemned them became a part of the equipment of the learned Christian."[8]

But in late antiquity, heresiographical concerns were hardly confined to a learned elite. Gregory of Nyssa's (d. c. 395) famous statement on the ubiquity of theological discussions on Arian propositions in the Byzantine capital is the most well-known illustration of this point: "If in this city [Constantinople] one asks anyone for change, he will discuss with you whether the Son is begotten or unbegotten. If you ask about the quality of bread you will receive the answer, 'the Father is greater, the Son is less.' If you suggest a bath is desirable, you will be told 'there was nothing before the Son was created.'"[9] W. H. C. Frend points out that this indication of the wide popularity of theological and heresiographical discussions is confirmed by other evidence from the capital as well as the provinces, east and west, and that "the more abstruse the doctrine in question the livelier the public interest."[10] But the public was not simply interested in theological doctrines and the outcome of theological disputes; it sometimes contributed actively to the process by which one doctrine was declared to be orthodox and its rivals condemned as heretical. For example, a letter written by Cyril of Alexandria (d. 444) "describes how the populace of Ephesus demonstrated night and day in favour of his vindication of Mary as *Theotokos* (God-bearing)."[11]

It might well be objected that the real or underlying issues involved in early Christian heresiographical controversies were political and social, not theological. It is certainly true that imperial and ecclesiastical politics, personal rivalries, and perhaps even class and ethnic conflict played significant roles in several of the great controversies such as those mentioned above. Yet we would be mistaken to hold that such great debates and mighty conflicts could not have been fought over "merely" religious issues.[12] In fact, the mightier the conflict and the more intransigent the combatants, the more likely it is to have been fostered by religious or ideological issues, as modern sociologists have discovered. Georg Simmel, for example, "claims that objectified struggles, which transcend the personal, are likely to be more radical and merciless than conflicts over immediately personal issues."[13] In other words, mere personal feuds or even power struggles usually cannot evoke such a high degree of intransigence and vituperation as can religious or ideological confrontations where the individual sees himself as the "bearer of a group mission."[14] When the group engages the total personality of its members, as is the case with religious sects as well as modern radical parties but is seldom the case with political factions or social classes, confrontations are apt to be more sharp and violent. Such a totalistic group is particularly sensitive to and vigilant of any danger from within, such as that posed by heresy. "Indeed, as Simmel suggests, the reaction may be stronger under these conditions because the 'enemy' from within, the renegade or heretic, not only puts into question the values and interests of the group, but also threatens its very unity."[15]

Since heresies and their refutation were such a matter of ultimate concern in late Roman and Byzantine society, it is small wonder that a large part of early Christian literature was dominated by antiheretical polemics.[16] This domination, moreover, was not simply a matter of quantity. For Christian theology itself was "to a large extent a reaction against heresies."[17] What is arguably the earliest work of Christian theology, the *Against All Heresies* (c. 180–c. 189) by Irenaeus (c. 125–c. 202), is also the first extant Christian heresiology. It was "the direct result not of any desire to produce a comprehensive theology, but grew out of the necessity to deal with a dangerous and persistent heresy."[18] The heresiographical orientation of early Christian theology is further attested by the conciliar statements that were the definitive expressions of orthodox theology. These statements mostly "assume a negative form; they condemn distortions of the Christian Truth, rather than elaborate its positive content."[19]

The creeds adopted by the great ecumenical councils were also devised principally to combat heresy and hence often conceal "a wealth of controversy."[20] Most of the creeds, like much of orthodox theology in general, "are mainly negative in their value, i.e., they prevent certain heresies."[21] Even the oldest Christian profession of faith, the so-called "Apostle's Creed" formulated around the middle of the second century A.D., appears to have been devised primarily in order to refute a heresy, Gnosticism, though the legend later developed that the Apostles produced the Creed as a group, with "each Apostle supplying a line or two."[22] This attribution might well be interpreted as a triumphant orthodoxy's attempt to mask its heresiographical origins, as well as an effort to increase the aura of sanctity surrounding the Creed. On the other hand, a later Byzantine theologian, Photius (d. 895), implicitly admitted the heresiographical character of Christian creeds in his statement that the only justification for an addition to the existing creed was the rise of a new heresy.[23]

Thus, the orthodox creeds and theological statements of early Christianity may be read as hidden heresiographies. The importance of creeds and theology in Christianity in turn illustrates the overriding concern with right belief in the Christian faith, which implies that wrong belief, heresy, is particularly objectionable. Christianity, the most credal of all the great religions, was also arguably the most heresiographical.

If Christianity is the most heresiographical religion, Islam runs a close second. Despite its undeserved reputation for monolithicity and conformity, Islam is among the most fractious of the world's great religions. According to the great Islamic heresiographer, al-Baghdadi (d. 1037), the Kharijite sect alone split into twenty different sub-groups.[24] Nor were the various Islamic sects reluctant to enter into theological conflict with one another. Thus "polemic is one of the most widely represented genres in the history of Islamic religious literature," to the extent that "Theology in Islam, more perhaps than in other religions, is a contentious science."[25]

Not only was Islamic theology often quite contentious, but much of it was formulated in the first place in the process of refuting or rejecting heresies.[26] According to al-Ghazali's (d. 1111) account of the origin of theology in Islam, "God brought into being the class of theologians, and moved them to support traditional orthodoxy with the weapon of systematic argument, by laying bare the confused doctrines invented by the heretics, at variance with traditional orthodoxy."[27] But theologians were not the only heresiographers in Islam. As the great modern student of Islamic heresiography, Henri Laoust, has remarked, "all Muslim thinkers, whether they belong to the category of canon lawyer, dogmatic theologian, traditionist, or philosopher, are also in their own way and to some degree heresiographers."[28]

By Islamic lights, the heresiographical role was by no means a mean one unworthy of a great philosopher or theologian. For the heresiographer was the heir of the holy warrior of yore, though he might conduct *jihad* "more against heresy inside the world of Islam than against the infidels outside its territories."[29] In Ghazali's words, heresiographers were the "protectors of religion through proof and demonstration, just as warriors were through sword and lance."[30] In medieval Islam, where sectarian identification, as opposed to ethnic, cultural, or even political associations, provided the chief means of understanding human differences, the heresiographers who determined and explained these differences played a vital social role. Their presence in each region and locale was so important that "if such a person comes to be lacking in a region, the inhabitants ought to all clamor for one just as they would if they lacked a doctor or a lawyer."[31]

Some of the heresiographical determinations by which the canonical one true sect was marked off from the seventy-two alleged heresies were, as in early Christianity, credal. It may be true that Islamic creeds do not have quite the same degree of authority as do Christian ones. For unlike their Christian counterparts, creeds in Islam were formulated not by Church synods and councils but by individual writers.[32] But the consensus of the community provided a powerful support for some of the historical Islamic creeds, even though they might have lacked official sanction.

Like the creeds of early Christianity, Muslim creeds are "full of hidden polemics."[33] The creeds of Islam are, however, evidently even more polemical, or perhaps hiddenly polemical, than Christian ones in that they frequently do not even bother to enumerate the chief articles of the faith, such as those concerning Allah, Muhammad, and the Qur'an, except where there is a polemical point to be made or a heresy to be opposed. Indeed, some Islamic creeds were specifically formulated to combat particular heresies.[34] The contents and sequence of the articles of such creeds "show which were the heresies deemed to be the most dangerous in the days when they were composed."[35]

From the foregoing, one might well conclude that Islam is an ultraheresiographical religion centered on the establishment and defense of dogma. However, dogma in Islam, as enshrined in creeds and doctrines, did not occupy such a central place as it did in Christianity. Nor in Islam did there exist any time-honored central ecclesiastical authority for determining and enforcing such dogmatic orthodoxy. In comparison with early Christianity, Islam was more a religion of practice than of belief, of law more than theology, of orthopraxy more than orthodoxy, as illustrated by the fact that only one of the five pillars of Islam focuses on matters of belief. Thus Joseph Schacht remarks that "whereas the early Christians fought one another (in the literal meaning of the word) in the streets of Alexandria and elsewhere over questions of theology, the Muslims did the same in the streets of Baghdad and elsewhere over questions of religious law."[36] But the distinction is not really so absolute as this statement might imply, since Islamic law, the *shari'a*, does not consist only of legal rules but contains some elements that might be classified as theological.[37] It includes "all that is in the Qur'an, including anecdotes about previous prophets, and also the non-legal part of Tradition."[38] Although Muslims make a distinction between orthodox schools of law and those of theology, the two are generally paired with one another.[39] At least one of the mainstream Sunni schools, the Hanbalite, has a dual character as a theological-juridical school. Thus in Islam, as in Christianity, "The dividing lines between doctrine on the one hand, and constitution, practice, ethos and ethics on the other, are very slender."[40]

In view of the sectarian character of ancient Judaism around the time of Jesus and the subsequent triumph of an orthodox "rabbinic" or "normative" Judaism in the early centuries A.D., Judaism might be expected to offer a fertile field for heresiographical enterprises. However, 'heresiography' was not exactly a household word in Jewish schools and synagogues through the centuries. Particularly for the obscure period from the destruction of the Temple in A.D. 70 to the rise of Karaism in the eighth century, the evidence for the existence of dissenting Jewish sects is sparse. Even for the late medieval era, the number and significance of dissident sects hardly matches those of Christianity and Islam of the same eras.

The relative paucity of certified heresies in medieval Judaism may reflect the comparatively small numbers of Jews, as well as the option available to medieval Jews of converting to Christianity or Islam: "as a minority community, they were less likely to develop internal heretical sects since dissatisfaction could be relieved by leaving the community altogether."[41] But the relatively small number of certified heresies and heretics in medieval Judaism might also reflect a wider tolerance for internal disputations by rabbis whose "sectarian consciousness was minimal."[42] As long as the debate was joined "in the name of heaven," the rabbis were loathe to condemn one of their number. The rabbis' limited sectarian consciousness might also indicate a sort of deliberate heresiographical amnesia in which rival sects or points of view were combatted by virtually ignoring their existence. As Alan Segal has pointed out, the rabbis of late antiquity "did little to characterize their enemies, especially when to do so would have had the effect of spreading the error further."[43]

The comparatively muted character and sparse appearance of early rabbinic heresiography might also be explained by a traditional Jewish emphasis on practice as opposed to belief, on orthopraxy over orthodoxy. Indeed, Judaism through the ages was not as concerned with dogma as were most ancient and medieval forms of Christianity. But this is less true of later rabbinic Judaism than of earlier forms of Judaism before the second century A.D. While the existence of 'orthodoxy' in first-century Judaism is debatable, in fact has been debated, it is less so for subsequent eras.[44] By the tenth century, the rise of Karaism, a theologically and philosophically sophisticated heresy that challenged rabbinic interpretations of Torah, forced rabbinic Judaism "to engage in the project of systematic theology." This is exemplified in the work of Saadiah Gaon (882–942), "the doughty opponent of Karaism and the first Jew methodically and rationally to expound the central beliefs of Judaism."[45] Saadiah's contemporary, the noted Karaite heresiographer, Ya'qub al-Qirqisani (fl. 930–940), in turn accused the Rabbanites of embracing doctrines "which amount to the wholesale abandonment of religion, and entail atheism and heresy."[46]

But even before the tenth century, the Mishnah Tractate Sanhedrin 10:1 (first or second century A.D.) posited an orthodox standard of belief as a requirement for salvation: "And these are those who have no portion in the world to come: (1) He who says, the resurrection of the dead is a teaching which does not derive from the Torah, (2) and the Torah does not come from Heaven; and (3) an Epicurean."[47] This passage, the only one in the Mishnah that links salvation to the acceptance of particular beliefs, was the *locus classicus* for later discussions of heresy in Judaism, and particularly for the formulation of rabbinic dogma by the great Jewish philosopher, Moses Maimonides (1135–1204), his famous Thirteen Principles of Judaism.[48] Maimonides went so far as to define a Jew as one who accepts these dogmatic principles, overriding questions of ethnicity.[49] In thus attempting to dogmatize Judaism, Maimonides did not, however, intend to downplay matters of practice; for he seems to have "truly believed that proper observance is impossible without an underpinning of correct belief." For example, "If a Jew has incorrect beliefs about God then every commandment which he fulfills is actually an act of idolatry."[50] Maimonides thus saw clearly the link between belief and practice in Judaism, something that has unfortunately escaped the notice of some modern students of the subject.

Maimonides' dogmatizing of Judaism was not universally accepted, though its wide influence is remarkable in view of the lack of any centralized authority in medieval Judaism to enforce orthodoxy.[51] Despite the lack of such authority, Maimonides took such a hard line on heresy that it is not difficult to imagine him assuming the role of a grand inquisitor, had the resources of an inquisition been available to him. Witness his condemnation of those who denied the Oral Torah, the touchstone of rabbinic orthodoxy: "He who repudiates the Oral Law is not to be identified with the rebellious elder spoken of in Scripture but is classed with the epicureans (whom any person has a right to put to death)."[52] Maimonides' opponents, for their part, accused him of heresy, leading to mutual bans and excommunications by both sides.[53]

Heresy hunting in Judaism, with its panoply of bans, excommunications, and persecutions, was not limited to this controversy. Even before Maimonides enunciated his principles, Rabbanites excommunicated and excluded those suspected of the Karaite heresy, stigmatizing them to the point of not accepting Karaite converts unless they first converted to Christianity before converting to Rabbanism.[54] Regarding the period after Maimonides, Rabbanites not only banned and excommunicated followers of the seventeenth-century Jewish messiah, Sabbatai Zvi (1626–1676) and the eighteenth-century Hasidim, but also persuaded the authorities to imprison their leaders and burn their books.[55]

The mere existence of religious persecution in medieval and early modern Judaism does not, in itself, prove the presence of developed conceptions of orthodoxy and heresy in that tradition (though where there is inquisitorial smoke, there is usually heretical fire). But when accompanied by dogmatic definitions of orthodoxy, such as the Thirteen Principles of Maimonides, and specific accusations of heresy, such as those charged against dissenting groups from the Karaites to the Hasidim, it does indicate that rabbinic Judaism, like the other two great monotheistic religious traditions of the West and Middle East, did have a significant heresiographical aspect.

The case for Chinese exceptionalism from the heresiographical pattern can be made even more strongly than for rabbinic Judaism.

Non-sinologists sometimes assume that heresy and heresiography are the products of Western monotheism and religious revelation, conditions not met by the religions of the East.[56] And even sinologists point to an uncanny Chinese ability to tolerate or reconcile apparent inconsistencies, to build bridges between various traditions, as opposed to digging ditches around them.[57] Following the well-worn path already trodden by modern students of Islam and Judaism, sinologists have also classified Chinese religion as more orthoprax (or orthopractical?) than orthodox, suggesting that "Chinese who fought against heterodoxy were perhaps more interested in reestablishing good practices than true beliefs."[58] According to Richard Smith, from the standpoint of the government in late imperial China, "heresy was less a matter of ideology per se than of practice."[59]

Such summary characterizations of Chinese religion as more syncretic, more tolerant of inconsistencies, and more orthopractical than were Western religions may be generally true of a wide range of Chinese religious phenomena. But there are a few strains in Chinese religion and philosophy, most notably the Ch'eng-Chu school of Neo-Confucianism, in which constructions of orthodoxy and heresy are surprisingly similar to those in the Western monotheistic religions of revelation, as explained in Chapters Three and Four below. The Ch'eng-Chu school, moreover, was not just another school of Confucian thought. It was the official orthodoxy of late imperial China, sanctioned by the state and written into the imperial civil service examination system from the fourteenth to the early years of the twentieth century, though it suffered from a sort of desertion of the intellectuals in the eighteenth century. This provides a capital opportunity for cross-cultural comparison of important intellectual phenomena, conceptions of orthodoxy and heresy, that have seldom been systematically compared in traditions not in historical contact with one another.

Assuming that "the question of orthodoxy was an endemic issue within Neo-Confucianism," as William T. de Bary has remarked,[60] was it also an important issue? In the opinion of several prominent Neo-Confucian scholars, the defense of orthodoxy and the refutation of heresy were matters of ultimate concern. According to Lu Shih-i (1611–1672), "The principal achievement of Mencius" (372–289 B.C), the second sage of the Confucian tradition, "was refuting Yang [Chu] and Mo [Ti]," the two archheretics of that tradition.[61] The noted Japanese Neo-Confucian, Yamazaki Ansai (1618–1687) held that the "myriad words of the Ch'eng-Chu schoolmen were solely intended to make scholars safeguard the orthodox Way and refute heresies."[62] Lu Lung-ch'i

(1630–1692), evoking a standard trope in Confucian and Neo-Confucian discourse, compared the harm done by alleged heresies and heretics such as Wang Yang-ming (1472–1528) to that caused by raging floods and fierce beasts.[63] Indeed, Mencius himself remarked that the dissemination of the heretical views of Yang and Mo would bring about a situation in which "animals are led to eat people, and people come to eat one another" (*Mencius* 3B. 9).

Although modern scholars have generally taken Mencius's claim that heresy leads ultimately to cannibalism with a grain of salt, they have affirmed the importance of heresy and heterodoxy in the Confucian and Neo-Confucian tradition, particularly for their having stimulated the rise of orthodoxy. According to Benjamin Schwartz, Mencius formulated his own philosophical position, which later developed into Neo-Confucian orthodoxy, by way of rejecting the contending views attributed to Yang Chu and Mo Ti.[64] Some 1400 years later, Neo-Confucianism arose primarily as a response to Buddhism and Taoism as well as alternate forms of Confucianism.[65] As K. C. Liu has remarked, "What seemed to be heterodoxy thus stimulated the struggle to defend orthodoxy,"[66] though he might have added that it also helped to create orthodoxy in the first place.

Ancient Definitions of Heresy

The issue of the significance of heresy and heresiography in the various traditions surveyed naturally raises the question of how heresy and related terms were defined in these traditions. Although the use of a modern vocabulary without any close correspondents in the traditions covered would not necessarily invalidate the comparative enterprise, the basis for comparison might be clarified by briefly relating the terms and categories used in early Christianity, Islam, rabbinic Judaism, and Neo-Confucianism for discussing heresy.

The modern English word 'heresy' is derived from the ancient Greek word *hairesis*, which had a considerably broader range of meanings, including "taking," "choice", "course of action," "election," and "discussion," all of which survived through the later periods of ancient Greek culture. But *hairesis* could also refer to any group or people having a clear doctrinal identity, such as a philosophical or medical school or a religious sect, a usage found in the Book of Acts in the New Testament.[67] In joining such a group, one naturally "took" a "choice," or followed a particular "course of action." The classical usage of the term carried no value judgment, and did not counterpose it to anything like "orthodoxy."[68] One could even refer to one's own school or sect, as well as others, as a *hairesis*. With some Greek philosophical schools, such as the Skeptics, the term even carried significant prestige. "To profess a *hairesis*, i.e., a coherent and articulated doctrine founded on principles grounded in reason, demonstrates that one is intellectually alert, fitted for reflection and philosophical discussion."[69]

Although this earlier, non-pejorative view of *hairesis* survived into later Christian antiquity, as evidenced by its usage in Eusebius (d. c. 340) and Clement of Alexandria (d. c. 215), early Christian authors used it increasingly "to refer to a body of false beliefs or believers."[70] Closer to this later Christian sense of heresy was the Greek word *heterodoxia*, which "meant the act of mistaking one thing for another."[71] For a time, *hairesis* and *heterodoxia* became virtually synonymous in Christian usage, both designating whatever diverges from the truth taught by the Church.[72] This might include pagan philosophical schools as well as Christian sects, at least in the usage of the great heresiologist, Epiphanius (315–402).[73] By medieval times, however, heresy, as opposed to heterodoxy, was generally conceived as having arisen from within the Church.[74]

Although some early Christian usages of the term *hairesis* employed it to refer to the moral faults of a group, Origen (184–254) and later Christian theologians and heresiographers used the word almost exclusively to denote doctrinal errors,[75] more so than was the case for similar terms in the other religious traditions surveyed here. While even Augustine found it difficult if not impossible to define heresy exactly, the medieval church was not so reticent, defining it more narrowly and precisely as "an opinion chosen by human perception, founded on the scriptures, contrary to the teaching of the church, publicly avowed and obstinately defended."[76] Understandably, the later medieval church stipulated that the *sine qua non* of heresy was a persistent or obstinate resistance to ecclesiastical authority, a characterization quite different from those in other traditions that lacked a strong central ecclesiastical organization.[77] Partly for this reason, I have concentrated in this study almost exclusively on pre-medieval Christianity (through the Great Schism of 1054), the heresiography of which is much more like that of Sunni Islam, rabbinic Judaism, and Ch'eng-Chu Neo-Confucianism.[78]

That heresiology as such was virtually unprecedented in the Western world before Christianity, and that the evangel brought to an end the relatively pluralistic intellectual world of classical antiquity may be signified by the Christian transformation of *hairesis*, outlined above. It is true that for Christian heresiographers of late antiquity, heresy still retained a grain of its classical root meaning of "choice." But whereas for the Greeks choice was praiseworthy, and for the Jews at least legitimate, for the Christians it was a stumbling block, as well expressed by Tertullian (c. 155–c. 222):

> The term 'heresies' in Greek has the sense of 'choice' (*ex interpretatione electionis*), the choice which one makes when one either teaches them (heresies) or accepts them for oneself. . . We, however, are not permitted to cherish any object after our own will, nor yet to choose what another has introduced by his own authority. We have the example of the apostles of the Lord who chose not to introduce any doctrine on their own authority but faithfully dispensed to the world the body of doctrines received from Christ.[79]

Clearly, a pro-choice position was not in keeping with the teachings of the church.

The noted scholar Marcel Simon was unable to locate any pagan precedent for the pejorative sense in which the Christians of late antiquity increasingly interpreted *hairesis*,[80] though this new usage did appear in Judaism at about the same time as in early Christianity. This invention of heresy and heresiography and the concomitant decline and fall of Hellenistic pluralism surely marks one of the great transformations in the intellectual history of the Western world, as does the supersession of the "hundred schools" in China at a slightly earlier date. In both civilizations, Chinese and Western, heresiography, conceived as the defense of orthodoxy, became one of the dominant intellectual and literary enterprises throughout most of the subsequent two millennia. This, in turn, gives rise to the question of how orthodoxy itself was defined. The Greek roots of the English word, *ortho* and *doxa*, mean "the right or correct opinion." This may seem auspicious unless one realizes that the classical Greeks counterposed *doxa*, mere opinion based on sense perception, to *episteme*, true knowledge of true reality.[81] Ironically, *hairesis* in pre-Christian antiquity had more favorable connotations than did *orthodoxia*.

Heresy was not the only recognized form of deviance or dissent in ancient and medieval Christianity. Other kinds of deviants included apostates, infidels, and schismatics. Although some ancient and medieval Christian writers frequently used these and other related terms rather inexactly, others, such as Basil of Caesarea (d. 379), devised a precise categorization of dissenting types and even suggested the appropriate forms of condemnation for each.[82] For the Christians of late antiquity, the category most directly related to heretics was schismatics. Augustine distinguished the two by remarking that "Heretics sully the purity of the faith itself by entertaining false notions about God, while schismatics withdraw themselves from fraternal charity by unlawful separation, though they believe the same things we do."[83] Heresy is thus more opposed to orthodoxy, defined as correct doctrine or right belief, than is schism, a phenomenon more closely tied to the centralized ecclesiastical organization of Western Christianity. Augustine, however, suggested that inveterate or long-standing schism might pass over into heresy.[84]

Although infidels might well be regarded as more clearly distinguished from heretics than are schismatics, in some cases ancient Christian writers depicted other religions as Christian heresies, thus connecting the two forms of deviation. The most well-known example of this from late antiquity is perhaps Augustine's treating Manicheanism as a Christian heresy. Indeed, Manicheanism was later contra-apotheosized in Byzantium as a sort of epitome of all Christian heresies, or as a generic term used for heresy in general.[85] Although Christians generally regarded Muslims as infidels, from the time of the great early medieval theologian John of Damascus (675–749) they sometimes called them heretics as well.[86]

There are several Islamic terms of rather different derivations that might reasonably be rendered as 'heresy.' One of the most common of these is bid'a, "meaning innovation, and more specifically any doctrine or practice not attested in the time of the Prophet."[87] According to a Muslim Tradition, Muhammad himself condemned innovation, remarking that "every innovation is an error and every error leads to Hell-fire."[88] To accommodate changing circumstances, however, some later Muslim legalists made a distinction between good or praiseworthy bid'a, which was acceptable, and bad or blameworthy bid'a, which ran contrary to the Qur'an or the Traditions (hadith) passed down from the Prophet.[89]

A kind of bid'a that orthodox Muslim heresiographers considered to be particularly dangerous and reprehensible was ghuluww, "excess" or "exaggeration." The primary type of those charged with such excess, the ghulat or "exaggerators," were the extremist Shi'ites who venerated their imams to the point of deifying them or regarding them as divine incarnations, thus compromising the oneness of God and committing the cardinal sin of shirk (polytheism). So heinous was this and other forms of ghuluww that orthodox heresiographers sometimes excluded the ghulat from the pale of Islam altogether.[90]

Another Islamic term for heretic was zindiq, an Arabic transliteration of a Persian word that was first used to designate Manicheans and other dualists. But the term "later comes to be applied to any extreme or seditious doctrine—to some forms of Sufi belief—or no belief at all."[91] A word more or less synonymous with *zindiq* in its later, more generalized usage is *ilhad*, "originally meaning deviation from the path," but later applied to "the man who rejects all religion, the atheist, materialist, or rationalist."[92] But the Islamic terms that best express the condemnatory force of the Christian notion of heresy are probably *Kaf-ir* and *Kufr*, "unbeliever" and "unbelief."[93] Not only are these words more "terrible and unequivocal" than the others, but they also seem to refer more directly to deviants in matters of doctrine and belief, as opposed to practice. In Muslim theological polemics, *'kafir'* is frequently used to designate one's opponent.[94]

In their classifications of various sects, Islamic heresiographers generally applied less polemical, more neutral terms. They referred to the groups into which the original Islamic community split as *firaq*, "a noun from the Arabic verbal stem *faraqa*, split, divide, differentiate."[95] The Arabic term for heresiography, *'ilm al-firaq,'* employs this more neutral word. To denote "a smaller group splitting off from a larger one," heresiographers used the word *'ta'ifa'* (sect), a term that appears more than a dozen times in the Qur'an.[96] Other related heresiographi-cal terms include *'milla,'* nation or law, and *'nihla,'* religion or religious order. Islamic heresiographers frequently used these words rather imprecisely. For example, they applied *'firaq'* to designate independent sects, schools of thought, and even minor doctrinal positions.

Some scholars, noting that in medieval Western Christendom heresy was determined by a supreme ecclesiastical authority the like of which Islam lacked, have questioned the existence of heresy, in the strict technical sense, in Islam.[97] Their case is buttressed by the observation that "among the very few loan-words of European or Christian origins used in modern literary Arabic are the words *'har-taqa'*—heresy, and *'hurtiqi'* (or *'hartiqi'*)—heretic."[98] Much of the difficulty, however, might be obviated by concentrating on Christian notions of orthodoxy and heresy in late antiquity, when religious conditions much more closely resembled those prevailing in Islam, rather than on those of the medieval church. In any case, tying basic cultural (and cross-cultural) concepts such as orthodoxy and heresy too closely to the circumstances of their manifestations in any one culture makes doing comparative intellectual history very difficult, if not impossible. At its worst, this procedure is a variation of the old cultural imperialist ploy, which first asserts that traditional non-Western cultures lack science, or philosophy, or reason, and then defines those terms in such a narrow, particularistic way that the assertion is "proven."

As already noted, *'hairesis'* took on a pejorative sense in Judaism about the same time as it did in Christianity, as an emerging rabbinic Judaism began to establish a form of orthodoxy following the great political catastrophe of A.D. 70.[99] But the word most commonly used to denote heresy in Judaism was not *'hairesis'* but *'minim,'* "a general term for heretics, applied at various times in the rabbinic period to different groups which presented doctrinal challenges to rabbinic Judaism while remaining from an halakic [or legalistic] point of view within the fold."[100] Although Talmudic references to the *minim* are numerous, it is very difficult in most cases to tell which specific group is meant—Samaritans, Sadducees, Gnostics, Christians (Jewish or otherwise), Philosophers, Epicureans, etc. The meaning of the word itself, which refers to "species" or "kinds" of people, especially those who differ from the majority in opinion or practice, offers little help in determining the specific group to which reference is made in any particular case.[101] But the same is true, of course, of most terms for heresy and heretic in other religious traditions as well.

'Min' was not the only rabbinic term for types of heretics. Another was the word *"apiqoros,'* apparently derived from the Epicureans "whose skeptical naturalism denied divine providence."[102] But *"apiqoros'* was later also applied to those Jewish groups that denigrated rabbinic and Talmudic authority, such as the Sadducees, on the suggestion that anyone who denied divine providence and retribution would feel free to flout divine law. *'Kofer,'* sometimes translated as "freethinker," was also used in rabbinic literature to denote heretics, particularly those who deny an essential *ikkar* or "dogma," like the *kafir* of Islam. While some medieval rabbis used the above terms, *'min,' "apiqoros,'* and *'kofer,'* interchangeably, "Maimonides attempted a precise and separate definition of each."[103] But there was no general agreement on how they were related to one another, or even on their basic meanings. Indeed, several rabbinic authorities devised imaginative or ingenious etymologies for some of these terms. For example, Abraham Bibago (d. c. 1489) derived *'min'* from the name of the Persian prophet, Mani, the alleged founder of Manicheanism.[104]

In ancient China, terms denoting a Chinese version of orthodoxy generally had an historical and linguistic priority over those related to heterodoxy or heresy. The character *'cheng'*, which means upright, correct, or orthodox in classical and modern Chinese, had already become an important term in the earliest period of recorded Chinese history, the Shang (1766–1122 B.C.), as revealed in the Shang oracle bone inscriptions. Words opposed to the meaning of *'cheng,'* including *'hsieh'* (depraved, unbalanced), *'ch'ü'* (bent, crooked), and *'yin'* (licentious, lewd), do not appear until later.[105] The master philologist of the Han era, Hsü Shen (d. c. A.D. 125), gave a definition of *'cheng'* close to the Western sense of orthodox: "to stop, to stand firm, and be content with one principle or high authority, and hence to be restrained by it."[106] According to Chi-yun Chen, the earliest usages of *'cheng'* denoted a governmental sanction backed by the power of the ruler.[107] Although a moral justification was later given for this sanction, even Neo-Confucian orthodoxy in late imperial China was more closely tied to political authority than was the case with orthodoxies in the other traditions surveyed here, with the possible exception of Byzantine Christianity.

While antecedents of the idea of ideological orthodoxy thus appeared in the earliest period of Chinese history, notions of heterodoxy and heresy were not articulated until the age of the classical philosophers. The primary *locus classicus* for a Chinese version of heresy is a highly ambiguous and problematic statement by Confucius in the Analects which was often interpreted by later Confucian commentators to mean: "To study heterodox doctrines; this is harmful indeed!"[108] The key term in this sentence, *'i-tuan,'* translated above as "heterodox doctrines," is more literally rendered as "strange shoots" or "monstrous sprouts." To these "monstrous sprouts" were opposed Mencius's famous four sprouts of goodness (*ssu-tuan*), which were normally inherent in everyone. Alternatively, one might interpret the *tuan* of *i-tuan* as the "beginning point" of a thread or line, instead of as "shoots" or "sprouts." This yields a different metaphor in which the *i-tuan* refer to threads that begin (and end) at odd points, and hence do not mesh with the total fabric.[109]

Whatever metaphor one prefers, botanical or textile, the *i-tuan* were to have a great future in later Chinese history and heresiography. They appear in all the surviving law codes of imperial times as well as in numerous writings by later Confucian scholars and philosophers condemning various heresies and heterodoxies ranging from Buddhism and Taoism to utilitarian Confucianism. Unfortunately (or perhaps fortunately) for these later commentators, the context (or lack of context) in the original passage from the Analects gives no clue as to which people or ideas, if any, Confucius meant. As Derk Bodde has pointed out in his meticulous examination of this passage, "we have no idea when or why Confucius made this utterance."[110]

As noted above, Confucian commentators also used other terms to condemn various heresies, including *'pu-cheng'* (unorthodox, incorrect), *'pu-tuan'* (improper, incorrect), *'hsieh'* (depraved, unbalanced), and *'p'ien'* (biased, partial). But most of these terms were used more loosely and diffusely than *'i-tuan'* to refer to various types of bad ideas and behavior that were not in many cases strictly heretical. Neo-Confucian scholars did, however, use the term 'tsa-hsüeh' (adulterated learning) to refer more particularly to heretical Confucians.

Having surveyed various definitions and renderings of heresy from the far West to the far East, we might ask how the idea of heresy at the furthest remove from the Western heresiographical hearth, that in Neo-Confucianism, might be compared to the most familiar, that of early Christianity. Several scholars have drawn a sharp contrast between the central institutional or ecclesiastical determination of heresy in the medieval West and the more private criteria of Neo-Confucianism.[111] But this contrast is much less stark or significant when one considers Christianity in late antiquity before orthodoxy was so entrenched and concentrated in Rome. Confucian and Neo-Confucian definitions of heresy do, however, differ significantly from those prevalent in Western traditions in that they were generally both intrasystemic and intersystemic in reference.[112] More specifically, they included Buddhism and Taoism, and even the classical philosophical schools of Mohism and Legalism, as well as heretical Confucians who claimed to adhere to the Confucian Way. Confucian heresy (and heresiography) is thus generally broader in scope than that of the other religious traditions surveyed here. It is often not distinguished clearly from what Western heresiographers might classify as heterodoxy or even apostasy.[113]

Of course, Christian heresiologists occasionally did incorporate non-Christian religions, such as Manicheanism and even Islam, into their heresiologies, as noted above. But in Christianity this was rather exceptional. The principal ideological basis for the broader, more inclusive Confucian idea of heresy was that there was one Great Way (Tao) that had been unified and whole in high antiquity, but which had later splintered into various deviant schools as "strange shoots" that branched off from the "Sage's Way of the Mean." Even Buddhism, a religion of non-Chinese origin, fell into the category of deviations from the Way; for this Way was not a particularistic creation of the ancient Chinese sages but prevailed throughout the world.

Nevertheless, Confucians and especially Neo-Confucians did present most other Chinese schools of thought as historical deviations from the Confucian Way, which was supposedly the source of all major strands of Chinese thought. The classical Confucian philosopher Hsün-tzu characterized the ancient school of Logicians or Dialecticians as purveyors of "unorthodox explanations and perverse sayings" that are "detached from the correct Way [cheng-tao]."[114] And the great Neo-Confucian philosopher Chu Hsi "maintained that the source of Chuang-tzu's philosophy was the Confucian school."[115] This Confucian heresiographical characterization of founders of rival schools of thought as deviant Confucians may not be altogether a fabrication. The classical philosopher Mo Ti, for example, may well have been at one time a follower of the Confucian school.[116] Further, the Confucian impression that Buddhism and Taoism were deviant offshoots (or "strange shoots") of the Confucian school may have been strengthened by Taoist and Buddhist controversialists' common custom of citing the Confucian classics to support their arguments.

It should be apparent by now that our usage of the terms 'orthodoxy' and 'heresy' is based not so much on modern definitions of these terms as on the judgments of orthodox heresiographers in the traditions surveyed.[117] This gives rise to the question of just who and what was orthodox in these traditions and how they became so. But before taking up this issue in the next chapter, it is appropriate to consider the development of the heresiographical literature that gave expression to these judgments. This will provide a brief survey of our most important primary sources, as well as an additional confirmation of the importance of heresiography in all of the great traditions surveyed.

Historical Development of Heresiography

Modern scholars' interpretations of heresies in most of the great religious traditions considered here rely heavily on the works of orthodox heresiographers in those traditions. Indeed, concern about the extent of this heresiographical influence on our picture of ancient heresies has driven scholars to redouble their efforts to isolate the heretical gold from the heresiographical dross. But heresiography, as one of the principal means by which orthodoxy defines, establishes, and perpetuates itself, is a worthy object of study in its own right, not just so much static to be blocked out so that the heretical thing-in-itself might sound forth in all its pristine purity.

Although the prehistory of Christian (and for that matter Jewish) heresiology may be traced back to Old Testament warnings against false prophets, Christian antiheretical writings first appear in the New Testament. Jesus, the purported founder of the new faith, was not particularly partial to polemics, and on occasion was even "silent when false witnesses spoke against him."[118] Other early Christian sages whose sayings or writings are preserved in the New Testament were not, however, so reticent. The New Testament Book of Acts, the oldest surviving account of Christianity's early years, condemns "false teachings" that had led to disunity in the community, though it does not use the word 'heresy' (*hairesis*) in the pejorative sense.[119] A protopolemic against protoheretics also appears in the Epistle of Jude. Even the Gospel of John's famous affirmation that the Word was made flesh (John 1:14) might be interpreted as an antiheretical statement directed particularly against the Gnostics.[120] But St. Paul's fulminations against dissenters and schismatics of various stripes, especially "those who create dissensions and difficulties, in opposition to the doctrine which you have been taught" (Romans 16:17), give him the clearest claim to the title of master protoheresiologist in the Christian church. As Edward Peters has observed, "St. Paul's argument for a single Christian truth gave the character of heterodoxy ('erroneous' teaching) to all other competing beliefs."[121] Although he may have striven to be all things to all men, St. Paul would never have called for a hundred flowers to bloom, unlike that wet liberal, Mao Tse-tung.

However immature and tentative were the New Testament beginnings of Christian heresiology, later fathers of the Church attributed to the New Testament writers, particularly St. Paul, a developed polemic against heresies that actually arose at a later date. Tertullian, for example, read into the Pauline epistles strictures against the Marcionites, the Valentinians, and the Ebionites.[122] As was the case with orthodox theology itself, later orthodox writers were often loathe to admit that their mature heresiology was not fully present at the creation.

Following the closing of the New Testament canon, the founder of the heresiological genre in early Christian literature was Justin Martyr, who was martyred in Rome in A.D. 165. His heresiological work, the *Syntagma* or *Compendium Against All Heresies*, was the first book to use the term '*hairesis*' to designate divergent tendencies within Christianity.[123] Although Justin's work, compiled in the middle of the second century, is now lost, it inspired some distinguished successors, most immediately that of Irenaeus of Lyons, "by far the most important of the theologians of the second century."[124] Irenaeus was not only the first systematic theologian in the Christian tradition but also the author of the first Christian heresiological work to have survived, the *Adversus omnes haereses* (Against All Heresies) (c. 185). This treatise, which borrowed from Justin's work, was directed primarily against the two most threatening heresies of his day, those of the Gnostics and the Marcionites.[125] Second in time and importance among surviving early Christian heresiological books is the *Refutation of All Heresies* (c. 230) of Hippolytus of Rome (170–236), which argued that all heresies are derived ultimately from pagan philosophy.[126]

The culminating work from Christian antiquity of the heresiological genre is the *Panarion* (Medicine Chest) of Epiphanius (315–403), "an historical encyclopedia of heresy and its refutation."[127] This book by the renowned "hammer of heretics" was "intended to offer a reliable antidote to those who had been bitten by the poison of heresy."[128] Later works in this heresiological genre, including the *De haeresibus* (428) of Augustine and the *Commonitory* (434) of Vincent of Lérins, copy much if not most of their material from earlier writers such as Epiphanius. The Christian heresiological literature of late antiquity was, in any case, a remarkably collective enterprise, even self-consciously so. For the systematic description and refutation of heresy was a task that required the efforts of successive generations.[129]

Christian heresiological handbooks and catalogs, moreover, were not simply the reflections of "savage minds" for whom heresiological classifications were "good to think." They provided church authorities throughout the Mediterranean world with the means to recognize and refute heretical opinions arising within their jurisdictions. As Judith McClure has remarked, "when it came to classifying heretics and being certain about heretical opinions, handy works of reference were indispensable."[130]

Writings in the heresiological genre, particularly the catalogs of heresies, are not, however, our only or even major sources for conceptions of orthodoxy and heresy in the early Christian centuries. Early Christian writers also composed more theologically informed tracts refuting particular heresies, such as Augustine's anti-Pelagian writings and Athanasius's (d. 373) treatises against the Arians. Christian ecclesiastical histories, especially Eusebius of Caesarea's (260–340) famous work on the history of the church, were also influential in constructing and establishing notions of orthodoxy and heresy in the early church. In fact, such notions may be found in practically every genre of early Christian literature, including "literary works obstensibly devoted to other ends that happen to take up the polemical task in midstream."[131] Heresiological cameos appear in works ranging in genre from scriptural commentaries to the letters and sermons of the Fathers of the Church.

Christian antiheretical writings tended to become more repetitious as late antiquity wore on. However, the general character of Christian heresiology did change from its inception in the apostolic age to its maturity in the golden age of heresy and heresiology, the fourth and fifth centuries. The earliest Christian heresiology was mostly directed at particular persons, such as the heresiarch Simon Magus, or at particular groups of heretics, such as the Gnostics.[132] As more heresies arose in the course of the third and fourth centuries, the concept of heresy was correspondingly broadened, and the historical and encyclopedic impulses began to assert themselves over the purely polemical: *Ketzerpolemik* was increasingly transformed into a kind of *Ketzergeschichte*.[133] The new "historical" focus was not entirely disinterested, however, as the heresiologists used history as a polemical weapon to link recent heresies with arch-heretical ones of the past, thus discrediting them more deeply.

Even as the later antiheretical writings broadened the concept of heresy, they also reflect a narrowing of the concept of orthodoxy, now more theologically or doctrinally oriented. "The area of tolerable diversity in teaching has shrunk."[134] This narrowing of orthodoxy may have been spurred in part by the need to present a united front against pagan attacks that sought to discredit Christianity by pointing to its internal contradictions and inconsistencies.[135] Conversely, the institutionalization of Christianity in the Empire after Constantine may have permitted the Church to concentrate more on internal dissidents since it no longer had to worry so much about external enemies.[136]

Did any of these dissidents, members of the groups branded as "heretical" by the more orthodox heresiologists of the emerging Great Church, develop their own counter-heresiology? Most "heretical" groups, such as the Gnostics, the Marcionites, the Arians, the Nestorians, and the Iconoclasts, did, after all, regard themselves as orthodox, as transmitting the true teaching of Christ and his apostles.[137] This is a difficult question to answer in view of the considerable destruction and neglect of heretical writings through the ages. But despite the discovery of some Gnostic heresiology in the Nag Hammadi materials, there remains a "curious scarcity of anti-orthodox polemics in the heretical literature. Although it seems that second-century heretical authors were far more prolific than their orthodox counterparts, they appear uninterested in refuting the orthodox position."[138] This raises the possibility that orthodoxy might owe its triumph in part to the superiority of its heresiography, which might give a new twist to the adage that history is the propaganda of the victorious: the victory is won in the first place by the most astute and prolific propagandists.

As in early Christianity, the heresiographical genre is a distinct branch of Islamic literature and a special object of study by modern scholars. But it is also more diverse as well as somewhat less polemical than its Christian counterpart (which might owe something to the Prophet Muhammad's having once condemned disputation itself as heretical).[139] The earliest heresiographical writings in Islam were composed not by the Prophet or his companions but by members of a school later generally regarded as heterodox, that of the Mu'tazilites, the rationalist theologians in early Islam who were particularly concerned with refuting anthropomorphic conceptions of God. The Mu'tazilites, in fact, were notorious for their contentiousness. "According to one early heresiography, there were more than a thousand questions on which the two main schools of Baghdad and Basra differed, and members of one school frequently accused members of the other of 'disbelief' (kufr)."[140]

Although the Mu'tazilites initiated the heresiographical venture in Islam, they did not survive to reap the full benefits of their heresiographical labors. Their heresiographical legacy passed to the Ash'arites, the orthodox Sunni sect that arose in reaction to some of the speculative philosophical excesses of the Mu'tazilites, but that relied heavily on their heresiography. In fact, the later Ash'arite domination of this particular genre is one of its main claims to the status of orthodoxy, both among Muslims themselves and among Western students of Islam.

The earliest heresiographical writing in the Ash'arite tradition is contained in the works of its eponymous founder, al-Ash'ari (d. 935), whose Maqalat al-Islamiyim includes a non-polemical account of the various sects known to him.[141] Ash'ari's main concern, it seems, was not to systematize or to refute, but simply to preserve as much of the earlier material as possible, much of it drawn from Mu'tazilite sources.[142] He was alleged to have "called disputation with the heretics 'innovation' [bid'a] and disliked it, because the ancients had regarded it as error and folly."[143] His illustrious Ash'arite successors, the most prominent and influential heresiographers in Islamic history, were al-Baghdadi (d. 1037) and al-Shahrastani (d. 1153). These three Ash'arite heresiographers came to represent the dominant Sunni orthodoxy.

Baghdadi's great heresiographical work is, however, more partisan and polemical than is that of Ash'ari, though it draws heavily on the latter. He is "an Ash'arite propagandist before he is a Sunni heresiographer; he is less interested in providing a history of the sects than in elaborating a normative classification of them in terms of their relationship to his own Ash'arite-Sunnism."[144] Shahrastani's Kitab al-milal wa 'l-nihal (The Book of Religions and Religious Sects) (1127), "the outstanding work in the heresiographical tradition," is not as polemical as Baghdadi's.[145] But while Shahrastani set out to avoid partisan polemic, he is "at times very much an Ash'arite in this work," particularly in his attempt to present the Ash'arite position as "the approved middle way" between two extremes of rationalism and fideism.[146]

As the most important work of Islamic heresiography, and indeed the best-known account of Muslim schools and sects in general, Shahrastani's book has exerted a wide influence in both the Islamic world and the West. Under the Ottomans, a Turkish recension of

Shahrastani's work was "promoted to the rank of an official manual of Islamic antiquities." It enjoyed "a career even more brilliant than that of its Arabic predecessor."[147] In the West, where the serious study of Muslim theology began with the translation and publication of the *Kitab al-milal* in the middle of the nineteenth century, Shahrastani has been celebrated as the first historian of religions.[148]

But neither Shahrastani nor the Ash'arites totally dominated the field of Islamic heresiography. Speaking of the heresiographical genre proper, two of the most notable works came from non-Ash'arite authors, al-Nawbahkti (b. c. 920) who wrote the oldest and most exhaustive survey of the Shi'ite sects, the *Firaq al-shi'a*,[149] and Ibn Hazm (d. 1064), the most celebrated scholar of Muslim Spain who also wrote on "the heterodoxies of the Shi'ites." Regarding the wider field of Islamic polemics, writers associated with the fundamentalist, traditionist, and anti-philosophical Hanbalite school excelled in composing creeds and tracts that are richer sources of antiheretical criticism than are most of the more descriptive and balanced works of the heresiographical genre proper. Outstanding among these are the writings of Ibn Batta (d. 997), Ibn Qudama (d. 1223), and particularly Ibn Taymiyya (d. 1328), who focused their attacks on the rationalist philosophers' characterizations of God, as well as on the Ash'arites to the extent that they were tainted by philosophical teachings at variance with fundamentalist tradition. But adherents of the schools and sects that the Hanbalites attacked themselves condemned the Hanbalites for their alleged anthropomorphism, literalism, and desertion of the family of the Prophet.[150] In sum, Islamic heresiography, broadly conceived, "proved capable of serving many masters, even the so-called 'heterodox.'"[151]

But if heresiography could indeed serve many masters in Islam, it served the Ash'arites, their close allies the Maturidites, and to some extent the more traditionist Hanbalites most faithfully. Not only did Ash'arite authors dominate the heresiographical genre proper, but they and the allied Maturidites are responsible for some of the most influential and popular Islamic creeds or treatises on the articles of belief, particularly that by al-Nasafi (d. 1142) with the commentary by al-Taftazani (1322–1389).[152] Although he is not known primarily as a heresiographer, the great Ash'arite theologian, al-Ghazali by his own account spent his life force in distinguishing between orthodoxy and heresy:

I have poked into every dark recess; I have made an assault on every problem; I have plunged into every abyss; I have scrutinized the creed of every sect; I have tried to lay bare the inmost doctrines of every community. All this have I done that I might distinguish between true and false, between sound tradition and innovation.[153]

As was the case in early Christianity (as well as Neo-Confucianism), the golden age of heresiography in Islam centered in the fourth, fifth, and sixth centuries after the founding of the new religion, lending some support to the view that there exists a natural heresiographical phase or stage in the development of a religion.[154] The work of al-Ghazali, in particular, "testifies to the engagement of the most brilliant minds of th[is] age in polemic and propaganda."[155] In the later premodern Islamic centuries, heresy as well as heresiography seem to have suffered a decline, at least to the extent that new sects arose less frequently. Increasingly, "it is not heresy which has to be met so much as simple unbelief, more or less frank."[156] Ibn Khaldhun (d. 1406), the encyclopedic historian who has been referred to as the "Tunisian Toynbee," claimed that there were no heretics left in his time, that "Heretics and innovators have been destroyed."[157] Although Ibn Khaldhun may have exaggerated on this point, the oppressive Ottoman empire that controlled much of the Middle East through the succeeding centuries helped to put an end to the creative period in the history of Islamic heresies.[158] Deprived of new subject matter, it is hardly surprising that heresiography, too, declined in these later Islamic centuries.

Jewish heresiography, unlike that of early Christianity and Islam, does not form a very well-developed branch of literature. Indeed, the rabbis combatted the first major heresy to confront normative Judaism in the early centuries A.D., that of "two powers in heaven," primarily through exegetical writings.[159] The closest approach in medieval Jewish literature to the heresiographical genre, Ya'qub al-Qirqisani's early tenth-century account of the Jewish sects, may well have been inspired by the works of contemporary Muslim heresiographers rather than by any precedent in the Jewish tradition.[160] However, some Talmudic tracts also have a heresiographical focus, such as the Tractate Kuthim, which deals with the Samaritans, and the Mishnah Helek, which polemicizes against Sadducees, Gnostics, and apocalyptic believers.[161] Among early medieval Jewish antiheretical writers, by far the most famous and important is Saadiah Gaon whose "many-sided literary activity was . . . dominated by his polemic against Karaism," as were his philosophical studies.[162] He was both the first and the last great teacher of Judaism who opposed the Karaite heresy by special writings, and in fact composed his first anti-Karaite tract at the young age of twenty-three.[163]

Moving on to late medieval times, the "Maimonidean controversies" (thirteenth–sixteenth centuries) over Maimonides' rationalist and allegorical interpretations of Torah generated a substantial quantity of heresiographical literature. But the most spectacular and bizarre heresy in the history of Judaism, that of the "apostate Messiah" Sabbatai Zvi that arose in the late seventeenth century, also provoked the emergence of the most professional heresiographers in the rabbinic tradition. Chief among them was Moses Hagiz (1671–1751) whose "exclusive focus on combating heresy as a mainstay of a rabbinic career is a virtual novum in early modern Jewish history."[164] According to Elisheva Carlebach's recent biography of Hagiz, the rabbinical campaigns against later heresies, including Hasidism and Reform Judaism, "borrowed freely from the arsenal of polemical techniques and ideological positions which Hagiz had formulated."[165] Jewish heresiography of early modern times, however, appears in a variety of different genres, including narrative, epistolary, poetic, and records of debates, making it rather difficult to trace. Its tone, moreover, ranges from the politely factual to the vituperative. This brings up the important distinction between non-heretical and heretical disputes in Judaism, between "controversy which is for the sake of heaven" and that "which is not for the sake of heaven."[166] Inasmuch as the rabbis generally allowed more latitude for the former than did their counterparts in other heresiographical traditions, it is important for us not to mistake controversies "for the sake of heaven," or what Mao Tse-tung called "contradictions among the people," for condemnations of heretics.

As is the case with the early Christians, not many non-orthodox heresiographical writings have survived from medieval Judaism. An important exception is the Karaite al-Qirqisani's account of the Jewish sects, which presents a heresiography at least as sophisticated as those of any of his Rabbanite opponents. In modern times, the works of the celebrated scholar Gershom Scholem have presented a very powerful and persuasive rehabilitation of medieval and early modern Jewish heresies, particularly Sabbatianism and apocalypticism, that has virtually transformed modern views of these once despised movements.[167] Much of Scholem's scholarly work may be classified as a sort of counter-heresiography in a modern key.

Heresiography in the orthodox Ch'eng-Chu school of Neo-Confucianism, as in the other religions surveyed here, engaged the energies of some of the greatest figures in the tradition. But these do not include the Sage, Confucius. Although the most specific term in classical Chinese used to designate heresy, '*i-tuan*' ("strange shoots" or "heterodox doctrines"), first appears in the Analects of Confucius, the Master himself seems to have deprecated debates, to say nothing of sectarian polemics. Indeed, the very sentence in which '*i-tuan*' appears can just as well be interpreted as "To attack heterodox doctrines; this is harmful indeed!" (Analects 2.16), though the more common Neo-Confucian interpretations would substitute something like "study" for "attack" in this sentence. The Sung Neo-Confucian commentator, Cheng Ju-hsieh, however, did render the meaning of the sentence in the way just translated, explaining that "since the distinction between our [orthodox] Way and heterodox doctrines is like that between black and white or east and west, so that everyone can see it, what need is there for an attack?"[168]

Nor was Cheng Ju-hsieh alone among Neo-Confucian thinkers in attributing a policy of verbal nonviolence to Confucius. The great Ch'eng I (1033–1107), one of the founders of the Ch'eng-Chu school, made a similar point in interpreting Confucius' advice to "Banish the tunes of Cheng, and keep specious talkers at a distance" (Analects 15.11), suggesting that it was better to avoid heresies than to combat them.[169] Modern interpretations of Confucius, too, depict him as a non-controversialist, not the sort of person who could be trusted with a dogma. According to C. Harbsmeier, "Confucius seems uncertain, even, whether he agrees with himself. He goes so far as to say that he does not know what to do with someone who is not as confused and puzzled as he so often is: 'There is simply nothing I can do with a man who is not constantly saying: "What am I to do? What am I to do?"'"[170] On the other hand, some accounts of disputational encounters between Confucius and Taoist (or protoTaoist) critics do appear in the Analects. But these accounts might well be the projection of later conflicts, unknown or unremarked upon in Confucius' own time, back into the Analects.

Confucians throughout history, even controversialist ones, have often applauded Confucius' deprecation of debate, at least in theory. "So glorious is the Tao, the Confucians would say, that its validity should be self-evident without the need for argument."[171] But the formation of alternative Ways, rival schools of thought in the era after Confucius, made debate necessary. This is particularly evident in the works of China's second sage, Mencius, who "lamented the need to resort to *pien*, 'dispute, argument, debate,'" remarking: "How could I be fond of disputing! It is simply that I have no alternative" (*Mencius* 3B. 9). Mencius did, however, apparently overcome his reticence long enough to engage in spirited polemics, the most famous and influential of which are his exchanges with the rival philosopher Kao-tzu on the question of human nature, and his condemnation of the "depraved doctrines" taught by Yang Chu and Mo Ti (*Mencius* 3B. 9). Not only is much of the material preserved in the book of *Mencius* of a polemical nature, but Mencius himself anticipated several of the major heresiographical arguments and strategies used by later adherents of the Ch'eng-Chu school of Neo-Confucianism.

However, Mencius's polemical achievements were not celebrated, or even widely appreciated, until the rise of the Ch'eng-Chu school of Neo-Confucianism in the Sung era (960–1279). Nor was the *Mencius* itself part of any canon, Confucian or otherwise, but merely one of the philosophers of the "hundred schools." Sung philosophers of the Ch'eng-Chu persuasion, however, rehabilitated Mencius and canonized his work as one of the Four Books. The extent of the role that Mencius's heresiographical achievements and polemical propensities played in this rehabilitation and canonization of his work some 1500 years after his death often goes unappreciated. In summarizing the chief merits of the greatest Confucian thinkers of antiquity, Ch'eng Hao (1032–1085), one of the founding fathers of Neo-Confucianism, remarked that "Confucius was quite clear and pure in disposition. Yen-tzu was quite happy and at ease. And Mencius was quite a vigorous debater."[172] And Chu Hsi wrote in his commentary on *Mencius* that "although Mencius did not attain his goals in his own time, yet because of him the harm done by Yang Chu and Mo Ti was extinguished, and as a result the Way of ruler and subject and father and son did not fall."[173] In the opinion of Han Yü (768–824), the great T'ang-era precursor of the Sung Confucian revival, the achievements of Mencius in quelling heresy in his day were of the same order as those of the legendary Yü the Great who supposedly tamed the great flood waters to make the land of China fit for human habitation.[174] To the later Korean Neo-Confucian scholar, Ki Taesung (1527–1572), Mencius was a sort of heresiographical saint whose name and memory he invoked to expose and refute the errors of the heretics of his own time.[175]

Mencius thus assumed an unrivalled primacy in the heresiographical hagiography devised by Neo-Confucian thinkers. Aside from the T'ang precursor of Neo-Confucianism, Han Yü, Mencius was practically the only antiheretical writer from pre-Sung times admitted into the Neo-Confucian genealogy of heresiography. The Neo-Confucians generally ignored Hsün-tzu's "aggressive denunciation of thinkers who deviated from the [Confucian] Way," principally because they regarded Hsün-tzu himself as unorthodox on the crucial question of the nature of human nature.[176]

But if master heresiographers are few and far between in the Confucian tradition before the Sung, the Sung and later Neo-Confucians created a heresiography unparalleled in the history of Asia east of the Indus. The greatest heresiographer of all was Chu Hsi (1130–1200), the grand synthesizer of Sung Neo-Confucianism and probably the most influential Chinese philosopher after Mencius. Although modern scholars have focused on this or that aspect of Chu's cosmology, ontology, or ethics as the key to his philosophy, for Chu Hsi himself, it seems, establishing the correct boundary between orthodoxy and heresy was of prime importance for reviving the Confucian Way.[177] As Chu himself remarked, "generally speaking, discussions of [schools of] learning ought first to distinguish their [respective] inclinations to either orthodoxy or heresy."[178] Later Ch'eng-Chu thinkers also ranked Chu's first priority and major achievement as heresiographical. As expressed by the early-Ming scholar, Hsüeh Hsüan (1392–1464):

> Master Chu's great achievement is to have caused the Way of Yao, Shun, Yü, Wen, Wu, the Duke of Chou, Confucius, Yen-tzu, Tseng-tzu, Tzu-ssu, Mencius, Chou Tun-i, the Ch'eng brothers, and Chang Tsai to shine gloriously for a myriad ages so that heterodox doctrines [or "strange shoots"] and heretical sayings could not adulterate them. Master Han [=Han Yü] said that the achievements of Mencius are not less than those of Yü [who supposedly tamed the raging flood waters]. I thereby say that Master Chu's merit is not less than that of Mencius.[179]

The later Ming scholar, Ch'en Chien (1497–1567), concurred that "refuting strange [doctrines] and putting a stop to heresies was Master Chu's great achievement."[180]

Chu Hsi not only formulated but also dominated heresiography in the Ch'eng-Chu school of Neo-Confucianism to an extent unmatched by any figure in any of the other traditions surveyed. His writings in this genre, scattered throughout his recorded conversations, literary collections, and scholastic genealogies and anthologies, are most widely known for their anti-Buddhist polemics.[181] But Chu's richest critique of fellow Confucian scholars and schools is probably his *Tsa-hsüeh pien* (Critique of Adulterated Learning), completed in 1166, which he wrote to refute other Sung Confucian scholars' interpretations of various classical texts.[182]

Chu's immediate successors, perhaps in awe of his heresiographical achievements, generally refrained from expounding further on the subject that Chu had treated so comprehensively. But among early Ming scholars of the Ch'eng-Chu school, Hu Chü-jen (1434–1484) and Hsüeh Hsüan rekindled the heresiographical torch, though Hu in particular was much more meticulous in his critique of Ch'an Buddhism than in his criticisms of Chu's philosophical rival, Lu Hsiang-shan.[183] The emergence in the mid-Ming of a major sympathizer of Lu Hsiang-shan's idealism, Wang Yang-ming (1472–1529), and the wide popularization of his teaching totally altered the heresiographical landscape. It presented a significant Neo-Confucian challenge to the primacy achieved by the Ch'eng-Chu school both in the political system and in intellectual life in general. To combat this new threat to orthodoxy, a new wave of heresiographers arose, the most famous and important of whom are Lo Ch'in-shun (1465–1547) and Ch'en Chien. Lo, whom Wing-tsit Chan calls "the most prominent Neo-Confucian of his time," was also the most influential of Wang's critics.[184] Lo, moreover, by no means regarded his heresiography as a sideline occupation. As he remarked in his major philosophical writing, *A Record of Knowledge Painfully Acquired* (K'un-chih chi), "To attack heterodox doctrines and expose heretical views is the traditional role of the Confucian school."[185] Lo's heresiographical achievements were equalled if not exceeded by those of his near contemporary, Ch'en Chien, whose major work, the *Hsüeh-pu t'ung-pien* (Comprehensive Critique of Scholarly Obscurations), is perhaps the most vigorous and thorough defense of Ch'eng-Chu orthodoxy and critique of Lu-Wang heterodoxy ever written by a Neo-Confucian scholar. This work, though completed in 1548, was not printed until 1606.

While neither Lo nor Ch'en managed to reverse the tide of Wang Yang-ming's popularity in the sixteenth century, the political catastrophes that engulfed China in the early seventeenth century contributed to a re-evaluation of Wang's legacy and stimulated a significant revival of the Ch'eng-Chu school in the early Ch'ing era. Several prominent scholars of this era attributed these catastrophes, particularly the fall of the native Ming dynasty and the Manchu conquest of the 1640s, to the influence of Wang and his school, a view rendered plausible by the close connection that was supposed to exist in imperial China between philosophy and the political order. The early Ch'ing scholar Lü Liu-liang (1629–1683) went so far as to attribute the fall of the last three native Chinese dynasties, the Northern Sung, the Southern Sung, and the Ming, to the influence of heretical Confucians who were supposedly under the sway of Ch'an Buddhism—Su Shih, Lu Hsiang-shan, and Wang Yang-ming.[186]

Lü was one of several prominent early-Ch'ing scholars of the Ch'eng-Chu school. Others include Chang Li-hsiang (1611–1674), Lu

Shih-i (1611–1672), and Lu Lung-ch'i, the latter of whom was the most partisan and focused in his antiheretical polemics. In his advocacy of the Ch'eng-Chu philosophy, he "would allow no room for any deviation."[187]

As the newly established Ch'ing dynasty reaffirmed and reinforced official support for the orthodox Ch'eng-Chu teaching in the late seventeenth and early eighteenth centuries, the leading scholarly supporters of Ch'eng-Chu increasingly assumed roles of house intellectuals. Among these, the most famous were probably Hsiung Tz'u-li (1635–1709), Li Kuang-ti (1642–1718), and Chang Po-hsing (1652–1725). Chang's greatest contribution to the defense of Ch'eng-Chu orthodoxy was not as a polemicist but as an anthologist. His most notable work along this line is his editing and printing of the huge collectanea of orthodox learning, the *Cheng-i-t'ang ch'üan shu* (1707–17) "which was done in honor of the Ch'eng-Chu school, and as a deliberate effort to ban Lu Chiu-yuan [=Lu Hsiang-shan] and Wang Shou-jen [=Wang Yang-ming]."[188]

The rise of new scholarly trends and fashions in the mid-Ch'ing era considerably thinned the ranks of Ch'eng-Chu heresiographers in the eighteenth and early nineteenth centuries. But the mid-nineteenth century saw a heresiographical last hurrah, marked particularly by the publication of Fang Tung-shu's (1772–1851) *Han-hsüeh shang-tui* (Exchanges of Views on Han Learning) (1831) and T'ang Chien's (1778–1861) partisan survey of Ch'ing learning, the *Ch'ing hsüeh-an hsiao-chih* (Brief Account of Cases in Ch'ing Learning). T'ang's work, one of a distinguished line of anthologies of scholarship and learning written in late-imperial China, was quite a notable departure from its two most famous predecessors, Huang Tsung-hsi's (1610–1695) *Sung-Yüan hsüeh-an* (Cases in Sung and Yüan Learning) and *Ming-ju hsüeh-an* (Cases in Ming Confucian Learning), in that it was openly and frankly partisan. T'ang himself complained that these two earlier works by Huang "mix up the pure with the impure and confuse the correct and the incorrect. . . . Thus the standards of Confucius and Mencius are lost."[189] Fang was even more partisan, condemning recent scholars' imputations that Ch'eng-Chu was heterodox as wreaking havoc as great as that caused by raging waters or wild beasts.[190]

As in the other great religious traditions surveyed in this book, the "heterodox" opponents of the orthodox Ch'eng-Chu school made a relatively poor heresiographical showing. The pretention and narrowness of the emerging Ch'eng-Chu orthodoxy or *"Tao-hsüeh"* (Learning of the Way) was the object of much derision and even condemnation in the late twelfth and early thirteenth centuries. Yet the opponents of

Tao-hsüeh "did not even devise a coherent theory to explain how their enemies had come to depart from the true way, other than through sheer perversity."[191] Even Lu Hsiang-shan, Chu Hsi's most celebrated philosophical rival, did not develop a heresiography to match Chu's, though he did accuse Chu Hsi of having unjustifiably applied the original Confucian term for heresy, '*i-tuan*' (strange shoots), to cover Buddhism and other heterodox teachings that did not even exist in Confucius' own day.[192] The other major Neo-Confucian *bête noire* of the orthodox Ch'eng-Chu school, Wang Yang-ming, was even less heresiographically inclined than was Lu Hsiang-shan. Rather than condemn Chu Hsi as a heretic, Wang argued in his *Chu Hsi's Final Conclusions of His Latter Years* (Chu-tzu wan-nien ting-lun) that Chu had reached a philosophical position quite close to that of Wang and Lu by the end of his life.

Thus, Ch'eng-Chu Confucians, like their orthodox counterparts in Western religious traditions, had the advantage of a more extensive and well-developed heresiography than did their nonorthodox rivals. In fact, the development of such a heresiography may well have helped to establish their orthodoxy in the first place. Yet, the actual contents and contexts of orthodoxies (as well as heresies) in various traditions vary widely, even though the signs by which orthodoxy and heresy are represented in these traditions share a basic grammar that operates cross-culturally. Before discussing the elements of this grammar in Chapters Three and Four, we should recognize the more particularistic variations in the lexicons of orthodoxy in the four traditions surveyed. In view of the significant differences in the historical processes by which orthodoxies were made, the subject of the next chapter, the convergence of their heresiographies is all the more remarkable.

2

THE MAKING OF ORTHODOXIES

If orthodoxies in early Christianity, premodern Islam, rabbinic Judaism, and Neo-Confucianism share any one common feature, it is that they were not fixed from the founding of their respective traditions; they were made, not born. But even this statement does not quite do justice to the dynamic character of orthodoxy, since orthodoxy, unlike the canon in some traditions, is never entirely made, fixed, or closed. Although modern scholars have generally reserved the term 'neo-orthodoxy' to describe re-inventions of orthodoxy in modern times, orthodoxies that were quite as "neo" appear frequently in ancient and medieval traditions as well. Since part of the genius of neo-orthodoxy, if not its main polemical strategy, is to conceal its newness, it is hardly surprising that the developmental aspect often passes unnoticed.

Ancient orthodoxies, moreover, did not develop in a vacuum or simply unfold by some inner logic. In most traditions, they arose in reaction to what was later called heresy or heterodoxy, though even this characterization does not do justice to the subtlety of the interactions between orthodoxy and its silent collaborator and public antagonist, heresy. For in responding to heresy, or perhaps protoheresy, orthodoxy framed its creed, canon, and theology around issues raised by the heretics, as noted above in Chapter One. Heretical terms and concerns, if not heretical ideas, lay at the heart of orthodoxy. As Rowan Williams has pointed out with respect to early Christianity, "modern scholarship has become increasingly aware of how the very vocabulary of orthodox theology is shaped by borrowing and reworking the terms and images of dissident groups."[1] For the orthodox, heresy was truly an enemy within to a greater extent than they could admit.

But even to speak of 'orthodoxy' versus 'heresy' is to impose a sharp dichotomy on a rather fluid situation in which emerging orthodoxies could hardly be distinguished from emerging heresies. Even after their emergence, orthodoxies in most of the traditions surveyed here were at one time or another considered to be heretical, both by the prevailing political powers and the majority of the faithful. Since orthodoxy was neither established from the beginning nor consistently triumphant once it had emerged, the determination of orthodoxy would seem to be more dependent on historical vicissitudes than on any comprehensive religious revelation or inescapable theological logic. This does not necessarily mean, however, that orthodoxy was determined by purely political means or that the intellectual position of orthodoxy was irrelevant to its triumph. This may be illustrated by examining the making of orthodoxy in four major religious traditions, beginning with early Christianity.

Early Christianity

If there is any issue that commands wide attention in modern studies of early Christianity, it is that of when and how what is later called orthodoxy as taught by "The Great Church" emerges and triumphs. While hardly any serious scholar supports the view that orthodoxy was fully formed from the beginning, some do argue that what was later determined to be orthodox doctrine is at least implicit in the New Testament. Harold Brown, for example, speaks of "an implicit trinitarianism—suggested, but not defined, by the language of Scripture and the liturgy."[2] A slightly more sophisticated version of this conception is the idea that later orthodox dogma "can be justified as an organic growth from New Testament shoots."[3] But the final fallback position for the argument that orthodoxy was implicit from the beginning is that this earliest orthodoxy, or proto-orthodoxy, is not to be found in the realms of ideas or doctrines at all, but in some form of practice or devotion. Thus Jaroslav Pelikan writes that "the authentic tradition of orthodoxy was not a matter to be decided by an intellectually formulated 'rule of faith' set forth by scholars and theologians, but by the 'rule of prayer' of 'the thousands of silent believers, who worshipped in spirit and in truth.'"[4] Empirical evidence and philosophical argumentation evidently being insufficient to support the case for the primacy of orthodoxy, Pelikan thus retreats to the last refuge of intellectual (and not so intellectual) rogues, the invocation of a great silent majority.

Unfortunately for its invokers, the majority in earliest Christianity was not always so silent, and it has left traces sufficient to suggest that the protoheretical, not the proto-orthodox, were in the majority at some points in the early Church. The leading proponent of this viewpoint is Walter Bauer, whose *Orthodoxy and Heresy in Earliest Christianity* (1934) is "possibly the most significant book on early Christianity written in modern times."[5] Bauer argues on the basis of a meticulous study of the historical geography of early Christianity that "in many regions heresy is the original manifestation of Christianity," and that protoheretics outnumbered the proto-orthodox in the Christian world as a whole.[6] In the second century, Bauer claims, what was later called orthodoxy was dominant only in the churches in Rome, Corinth, Antioch, and western Asia Minor.[7] Bauer thus stood on its head the traditional conception that orthodoxy was both historically prior and numerically superior to heresy. He also virtually deconstructed the ideas of 'orthodoxy' and 'heresy,' using the terms to refer to social groups without implying any value judgment as to which was right and which was wrong, which authentic and which inauthentic.[8]

While Bauer's historical geography of early Christianity stood traditional Christian historiography on its head, more textually oriented scholars were discovering heretical tendencies in the canonical source of orthodoxy, the New Testament. The most widely heralded and debated such tendency is the Gnostic element in Paul, which was so evident and troublesome to the fathers of the Church that they "were only able to retain Paul within the great Church by misinterpreting him."[9] But Paul is not the only New Testament writer with protoheretical leanings. The Docetic tendencies in the Gospel of John, which at times all but efface the historical Jesus behind "the bold presentation of the divine son of God," are even more disturbing in that they directly concern the Christological issue, the touchstone of later theological orthodoxy.[10]

To scan New Testament writers, as well as the works of the early fathers of the Church, for expressions of what later came to be recognized as orthodoxy and heresy, however, somewhat misses the point. This is because orthodoxy and heresy as both we and later Christian writers understand these terms are relatively late developments. What preceded orthodoxy and even heresy was, for lack of a better term, "heterodoxy, i.e., an open and eclectic situation allowing for wide-ranging theological speculation, and tolerating diversity."[11] Indeed, even "contemporary Christianity, diverse and complex as we find it, actually may show more unanimity than the Christian churches of the first and second centuries."[12]

Just how orthodoxy and heresy eventually emerged from this stage of tolerable diversity is a question on which there is no consensus among scholars of Patristics. But it appears that the first moves in the direction of exclusion and rigidification were made by those later condemned as heretics. For example, Gnosticism, "the first and most dangerous heresy among the early Christians," was "incapable of—and perhaps uninterested in—representing a mainstream position."[13]

A second major early Christian heresy, that of the Marcionites, rejected the Old Testament with its tales of the escapades of an immoral Demiurge, as well as most of the New. Marcion, moreover, was probably the first great systematizer in Christian history, in a tradition in which systematization generally entailed exclusion. Finally, many of the early Jewish Christians, stigmatized as "Ebionites" by later heresiographers, insisted that even Gentile converts adhere to the rather restrictive Jewish law.[14] The party (or parties) later recognized as orthodox rejected these exclusions and particularisms, though they were certainly not averse to polemicizing against the exclusionists. Following this line of interpretation, not only was proto-orthodoxy more catholic than its rivals, but the drive toward catholicity was one of the main forces that brought about the initial formation of orthodoxy. Ironically, the defense of catholicism necessitated the exclusion of the uncatholic, which made Catholicism itself less catholic. By the fifth century, orthodoxy in both East and West had grown to be as rigid and almost as exclusionary as were some of the early Christian heresies. Thus heresy in early Christianity may have been as much a matter of timing as of theological concept and precept.[15]

Not only heresy, but also heresiology, seems to have preceded orthodoxy in the history of early Christianity. The earliest Christian heresiologists, particularly Justin Martyr (d. 165), wrote before orthodoxy as a uniform belief system had been established in the form of creeds, canons, theology, or the strictures of a universally recognized ecclesiastical authority. The early heresiologists are, moreover, much clearer on what they rejected than on what they affirmed.[16] Thus Irenaeus (c. 130–c. 200), the author of the earliest Christian heresiology to have survived, offered not a set doctrine, but rather "various conceptual formulations, depending on what heresies [he] is combating in a given part of *Against Heresies*."[17] But once having created a dichotomy between orthodoxy and heresy, and having identified the latter with specific ideas and principles, the early heresiologists were obliged to give a more stable and positive content to orthodoxy. Thus it is perhaps no accident that Irenaeus was the first Christian theologian, as well as the most influential early Christian heresiologist.[18]

Although a "tendency" to orthodoxy, with its collections of "apostolic" books and creeds and its institutionalized hierarchal continuity, may be traced back to about the end of the second century,[19] the question of when and how orthodoxy attained a position of hegemony remains unsettled. Unlike the Roman emperor Constantine, the humble historian is not given any sign indicating that whereby orthodoxy conquered. But most would probably agree that the making of orthodoxy proceeded over a rather extended period, from around the middle of the second century to the middle of the fifth, and that orthodoxy through this process became more and more a matter of right belief. The Council of Chalcedon (451) is often taken as the point of culmination and closure in the establishment of orthodoxy on the crucial Christological and Trinitarian questions, though it certainly did not settle all outstanding theological disputes even in its own time.

But what happened during this three-hundred-year period between the earliest Christian theologians and Chalcedon to bring about the establishment of an orthodox authority and theology that prevailed throughout most of the Christian world? Was it simply that orthodoxy presented the truest and most compelling interpretation of the evangel, or that its proponents were more intellectually gifted and brilliant than were their rivals? While determining theological truth is beyond the scope of this study, we may point out that even Augustine, the greatest Christian philosopher and theologian of antiquity, affirmed the brilliance and even genius of some of his heretical opponents. Moreover, some of the major ideas condemned as heretical in antiquity, such as those of the Gnostics, seem to have quite a perennial appeal. They have reemerged repeatedly in Christian history, showing a surprising resilience in the face of repeated orthodox efforts to suppress them.

Further, if the truth of orthodoxy and the brilliance of its defenders were so compelling, one might expect orthodoxy to have enjoyed an uninterrupted progress from its conception in the second century to its triumph at the end of the ancient world. But such was not the case. Indeed, "At times, in the great movements such as Arianism and Gnosticism, heresy seemed to overshadow the Church altogether."[20] Bauer's claim that Christian beliefs later denounced as heretical were dominant in large geographical areas during the second century has already been noted. More specifically, the Marcionite rejection of the Old Testament was apparently quite popular among second-century Christians, perhaps even becoming for a time the majority view.[21] Nor did heresy pass into the state of being a permanent minority with the formation of a nascent orthodoxy and heresiography by the end of the second century. In early fourth-century North Africa, the Donatists, not the "Catholic" church, represented the main line of local orthodoxy both socially and intellectually.[22] In the middle of the fourth century, Arianism, which postulated the inferiority and posteriority of the Son to the Father, "seemed to have become for all time the only permissible Christian faith."[23] For a brief period, the Arians even won the support of the Roman state and the emperor, prompting Jerome (c. 340–420) to make his celebrated remark: "The world groaned and was amazed that it had become Arian."[24] Near the end of the fourth century, Epiphanius (315–402), the seal of the heresiographers of Christian antiquity, was in a distinct minority in condemning the Apollinarian heresy, at least in the Greek East.[25] Even after the council of Chalcedon (451), heresies continued not only to prosper, but even to triumph temporarily in the Byzantine empire. The Monophysite heresy, which opposed the Chalcedonian formula that imputed two natures to Christ, not only won imperial support for a time but by the end of the sixth century was "dominant in a great band of territory extending from the Black Sea to the sources of the Nile."[26] That territory was more extensive than that of Byzantine and Latin Christianity combined. Had Islam not conquered most of these lands, the Monophysites might have remained the majority party in Christianity.

This abbreviated tale of early Christian heresies' temporary triumphs brings up the significant point that had the triumph of any one of them been more than temporary, it would probably have been recognized as orthodoxy. Indeed, most of those later branded as heretical regarded themselves as orthodox. "Arians," for example, "thought of themselves, naturally as Catholics . . . as mainstream Christians," and looked upon their "orthodox" opponents as "isolated extremists."[27] This would seem to complete the ideological deconstruction of orthodoxy advanced by Bauer and others, and to reduce it to meaning little more than the doctrine of the party that emerged as victorious in the long run. The credibility of this view is enhanced by the consideration that some of the early fathers of the Church are just as plausible precursors of later heresies as of later orthodoxy. Even orthodox apologists and heresiologists may have recognized this at least implicitly. For they often found it necessary to explain away heretical-sounding language in the works of some of the early fathers.[28] In sum, the statement that orthodoxy triumphed is apparently tautological; for it seems that orthodoxy became such by virtue of its triumph.

This triumph might be more plausibly explained by political and social factors broadly conceived, than by theological considerations. The first of these factors to come into play was the superior administrative prowess, material resources, and prestige of the Church at Rome.[29] The institutional charisma of Rome was greatly enhanced toward the end of the second century by such popular figures as the heresiologists Justin Martyr and Ireneaus, the latter of whom celebrated the bishops of Rome as the rightful guardians of the true ecclesiastical tradition.[30] Rome's position as the arbiter of orthodoxy was finally formalized in the fifth century by Pope Leo I, who declared that the Pope's authority rested in the papal succession from St. Peter.[31] The orthodoxy of Rome was exalted not only by virtue of its association with some of the great apostles, martyrs, and saints of the Church, but also by dint of its primary role in the suppression of heresy. For it was at Rome that the semi-legendary heresiarch, Simon Magus, had supposedly been confronted by St. Peter himself. And it was also at Rome that the venerable Polycarp (d. 156) had denounced the first great historical heretic, Marcion, as the "first-born of Satan."[32] The works of the early Christian heresiologists, Justin Martyr, Hegesippus, Irenaeus, and Hippolytus of Rome, moreover, all "stood in close relation to Rome."[33] By their reportedly unparalleled capacity for identifying and exposing heretics, Roman authorities thus acquired a nearly spotless reputation for orthodoxy, which is not surprising in view of the fact that Rome was to a great extent the arbiter of orthodoxy in the first place. Even the ecclesiastical authorities of the Greek East appealed to Rome to settle theological disputes.

In the Roman Empire following the conversion of Constantine, especially in the East, political authorities contributed as much to the constitution of orthodoxy as did the See of St. Peter. The most prominent and well-known instance of the establishment of orthodoxy and suppression of heresy by a political authority is the imposition of Nicene trinitarian theology in the empire by the Emperor Theodosius. In his celebrated edict *Cunctos populos* of 28 February 380, Theodosius decreed that only the adherents of the Nicene confession were worthy of the name of Catholic Christians: "the rest were branded with the infamy of heresy."[34] The Emperor, moreover, not only condemned those who departed from Nicene trinitarianism as heretics, but also repressed them with the force of secular law.[35] Although Theodosius was no doubt a sincere Nicene Christian, both he and later emperors had political as well as religious reasons for proclaiming an orthodoxy and suppressing those who dissented from that orthodoxy: a uniform orthodoxy could serve as "a unifying force in an empire under pressure."[36] This political motive played a significant role in the decision to summon ecumenical councils to adjudicate disputed doctrinal questions and to make peace between warring factions holding different beliefs.[37]

The appeal to church councils to mediate conflicts of opinion in Christianity may be traced back to the Book of Acts in the New Testament.[38] But the first and most famous ecumenical council, that of Nicea (325), did not take place until after the conversion of Constantine. These councils were primarily concerned with the definition of orthodoxy and the identification and condemnation of heresy. In fact, later Christian authorities, including Gregory the Great (c. 540–604), associ-

ated each of the four great ecumenical councils of late antiquity with
the condemnation of a particular heresy: "at Nicaea (325), he says, 'the
perverse dogma of Arius was destroyed'. At Constantinople (381), the
error of Eunomius and Macedonius was condemned. At Ephesus
(431), the wickedness of Nestorius was condemned. At Chalcedon
(451), the wickedness of Eutyches and Nestorius was made apparent."[39] The atmosphere of these councils was evidently not always
conducive to free and disinterested theological speculation. As Harold
Brown puts it, "It is a potentially embarrassing fact that the central
doctrines hammered out in this period often appear to have been put
through by intrigue or mob violence rather than by the common consent of Christendom led by the Holy Spirit."[40] But who is to say that
the Holy Spirit may not work its way through intrigue or violence as
well as through rational dialogue?

The above account of Christian orthodoxy as having been determined by the power and pretentions of Rome, the political priorities
and religious idiosyncracies of emperors, and the quarrelsome in-
trigues of councils would seem to allow little scope for the religious or
intellectual dimension. To mere empirical historians, oblivious to the
cunning of reason and blind in the eye of faith, it might seem as though
the search for such a dimension is best left to theologians. But there are
some points in the making of Christian orthodoxy that a comparative
study suggests might be influenced by the temporal workings of intellect or spirit, if not necessarily of the Holy Spirit. One of these, already
mentioned, is that orthodox doctrine is never fixed or even formulated
by the original revelation or sagely teaching that established the foundations for a new religion. What is perhaps the most basic Christian
dogma, the doctrine of the Trinity, did not receive its final formulation
until the latter years of the fourth century.[41] And the related but equally basic Christological issue was not authoritatively settled until
Chalcedon (451). Even the skeptical historian, moreover, must acknowledge the intellectual grandeur and subtlety of these orthodox
dogmas, however untidy the historical process by which they were
reached. They were indeed worthy of the spirit of the Holy Spirit
which is said to have guided their formulation, as well as probably beyond the intellectual horizons of Jesus, if not of Christ. Like the
Buddha, Christ may well have realized that "had he not first preached
the Common Truth . . . , but preached right away the Supreme Truth,
he would have given rise to heresy."[42]

The working of intellect, if not the guidance of the Holy Spirit, may
also be found in the trajectory of orthodoxy from its open-ended inception in the second century toward increased narrowness and precision.

To gainsay an old Protestant hymn ("The Old Time Religion"), what was good enough for Paul and Silas was not good enough for later theologians. A particular illustration of this narrowing even over a relatively brief period of time appears in R.P.C. Hanson's tome on the Arian controversies: "In the middle of the third century, Dionysius, bishop of Alexandria, produced in a treatise an account of the Son as created which evoked a rebuke from the bishop of Rome but no more. At the end of the fourth century such a sentiment would have cost him his see."[43]

This progressive constriction of orthodoxy is a world-historical phenomenon that appears in all of the orthodox traditions surveyed below, including Sunni Islam, rabbinic Judaism, and Ch'eng-Chu Neo-Confucianism. Its generality may be further confirmed by Paul Ricoeur's oracular pronouncement that "ideology [including religion] effects a narrowing of the field in relation to the possibilities of interpretation which characterize the original momentum of the event."[44] When the original event carries eschatological expectations, as was the case with early Christianity, the failure or frustration of these hopes may accentuate the narrowing: "If one has to prepare for a lengthy stay, he longs for orderliness and harmony in the house."[45]

Although the early fathers of the Church can hardly be called pluralists, they accommodated and even expressed views that at times looked remarkably heretical from the perspective of post-Nicene orthodoxy.[46] But as the Great Church grew more universal in scope and power, it became more like a sect in mentality, somewhat like the Chinese Communist Party under Mao from the Second United Front to the Cultural Revolution. Although Christian heresiologists as early as the second century drew lines between orthodoxy and heresy, the great leap forward in the direction of sectarianism, with its "need for uniformity and homogeneity," came in the fourth century, inspired particularly by the Arian controversy.[47] But the real culmination of constriction came with the Chalcedonian creed which "narrowed the definition of orthodoxy so much that it excluded many who really belonged within it,"[48] just as Mao expelled his cohorts from the Party during the Cultural Revolution. This exclusion, moreover, provoked more than verbal violence between the parties involved. A slight miscue on a particularly sensitive doctrinal issue could have disastrous consequences.

A curious counterpart of this narrowing of the acceptable range of orthodox doctrine is the narrowing of the range of issues on which alleged heretics were criticized. In the early Church, before the heresiographical habit of reducing practically every heresy to a Christological or Trinitarian error took hold, such heretics were faulted on many grounds, including having "introduced prophets after the Lord" (the Montanists),[49] exclusion of the Old Testament from the Christian canon (the Marcionites), and a misapprehension of the relationship between divine grace and human free will (the Pelagians). But by the fourth century, these diverse doctrinal issues were giving way to Trinitarian and Christological concerns, the primary reference points for later Christian orthodoxy. The major focus of the so-called Arian controversies of the fourth century was Trinitarian, specifically the relationship of the Son to the Father. After this dispute was settled in favor of the emergent orthodox party at the Council of Constantinople in 381, interest shifted to Christological questions concerning the relation of the human to the divine in Christ.[50]

So narrow and even obsessive was orthodox concern with these issues that orthodox heresiologists tended to recast heresies of the most diverse origins into a Trinitarian or Christological mold. For example, later heresiologists accused the afore-mentioned Montanists of "holding heretical doctrines regarding Christ or the Trinity."[51] Thus Jerome (c. 340–420) claimed that the Montanists "compress the Trinity into the restrictedness of one person."[52] But "there is no evidence such charges were levelled at them in the earliest period."[53] Even the illustrious "hammer of heretics," Epiphanius (315–402), acknowledged that the Montanists "hold the same view of the Father, Son, and Holy Spirit as the holy Catholic Church."[54] During the same period, Augustine tried to make Christology an issue in his anti-Pelagian writings, even though Christology was not an area of controversy for Pelagius.[55] For a time, Byzantine theologians even interpreted the new religion of Islam as a Christological heresy.[56]

The progressive narrowing of the acceptable range of orthodox belief, and of the issues on which orthodoxy hinged, need not, however, be regarded as a purely negative development. Following recent church historians, we might look upon the making of orthodoxy as "a process of trial and error in which the error was not all on the side of the 'heretics', but was shared by the 'orthodox' too. . . . Men learnt by experience, by controversy, by seeing their own mistakes and the mistakes of others."[57] Some of these mistakes may have entailed confusing secondary issues with primary ones. In sum, if we assume that men make mistakes and that both they and their successors can identify and learn from these mistakes, then there is perhaps an intellectual process at work in the making (and narrowing) or orthodoxy.

Heretics, by this measure, might be those who failed to learn from the errors of the past, remaining fixated on a previous position or issue. As expressed by John Henry Newman, "one cause of corruption in religion is the refusal to follow the course of doctrine as it moves on, and an obstinacy in the notions of the past."[58] Recent historians have confirmed Newman's judgment on this particular point, speaking of "archaism as a cause of heresy" and referring to heresies as "premature and partial formulations."[59] Regarding particular heresies, Thomas A. Robinson characterizes Arius's position as "more conservative than that of his major adversaries," and Walter Bauer refers to the Judaists (or Ebionites) as "an instructive example of how even one who preserves the old position can become a 'heretic' if the development moves sufficiently far beyond him."[60] Thus, the statement with which we began this chapter, that orthodoxies are made, and not fixed from the outset, seems to have received a negative confirmation: heresies, in contrast to nascent orthodoxies, often *are* so fixed, or at least fixated. So, *eventually*, are orthodoxies. The key trick in the development of an orthodoxy, as in the development of individual psychology, is not to become fixated until maturity is attained.

Premodern Islam

Although scholars differ on just when and how orthodoxy emerged and triumphed in Christendom, there is at least a general consensus that a Christian orthodoxy did exist and prevail by the end of the fifth century. But in Islamic studies there is no such consensus. On the contrary, prominent scholars have suggested that "The word 'orthodox' is out of place in an Islamic context," that "the question of the 'orthodoxy-heterodoxy' dichotomy creates a false distinction in the case of Islamic doctrinal developments," and that in Islam "It is difficult to see who 'the orthodox' would be."[61]

These authorities give several reasons for their reluctance to apply the term 'orthodox' to any branch of Islam. First, there was no central ecclesiastical authority in Islam comparable to the ecumenical councils or the Papacy which could state authoritatively what constitutes "right doctrine."[62] Second, Islam puts more emphasis on law and practice that it does on doctrine.[63] Third, branches of Islam that have been condemned or categorized as heretical have in some cases an arguably more ancient and distinguished pedigree than does alleged orthodoxy. Some of these "heresies" have not only survived through the centuries but have even flourished in modern times. These Islamic sects, moreover, regarded themselves as the true believers and their opponents as heretics and infidels.[64] Finally, if one takes political support or patronage by the powers that be as a criterion or determinant of orthodoxy, then there appears to be little upon which to choose among several divergent Islamic schools and sects, some of which were sponsored by various caliphates and other potentates for rather long periods of time. In sum, even the convinced comparativist might be persuaded to steer clear of Islam when discussing questions of orthodoxy and heresy.

However, the Islamicists whose views are noted above may have been a little hasty in dismissing the possibility of applying the concept of orthodoxy to any branch or aspect of Islam. Part of the problem may stem from a tendency to take the medieval Christian regime as the paradigm for the proper application of the ideas of orthodoxy and heresy. But, as already noted, this regime gives a somewhat atypical standard of orthodoxy and heresy when measured against those of other great religious traditions. Some of the very points made by modern Islamicists to establish that orthodoxy did not exist in Islam might as well be applied to Christianity in late antiquity, or to rabbinic Judaism and Neo-Confucianism. This would leave medieval (and perhaps early modern) Christendom as the only major religious tradition to have developed a bona fide orthodoxy, not a very bright prospect for a comparative study of the subject.

That a case can be made for the existence of an 'orthodoxy' (or perhaps orthodoxies) in Islam is suggested by the fact that some Islamicists do apply the term in their studies. As Alexander Knysh has pointed out, "There is hardly a scholarly work dealing with Islamic subjects that does not emphasize dramatic cleavages between the 'orthodox' and the 'heterodox.'"[65] But wherein is such an orthodoxy to be found? In view of the close association between religion and politics in Islam, particularly the confluence of religious and political authority in the imam or caliph, one might expect to find orthodoxy in Islam, more than in any other major world religion, to be determined by political authority. This is all the more so since the political question of the succession (or of the imamate) was the most important source of sectarian division in early Islam, even "the single most contentious issue in Islamic history."[66] But, as already mentioned, several divergent sects, some of which were regarded as heterodox by most Muslims of later times, enjoyed official support and even the position of state orthodoxy at various times in Islamic history.

The most famous example of this from early Islam is the hegemony of the Mu'tazilites, the speculative theologians, in the early years of the Abbasid caliphate.[67] For a time during the reigns of the caliphs al-Ma'mun, al-Mu'tasim and al-Wathiq (827–847), officials were required to affirm a belief in Mu'tazilite dogma, particularly the doctrine that the Qur'an was the created, not the uncreated, speech of God. Persecutions and an inquisition (*mihna*) were even initiated in an attempt to impose Mu'tazilite views on the populace.[68] Under the subsequent caliph, however, Mu'tazilism lost its favored position as state orthodoxy and was thereafter generally regarded as heretical until it gradually faded away into insignificance.[69] The other most celebrated instance of heretical political hegemony in early Islamic history was under the Fatimid "anti-caliphate" (909–1171), centered in Egypt, which adopted a form of Isma'ilism (an "extreme" form of Shi'ism) as the state religion for a period of about two centuries. Finally, Shi'ism, a type of Islam that occupies a distinctly minority position in the Islamic world today, was predominant in several times and places, such as the tenth century throughout much of Islam and in Iran through most of its Islamic history.

In sum, the political history of *early* Islam does not offer very substantial support for designating any branch or school of Islam as orthodox, less than is the case with either early Christianity or Neo-Confucianism. Nor, as already mentioned, did ecumenical councils exist in Islam to formulate authoritatively the articles of right belief. Yet a large body of heresiographical literature did develop in Islam, which would be difficult to explain had there been no conception or criterion of orthodoxy, however conflicted and unstable. Such a conception did exist, though it was hardly as precise or as institutionalized as the rather intricate theological formulas developed in the Christian tradition. This criterion of orthodoxy was, in a word, *ijma'*, the agreement or consensus of the community of the faithful in any generation, particularly of the scholars or legal specialists, based on the famous saying attributed to Muhammad: "My Community does not agree on an error."[70] According to Montgomery Watt, Muslims in fact "showed considerable skill in reaching a common mind or consensus" on legal and theological matters.[71] This consensus, however, need not be audible or explicit. "Agreement may be tacit," and "consensus was considered to exist when there was *no known authoritative dissent*."[72] Such a negative method of determining consensus made it easier to support the claim that *ijma'* existed on any given question. Even when an explicit challenge did arise, one could always argue, with al-Baghdadi (d. 1037), that it emanated from a nonauthoritative source, since the heretics had never produced "a leading jurist, or a leading traditionist, or an outstanding rhetorician and grammarian, or a person credible in transmitting deeds of heroism or Lives of the Prophet or histories. . . . But the leaders in these sciences, whether specialized or general, have all been from the Orthodox group."[73]

This broad criterion of orthodoxy in mainstream Islam, in contrast to that of early Christianity, was more concerned with the process

by which dogma was formulated or judged than with the actual doctrines themselves. This raises the question of how such a differential
diagnostic of dogma came to be established. In the first place, however
ecumenical the doctrine of *ijma'* might sound in the abstract, it did not
apply to all who called themselves Muslims. On the contrary, it seems
to have been framed initially to oppose those Muslims, particularly the
Kharijites, the Mu'tazilites, and the Shi'ites, who adhered to other
sources of authority or criteria of orthodoxy, such as the Qur'an alone
for the Kharijites, rational theology for the Mu'tazilites, and the charismatic imams for the Shi'ites.[74] The framers of the doctrine of *ijma'* were
of the party that became known as the Sunnites, those who claimed to
be adherents of the correct or standard prophetic practice, those who
followed the *sunna* ("beaten path") of the Prophet.[75] This "standard
practice" of Muhammad was primarily revealed through Traditions
(*hadith*) which related the words, deeds, and tacit approvals of the
Prophet. It was diametrically opposed to *bid'a* or "innovation." In rejecting both the rational theology of the Mu'tazilites and the
charismatic authority of the Shi'ite Imams, the Sunnites posed as a conservative movement that looked back to the original sources of
revelation, the Qur'an and the *hadith*, as the bases of right belief and
practice. They were conservative even in the etymological sense, in
that the word *sunna* in pre-Islamic times referred to the "normal and
normative custom" of a tribe; to forsake it was to transgress against
"the inviolable rules of hallowed custom."[76]

   Like most conservative ideologies, Sunnite Islam was a relatively
late development in the history of the tradition. It arose in reaction to
perceived threats to the integrity of the tradition, which was relatively
inarticulate as long as it required no defense. Just when the various
doctrines and practices that constitute Sunnite Islam developed is difficult to determine, particularly since Sunnism at large is rather diverse
and even divided.[77] It managed eventually to absorb many of the
cross-currents of early Islam into its grand synthesis.[78] By the time of
the Mongol invasion of the thirteenth century, the great majority of
Muslims were professed Sunnites, as the extremist Shi'ite sects fal-
tered.[79] So deeply rooted did Sunnism become that it easily maintained
itself even under Shi'ite rulers, such as the Fatimids.[80] In modern
times, the Sunnites have grown to be the preponderant majority, claiming the allegiance of ninety percent of the world's Muslims. Sunnite
Islam is thus orthodox in the sense that "the overwhelming majority in
Islam constitutes its membership."[81] Indeed, Sunnism has even been
compared to "the undivided Christian church of the first ten centuries."[82] The widespread adherence to the *sunna*, the "standard

practice" of the Prophet, in Islamic lands ranging from Morocco to Indonesia has helped to give a worldwide unity to Islamic culture.

In view of its relative conservatism, Sunnite Islam can make a greater claim than can Christian orthodoxy to having developed from the implicit, inchoate pre-orthodoxy of the early community that rose to self-awareness and self-definition in response to heretical challenges. Although some protoSunnite tendencies and sects have been identified, there was no Sunnite self-consciousness until at least the latter years of the ninth century when the phrase "people of the Sunna" (*Ahl as-Sunna*) first appears.[83] But even then there was no recognition of the solidarity of all Sunnites, as the name was applied only to local groups.[84] Full Sunnite self-awareness and mutual recognition did not come about until the late eleventh century, though the essential polarization of Islam into Sunnite and Shi'ite can be dated from the early tenth century.[85] One result of the lateness of Sunnism's full development is that the later Sunnites "have an embarrassing time finding good Sunnis in the early generations,"[86] just as later Christian theologians found heretical-sounding language in the works of the early church fathers.

Whereas the Sunnites held to the *sunna* of the Prophet, transmitted through the *hadith* correctly interpreted by the community, as their main authority, the Shi'ites in general put their faith in an infallible imam who is chosen by God to rightly guide the community. The authority of the imam, "the authorized interpreter of God's will," may overshadow even that of the Qur'an and the Prophet.[87] Unlike Sunnism, which has throughout much of its history been identified with the consensual and conciliatory tendencies in Islam, the Shi'a generally took a dim view of their sectarian rivals. "Strong in its loves and hates, the Shi'a looked on itself as a saved remnant in a corrupt world, as did some of the prominent early Christian heresies."[88]

Shi'ite imamology, however characteristic of later Shi'ism as its most distinguished feature, was actually a rather late development. The name '*Shi'a*' means literally "party" or "followers" but was used specifically to designate the party of 'Ali (d. 661), the cousin and son-in-law of the Prophet.[89] Following the murder of Muhammad's third successor, 'Ali's party unsuccessfully sought to assert the political claims of 'Ali to the leadership of the community. In the course of a series of uprisings against the dynasty that supplanted 'Ali, who was himself murdered in the year 661, the Shi'a developed a sort of perennial oppositional stance as well as a vague longing for a charismatic leader, a successor to 'Ali.[90] Around the year 900, the mainline of the Shi'a developed a more coherent imamology expressed in the doctrine of the twelve imams, all hereditary successors to 'Ali. The twelfth and last of these imams had supposedly entered into a state of occultation following the death of the eleventh in 874, and will return as the Mahdi to restore order and justice to the world.[91] This new imamite doctrine, which appears to have been mainly the work of the great Shi'ite heresiographer, al-Nawbakhti (d. 923), gave form and unity to what had been a rather fluid and fragmented movement.[92]

Aside from the "Twelvers," now dominant in Iran, the most prominent branch of the Shi'ites consists of the Isma'ilis, whose imamology revolves around the number seven instead of twelve, and who hold that prophecy did not cease with the "seal of the prophets," Muhammad.[93] Indeed, Isma'ilis go so far as to exalt the imam *above* the Prophet, and even attribute to him divine qualities, thus committing (in the eyes of other Muslims), the cardinal sin of *shirk*, "the heresy that associates God with others and thus denies His radical uniqueness."[94] This "error," so reminiscent of Christian incarnationism, is enough to raise a heresiographical eyebrow, if not turn a heresiographical stomach. Partly for this reason, Isma'ilis are often classified as "extremists" (*ghulat*), even by other Shi'ites, and by some accounts excluded from the pale of Islam altogether. In the words of a contemporary Sunni polemicist, "The majority of the [Sunni] Muslim scholars consider whoever believes some human beings better than the prophets as '*kafir*'—unbelievers."[95]

Yet various forms of Shi'ism have survived the force of such condemnations. Unlike the ancient Christian heresies, all of which have disappeared, both the Twelvers and the Isma'ilis claim millions of adherents in such countries as Iran, India, and Lebanon. Thus, modern historians sympathetic to the Shi'a reject Sunni heresiographers' categorization of the Shi'ites as heretical, instead classifying Sunnism and Shi'ism as two parallel orthodoxies.[96]

Apart from Sunnism and Shi'ism, the other major form of Islam known to many Westerners is Sufism, which is also difficult to classify by the familiar categories of 'orthodoxy' and 'heresy.' Just as Christian mysticism and Jewish Kabbalah both attracted and repelled the guardians of orthodoxy in their respective traditions, so has this mystical form of Islam.[97] Mystical Sufism, as the great Sunni polemicist Ibn Taymiyya (d. 1328) recognized, could be either a friend or foe to orthodoxy.[98] Certain "extremist" tendencies in Sufism, such as its alleged antinomianism and incarnationism, evidently threatened to shake some of the chief pillars of Islam, particularly the adherence to the Islamic law (the *shari'a*) and the doctrine of the unity of God, as the heresiographer al-Razi (d. 1209) pointed out.[99] But even the mystical core of Sufism was suspect to the extent that it substituted subjective illumination for the "objective" revelation contained in the texts of the Qur'an and the records of the *hadith*. Orthodox theologians also condemned the ascetic life followed by some Sufis as an abandonment of social obligations prescribed by Islamic law and tradition.[100]

Yet Sufis and Sufism were never the objects of universal heresiographical condemnation. Even the heresiographer al-Razi, while condemning Sufi excesses, remarked that among the Sufis one might find the best and most disinterested of men.[101] Al-Baghdadi, one of the most passionate and militant of orthodox heresiographers, went so far as to categorize Sufis as orthodox Sunnis.[102] In early Islamic Iran and Iraq, moreover, Sufis were linked with the most orthodox of the Sunni theological schools, those of the Ash'arites and the Maturidites.[103] Even those heresiographers who condemned the Sufis generally directed their criticisms at its more extremist representatives, sparing the moderates.[104] In any case, Sufism could hardly be an object of blanket condemnation, since it contained so many variations and inasmuch as it presented no unified creed or theology to be argued against. Sufism in Islam, even more than mystical movements in other world religions, functioned as a sort of religious Rorschach test: it seems that every shade of Islamic orthodoxy and heresy, from the Sunni Ash'arites to the more extremist Shi'ites, found some congenial element or aspect in Sufism (as well as something to criticize).[105] Its highly ambiguous status is a good reflection of the relative imprecision and instability of the boundaries between orthodoxy and heresy in Islam.

Some medieval Muslim heresiographers as well as modern historians have, however, attempted to draw these boundaries more narrowly or precisely. The Sunni theological school that they most frequently identify as the orthodox, or at least the most orthodox, is the Ash'arite, supposedly founded by the seminal theologian, al-Ash'ari (873–935). As the most renowned Islamic heresiographer, al-Shahrastani (d. 1153), put it, "Ash'ari's views and methods were adopted by the Orthodox."[106] Not only did the Ash'arites receive official patronage under the Abbasid caliphate, but many if not most of the great theologians as well as heresiographers in Islam from that era forward associated themselves with the Ash'arites.[107] Thus modern Islamicists have spoken of the "triumph of al-Ash'ari," crediting him with having "founded the system which today is that followed by the great majority of orthodox Muslims," which "spread with remarkable speed through all the lands of Islam," and which "for several centuries . . . has almost totally dominated Sunnite Islam."[108] An analogue to the perceived primacy of Ash'arism among the six orthodox (or semi-orthodox) Sunni schools of theology is that of Vedanta among the six orthodox schools of Hinduism. Just as Shankara (788–820), the great philosopher of advaitic (non-dualist) Vedanta, has been lionized in both medieval and modern India, so al-Ash'ari was credited with having accomplished a great intellectual revolution virtually single-handedly.[109] He supposedly not only "formulated the doctrinal position of orthodox Islam," especially on the vital theological issue of the unity and attributes of God (*sifat*), but also "is credited with having saved the faith from corruption and having silenced the heretics." In view of his position in the formation of Islamic orthodoxy, as well as the fact that he lived approximately three hundred years after the death of Muhammad, Ash'ari is said to have occupied "in Islam a place comparable in the history of Christian doctrine to that of the Council of Nicaea."[110]

However great were Ash'ari's accomplishments, his revolution was hardly a one-man affair. Ash'ari's chief innovation was supposedly his adaptation of the rational theology (*kalam*) of the Mu'tazilites to defend traditionist non-Mu'tazilite positions. But, as recent historians have pointed out, Ash'ari was not the first to use Mu'tazilite methods to support such traditionist or fundamentalist theological views as the literal interpretation of the attributes of God as recounted in the Qur'an.[111] Although he was one of the most distinguished pupils of a great Mu'tazilite master, Ash'ari dramatically renounced the extreme rationalism of Mu'tazilite beliefs in his middle age in about the year 912, and turned to the more traditionist faith associated with the name of Ahmad b. Hanbal (780–855), who had "led a reactionary movement that insisted on a literal interpretation of the Qur'an and abhorred rationalizing."[112] But even though Ash'ari may have set out to defend Hanbalite fundamentalism, he in fact subtly enlarged upon its fundamental ideas, such as the literal interpretation of the rather anthropomorphic Qur'anic descriptions of God.[113] Even in his willingness to argue, Ash'ari departed from Hanbal's uncritical "adherence to text and tradition which allows of no argumentation."[114] Thus the Ash'arite position is sometimes spoken of as one of "compromise between the men of traditions and those who tried to establish faith by reason."[115] As Ibn Khaldhun put it, "He mediated between the different approaches."[116] This formula has not, however, ended speculation on just what was Ash'ari's definitive theological position on the spectrum of views ranging from Hanbalism to Mu'tazilism, an issue complicated by the difficulty of dating his various works.[117]

A matter that has elicited even more speculation is that of Ash'ari's relationship to the orthodox movement and theological school that bore his name, Ash'arism. Just as Jesus was arguably not a Christian and Confucius not a Confucian, so Ash'ari does not seem to be very Ash'arite when measured by the standards of a later age. While still paying homage to Ash'ari's name, later Ash'arite theologians frequently adopted positions closer to those of the founders of other Sunnite theological schools, such as al-Maturidi (d. 944), than to al-Ash'ari.[118] Some later Ash'arites, moreover, carried the method of philosophical argumentation further than did Ash'ari, thus provoking the ire of later Hanbalite fundamentalists, who opposed the "spirit of inquiry" (takyif) in religious matters.[119]

Although the early develoment of Ash'arism is not well understood, there is good evidence that it had already risen to a position of prominence within sixty years of Ash'ari's death.[120] Under the rule of the Seljuq Turks, the Ash'arite creed was propagated as the "official doctrine of orthodoxy."[121] But the orthodox position of the Ash'arites was in the long run more dependent on the consensus of the scholarly community than on any state sponsorship. The most notable contributor to winning this consensus was the most famous and revered Islamic philosopher and theologian, al-Ghazali (d. 1111), called "the proof of Islam" by his admirers: "To him is ascribed the final triumph of the Ash'arite system in the East."[122] However, Ghazali also contributed to winning state sponsorship for Ash'arism, even serving as an "official theologian" for the Seljuqs.[123] Indeed, the caliph even charged Ghazali with the responsibility of writing a heresiographical treatise against the Isma'ilis.[124]

While both medieval Islamic heresiographers and modern Western Islamicists have celebrated the Ash'arite school as the orthodox one, there was in medieval Islam a second orthodox theological school whose origins and development are much more obscure, the Maturidite, named after its eponymous founder and systematizer, Abu Mansur al-Maturidi. Like his more famous contemporary, al-Ash'ari, al-Maturidi was concerned with meeting the challenge posed by the rational theology of the Mu'tazilites, although his antagonism toward the latter was probably less extreme.[125] But in contrast to the Ash'arites, who constituted a significant movement within fifty years of their master's death, the Maturidites remained so obscure that they are not mentioned in Ash'arite writings until around 1200.[126] They flourished particularly in the East, the region of Samarqand in Transoxania. The Maturidite school reached the height of its power under the Ottomans, attaining the status of a second orthodoxy in Sunnite Islam. The main reason why the Ottoman rulers favored the Maturidite theological school was its close association with the Hanafite legal school, to which the Ottomans gave preference as the official law of the state.[127] Although some theological differences do exist between the Ash'arites and the Maturidites, the heresiographers associated with the two schools do not condemn each other as heretics. Indeed, some later "Ash'arites" have found the views of al-Maturidi and his school more congenial on some issues than those of al-Ash'ari.[128]

Inasmuch as these two parallel orthodoxies, Ash'arism and Maturidism, predominated in distinct geographical regions, they might be very roughly compared to Western Catholicism and Eastern Orthodoxy in the European middle ages. However, these Islamic orthodoxies experienced no great schism such as that which occurred in Christianity in the year 1054; nor did their adherents polemicize against one another. In Islam, it seems, orthodoxy was less absolute, somewhat more a matter of degree, than in Christendom.

This rather pat picture of two parallel orthodoxies within Sunnite Islam is not above challenge. In the first place, one might ask what proof there is that they really won the consensus of the community, even of the scholarly community. Some hints that they did not win such a consensus appear even in the writings of Ash'arites. For example, Ibn 'Asakir (1106–1176), a noted Ash'arite apologist, wrote that "Someone may object that the great majority of men, in different times and countries, have not followed the teaching of al-Ash'ari. The answer to this is that the men who really count did follow al-Ash'ari."[129]

Second, the supposed founder of Ash'arism, al-Ash'ari, presented himself as a defender of the fideism of Ibn Hanbal, the eponymous founder of another Sunnite school of theology (and of law) that in later centuries was frequently at odds with Ash'arites. Some Ash'arite heresiographers have portrayed this school as "a small group of backwater theologians."[130] But Hanbalism was much more a force to be reckoned with than these heresiographers admitted. It may have arisen in reaction to Mu'tazilite efforts to strip God of the anthropomorphic attributes ascribed to Him in the Qur'an. But it grew into "an attempt to transcend the regional traditionalist schools and currents and to create a uniform religious and legal doctrine."[131] Its fideist minimalism and reliance on the word made Hanbalism especially appropriate for popular preachers. Indeed, "Hanbalite histories are replete with accounts of Hanbalite preachers, and the Hanbalite Ibn al-Gawzi was possibly the greatest preacher in Islamic history."[132] On the other hand, the theological authority of Ibn Hanbal was not nugatory. In fact, it was so respected that it proved decisive in winning general consent on such finely disputed points in Sunnite theology as the doctrine of the eternity of the Qur'an.[133] The Hanbalite school even developed its own heresiography, though it appeared more in commentaries on creeds or articles of belief than in the conventional heresiographical treatises favored by Ash'arites.

In sum, the Hanbali school has quite a respectable claim to orthodoxy, even though it "never succeeded in gaining any real territorial dominion until its tenets were adopted by the Wahhabi movement in the eighteenth century, so that today the Hanbali school is the official law of Saudi Arabia."[134] But this does not necessarily mean, as George Makdisi has argued, that it was the Hanbalites rather than the Ash'arites who were the truly orthodox in Sunnite Islam. It may be true, as Makdisi asserts, that "the place of Ash'arism in the historical development of Muslim theology has been allotted an exaggerated importance," while that of traditionism has been overlooked.[135] But Makdisi overreaches himself in claiming that "Ash'arism failed as a school of theology" because of its inclusion of a rational element, and in arguing that Ash'arite appeals to tradition indicate that "the Ash'arites were still struggling for recognition."[136] While debunking Ash'arite heresiographical claims that Ash'arism was *the* orthodox sect, Makdisi ironically seems to have embraced other articles of heresiographical propaganda, particularly that there can be but one orthodoxy and that orthodoxy must be stable.

That there may have been more than one orthodoxy is suggested by another analogy with the history of Christianity in the West: "The Hanbalite movement may be described as a protestant reformation" which looked back to the primitive Community, the companions of the Prophet, for guidance.[137] If a triple orthodoxy of Catholic, Greek Orthodox, and Protestant may be admitted in post-Reformation Europe, a triune orthodoxy in three persona may have inhabited Islam as well—Ash'arite + Maturidite + Hanbalite. Eventually, however, these sectarian identifications faded with the formation of a "doctrinal synthesis that, from the fourteenth and fifteenth centuries on, encompassed most of the attested ritual, spiritual, and intellectual tenets within Islam."[138]

If the bounds of Islamic orthodoxy are more difficult to define and delineate than is the case with post-Nicene Christianity, the same general historical trend toward the narrowing of orthodoxy appears in Islam as well as in early Christianity. For example, the Qadarites who generally affirmed the doctrine of man's responsibility for his actions (*qadar*), were "respected members of the general religious movement" in the seventh and first quarter of the eighth century. But by the middle of the ninth century, "Qadarism had become something reprehensible in the eyes of most religious scholars,"[139] mainly because it seemed to question God's omnipotence. Similarly, the Murji'ites, the earliest of whom were "forerunners of the Sunnites," were totally suppressed in Sunni tradition of the ninth century.[140] The Shi'ites also gradually fell from Sunni favor through the centuries, finally to the point where some of them were branded as outright infidels. The Sunnite heresiographer Ibn Hazm (994–1064) set out in his work on the heterodoxies of the Shi'ites to "describe their detestable tenets," as well as those of other non-Sunni sects.[141] Orthodox heresiographers generally reserved their choicest condemnations for the *ghulat* among the Shi'ites, the extremists or exaggerators who held such beliefs as that imams were divine incarnations. But this too is a later development: "there is nothing to indicate that *ghulat* speculation was considered extremist or immoderate by the Muslims in the second century (A.D. 718–815)."[142] Indeed, so "mainstream" were *ghulat* views among the Shi'ites during the early years of Islam that the later, more "moderate" Twelver Shi'tes opposed to the *ghulat* had difficulty in finding early representatives for their own views.

On the other hand, Sunni orthodoxy, particularly that of the Ash'arite-Maturidite varieties, was doctrinally more latitudinarian than was that of post-Nicene Christianity. It was also more liberal than were some of the sects its apologists categorized as heretical, such as the autocratic and inquisitorial Mu'tazilites who "came to set up rigid standards of orthodoxy branding any deviation as a form of polytheism."[143] One of Ash'arism's greatest exponents, the philosopher al-Ghazali, even went so far as to call into question any (latter-day) claim to a monopoly of truth:

> If you are fair, you will soon realise that whoever makes truth the preserve of any one theologian is himself nearest to heresy . . . because he gives his master a rank that belongs only to the Prophet, considering him immune from error, so that orthodoxy consists in following him and heresy only in opposing him."[144]

Rabbinic Judaism

The making of Jewish orthodoxy, of what is called normative or rabbinic Judaism, is an even more mysterious process and disputed question than is the case with either early Christian or Islamic orthodoxy. Like scholars of Patristics, Judaists are concerned with the issue of by what right (or might) the "orthodox" won the crown of orthodoxy. But as in Islamic studies, the question of whether or not there *was* a medieval Jewish orthodoxy worthy of the name has also stirred debate. To complicate matters further, the available source materials are less informative on both of these issues than is the case with either early Christianity or Islam.

As indicated above, historians of early Christianity and Islam have located the origins of orthodoxy in these religions not in any specific sect, but in a sort of inchoate preorthodoxy that did not rise to self-consciousness or self-assertion until threatened by various heresies. Sectarian divisions supposedly appeared only after the fall from this state of inchoate innocence. In contrast, historians of Judaism in late antiquity have identified specific sectarian precursors of the "normative" rabbinic Judaism that emerged to attain a position of dominance in the early centuries A.D., particularly the sect of the Pharisees. That such earlier sects preceded and contributed to the rise of rabbinic Judaism is really not very surprising, since Judaism, in contrast to Christianity and Islam, had been in existence for several centuries before its normative form began to develop in the first and second centuries A.D. It is to be expected that a religion that had lasted for several hundred years should have developed some sectarian divisions.

Although some commentators have imaginatively traced the origins of Jewish sectarianism back to Sinai, and even to Cain and Abel, by Roman times three sects in particular commanded the attention of historians such as Josephus (d. c. 100): the Pharisees, the Sadducees, and the Essenes. Of these three, the most likely candidate for the pre-rabbinic one that eventually developed into orthodoxy of a sort is Pharisaism. The origin and orientation of the Pharisees in antiquity is obscure. As Jacob Neusner has pointed out, "We know very little about the Pharisees before the time of Herod."[145] Even the significance of the term 'Pharisee' is uncertain and disputed. As Anthony Saldarini has explained, "The name seems to come from the Hebrew and Aramaic root 'prs' which means 'separate' and 'interpret.' The most common etymological rendering of Pharisees is 'separate ones,' though from whom or what is disputed."[146] One possible explanation is that the Pharisees were those rigorists who went out of their way to separate themselves from either the pagans of Maccabean times or the ritually impure among their own people, or both.[147] But the term was also occasionally used in the negative, pejorative sense in later rabbinic literature to mean something like "heretics," "renegades," or "people who separated themselves illegitimately from society at large."[148] The other major rendering of Pharisees as "interpreters" has more positive connotations. It also accords well with the role assumed by later rabbis as interpreters of the Jewish Law, particularly the "Oral Torah," the more esoteric part of the divine revelation supposedly given to Moses at Sinai and later codified in the Mishnah (c. A.D. 200) and the two Talmuds (c. A.D. 400 and 600).

Although modern historians have traced the Pharisaic movement as far back as the fourth century B.C., a "Pharisaic Revolution" appears to have taken place in tandem with the Hasmonean Revolt (c. 167–142 B.C.), making Pharisaism one of the main Jewish sects.[149] But just how important or dominant the Pharisees were during the Second Temple period up to the time of the destruction of the Temple in A.D. 70 is an area of wide disagreement. On the one hand, Ellis Rivkin asserts that the Pharisees of this period "sat in Moses' seat" and that "Pharisaism was . . . adhered to by all but a handful of Sadducees, a smattering of Essenes, and by a minority . . . of malcontents." It was "the definitive form of Judaism long before Paul was born."[150] More recent scholarship, however, has called into question this characterization of the Pharisees as the dominant political and religious party in Judaism of the Second Temple period. Neusner, for example, asserts that although the Pharisees were probably more numerous and ultimately more influential than either the Sadducees or the Essenes, they "numbered only about 6,000, [and] had no real hold either on the government or on the masses of the people."[151] They owe their prominence in later literature not to any domination of Judaism of the Second Temple period, "but to two later historical developments, the Christian interest in them as opponents of Jesus and the rabbis adoption of them as their own predecessors."[152] A judicious compromise between these two positions on the question of Pharisaic domination is that they enjoyed considerable popularity and widespread support during the Second Temple period, even though they constituted only a small fraction of the population.[153]

The divergence of scholarly opinion on the question of the religious orientation of the Pharisees parallels that on the issue of their relative power and influence. Again, older views seem to adhere more closely to traditional rabbinic historiography in attributing to the Pharisees some of the characteristics of the later rabbis, particularly dedication to the Oral Law and a constitution as a class of scholars.[154] In contrast, their main rivals, the Sadducees, are supposed to have adhered to the concept of the single written law recorded at Sinai in the form of the Pentateuch and not supplemented by any oral tradition, as well as to have been centered on a hereditary priesthood. The Pharisees, by this interpretation, were the true revolutionaries or innovators, though they cleverly cast themselves as the traditionalist conservative party, much as did early Christian orthodox in the early centuries A.D.[155] Again, more recent scholars have questioned this account of the religious orientation of the Pharisees, particularly the attribution to them of a belief in an Oral Torah revealed to Moses and passed down to later ages through a rabbinic chain of transmission.[156] Since this was the single most significant identifying mark of later rabbinic orthodoxy, the lack of a clear Pharisaic commitment to the Oral Law undermines considerably their claim to the status of preorthodoxy.

If an unwavering line of descent cannot be drawn between the Pharisaism of the Second Temple period and the later rabbinic orthodoxy, or "normative Judaism," that prevailed from late antiquity through the eighteenth century A.D., then how did this orthodoxy emerge? And what was its relationship to its sectarian predecessors, particularly Pharisaism? Even more so than does orthodoxy in any of the other religious traditions surveyed here, rabbinic Judaism appears to owe its formation and eventual triumph to a political event, namely the fall of Jerusalem and the destruction of the Temple by Roman armies in A.D. 70. Inasmuch as the Temple had provided the focal point for Jewish sectarianism, the sectarian landscape of Judaism was thereby altered almost beyond recognition. "The world which produced Jewish sectarianism, nurtured it, and gave it meaning, disappeared in 70."[157]

However, not all of the pre-Destruction sects were equally affected by the demise of the Temple and its cult. While the Sadducees, reputedly the chief celebrants of this cult, were mortally wounded, as were the more militant sects such as the Essenes, the Pharisees were poised to profit from this catastrophe. For in pre-Destruction times, "The Pharisees were a particular set of people who pretended, in their homes, that they were priests in the Temple." Thus, "When the Temple itself was destroyed, it turned out that the Pharisees had prepared for that tremendous change in the sacred economy."[158] For these "lay people" now had a much better reason for pretending to be priests: in the absence of the Temple and its cult, they were the new repositories of holiness in Israel, whose ultimate task it was to build a new holy temple in the form of a holy people.

However, Pharisees did not evolve into rabbis after A.D. 70 in such a simple and straightforward manner as the above account might suggest. For one thing, it leaves unexplained the later rabbinic reverence for the Oral Torah, belief in which was the touchstone of later rabbinic orthodoxy to the extent that rabbinic polemicists tended increasingly to reduce all other disputes within Judaism to this issue. This, as well as other facets of the new Judaism that developed after A.D. 70, are best explained by considering later rabbinic Judaism as a synthesis of pre-Destruction Jewish movements and tendencies, and not simply as the triumph of one particular sect, that of the Pharisees. Although this synthesis took place over a period of several centuries, its origins may be traced back at least as far as the grand convocation of Yavneh, which occurred around A.D. 90, about twenty years after the Destruction. In addition to fixing the Hebrew canon, Yavneh has also been credited with helping to establish "a grand coalition of different groups and parties, held together by the belief that sectarian self-identification was a thing of the past."[159]

But if the Pharisees and their descendants were a significant element in this coalition, what was the origin of the other parties, and how did they contribute to the emergence of rabbinic Judaism? Apart from the Pharisees themselves, the most important contributors to the new orthodox synthesis were the scribes. The scribes of pre-Destruction times were not, of course, so much members of a sect as of a profession. But they were also purveyors of an ideology, based on the study of the Torah, that goes back to the fourth century B.C. This ideology began with the view that "the law given by God to Moses was binding and therefore has to be authoritatively interpreted and applied to daily affairs."[160] The custodians and teachers of this law, the scribes, thus had direct access to a source of authority and knowledge at least potentially as great as that commanded by the Temple priests. With the Destruction of the Temple and the demise of the priestly vocation, the field was cleared for the realization of this potential, and more specifically for the synthesis of Pharisaism's domestic practice of priestly religion with the scribes' focus on Torah study. As the prospect of restoration faded further from the realm of historical possibility, Torah study and the "deeds of lovingkindness" it supposedly inspired were substituted for the Temple and its sacrificial rites as the means through which Israel might achieve atonement and live a holy way of life. In the words of an oft-quoted Talmudic text, *The Fathers According to Rabbi Nathan*:

> Once as Rabban Johanan ben Zakkai was coming forth from Jerusalem, Rabbi Joshua followed after him and beheld the Temple in ruins.
>
> "Woe unto us," Rabbi Joshua cried, "that this, the place where the iniquities of Israel were atoned for, is laid waste!"
>
> "My son," Rabban Johanan said to him, "be not grieved; we have another atonement as effective as this. And what is it? It is acts of lovingkindness, as it is said, *For I desire mercy and not sacrifice*" [Hos. 6:6].[161]

Thus there gradually developed the motifs characteristic of later rabbinic Judaism, including "the centrality of the oral Torah, the view of the rabbi as the new priest and of study of the Torah as the new cult, . . . and the goal of turning all Israel into a vast academy for the study of the (rabbinic) Torah."[162] These motifs not only superseded the older forms of Judaism centered on the Temple and its cult, but also messianic Judaism, such as militaristic zealotry, which was not only discredited but also either scattered or destroyed by the unsuccessful Jewish revolts against Rome. But even here, the rabbis did not so much displace an older sectarian form of Judaism as transvalue and synthesize it: the Messiah came to be represented as a learned rabbi, just as had the Temple priest.[163] The rabbi, the "ideal type" of this new "normative" form of Judaism, was thus both a priest *manqué* and a messiah *manqué*; and God himself was eventually transformed into a rabbi *manqué*. Orthodoxy in rabbinic Judaism, as in early Christianity and Sunni Islam, thus began as a sort of united front operation, one that was broad enough to include even God.

That the Pharisees were precursors of rabbinic Judaism has sometimes been obscured by condemnations of them that occasionally appear in later rabbinic literature.[164] There are several possible explanations for this lapse of rhetorical continuity between Pharisees and rabbis that might help to illuminate the mind of rabbinic orthodoxy. In the first place, few religious sects, especially those that manage to win some credible claim to orthodoxy, are anxious to be identified as such. Not only were the Pharisees rather irredeemably identified as a sect in pre-Destruction Judaism, but their very name, which means "separatists," accentuated their apartness and aloofness from the mainstream.[165] However, not all of the references to the Pharisees in later rabbinic literature, particularly the Babylonian Talmud (c. A.D. 600), are negative; some, in fact, are rather laudatory, particularly the ones to the Pharisees of the pre-Destruction era.[166] As precursors of Rabbinism and vital links in a genealogy of orthodoxy reaching back to Sinai, it is understandable that these Pharisees received rabbinic rehabilitation once rabbinic orthodoxy was firmly established. But the dissident or reactionary rabbis who opted out of the post-Destruction synthesis that developed into rabbinic Judaism could not be dealt with so benignly. Their "exaggerated piety" constituted a threat to the emerging rabbinic united front.[167] It was too reminiscent of the old sectarianism that was held to be partly responsible for the great catastrophes of A.D. 70 and 135, and which was evidently unviable in the post-Destruction diaspora. Thus those Pharisees who resisted change apparently suffered the typical fate of orthodoxies (or protoorthodoxies) that fail to move with the times: they became heretical.

But was Rabbinism of the post-Destruction period orthodox simply by virtue of its having adapted to the new historical circumstances, or by its supersession of its more sectarian predecessors? There are some grounds for questioning the dominance of the rabbis in Jewish culture and society of late antiquity. Although the religious or sectarian orientation of Jews in late antiquity and the early middle ages is difficult to gauge, at least one scholar has asserted "that most Jews of the 'Rabbinic Period' were not rabbinic."[168] The anti-Rabbanite Karaite movement which peaked in the ninth century is supposed to have claimed the allegiance of as many as one-third of all Jews for a time.[169] Moving on to a much later period, the popularity of the seventeenth-century apostate messiah, Sabbatai Zvi (1626–1676), was for a time so great that "most Jews accepted his authority."[170]

Yet, even if all of these accounts of heretical hegemony (or near-hegemony) are accurate, the theory that Rabbinism constituted an orthodoxy in Judaism is not necessarily refuted. The temporary hegemony of 'heresy' is a phenomenon common to the history of all the orthodox traditions surveyed here, and is less pronounced in the history of normative Judaism than it is in early Christianity, Islam, and Neo-Confucianism. Further, the rabbinic domination in the longer term was not confined to the intellectual and educational spheres but was institutionalized, at least in Talmudic times, in a central Jewish administration residing in Babylonia which claimed authority over Middle Eastern Jewry.[171]

However, for the first few hundred years of its existence, rabbinic Judaism did lack a formal creed or dogmatic statement of the articles of faith, such as those which appear prominently in early Christianity and Islam. The closest approach to such a statement of obligatory beliefs in early rabbinic Judaism is the famous passage in the tenth chapter of the Mishnah Sanhedrin, quoted above in Chapter One, which states that "All Israelites have a portion in the world to come. . . . But the following have no portion in the world to come: he that claims that the Resurrection is not taught in the Torah, he that denies the Torah's divine origin, and the Epicurean."[172] However important and influential was this brief statement, it was rather isolated. Although Saadiah Gaon (882–942), the great opponent of Karaism, did expound a set of Jewish beliefs in the tenth century, one must await the appearance of the great Maimonides (1135–1204), the second Moses, for a detailed and systematic statement of the articles of rabbinic Jewish belief.

Maimonides was distressed that even those Jews of his time who observed the Jewish law might negate the efficacy of their observances through their incorrect habits of thought, particularly their beliefs about God, which might render their worship idolatrous. He sought to correct this situation in his commentary to the tenth chapter of Mishnah Sanhedrin, quoted in the previous paragraph, by positing a set of thirteen principles or beliefs that he designated as "foundations of the Torah."[173] Failure to accept these beliefs, Maimonides warned, will lead to dire punishment: the loss of a portion in the world to come.[174] This "definition of a Jew by virtue of his beliefs," according to Menachem Kellner, "is an absolute innovation in Judaism."[175] While this innovation was perhaps not quite so absolute as Kellner suggests, it did provoke much discussion and debate, as well as inspire quite a number of later imitations. Despite its innovativeness and arbitrariness, Maimonides' set of thirteen principles met with a surprising degree of acceptance from Jews all over the world, which is all the more amazing in view of the fact that Maimonides lacked any formal authority through which he might impose his dogmas. Perhaps even more influential was Maimonides' establishment of the commitment to Torah and Torah study as Judaism's defining feature.[176] For these achievements, Maimonides became known as the lawgiver to future generations, "a fact to which his admirers gave expression in the well-known saying, 'From Moses to Moses, there arose not like Moses.'"[177] On the other hand, some of Maimonides' Mosaic claims did provoke opposition from conservative Rabbanites, who accused him of trying to replace the Talmud with his own *Mishneh Torah*.[178]

While Maimonides' position as a lawgiver may have been unprecedented in medieval Judaism, his declaration of thirteen dogmatic principles as requirements for salvation is indicative of a general trend in the history of rabbinic Judaism which we have already seen at work in early Christianity and Islam, the narrowing of orthodoxy. The beginnings of a movement toward a more "specific and detailed" form of orthodoxy may be dated all the way back to the first century A.D.[179] But it is more clearly manifested in the centuries following the Destruction of A.D. 70, when the Sadducees are "moved further and further from the mainstream of Judaism until they became an heretical or quasi-heretical sect" before finally disappearing.[180] Inasmuch as Maimonides threatened with extinction anyone who denied any one of his dogmas, he too made a significant contribution to the constriction of orthodoxy in his day. So did Isaac Abravanel (1437–1508), who remarked that "a false opinion about any one of the principles of faith turns the soul from its true felicity and will not bring [one] to life in the world to come, even if the opinion is held without intention to rebel."[181]

As in early Christianity, the narrowing of orthodoxy in rabbinic Judaism also took the form of the narrowing of the range of issues on which orthodoxy hinged. This is especially evident in the retrospective and anachronistic interpretation of early sectarian conflicts in Judaism as pivoting on the issue of the Oral Torah. While the Samaritan schism evidently arose over the location of the Samaritan temple at Gerizim (rather than Jerusalem), the conflict between the Sadducees and the Pharisees over ritual and cultic issues, and the Karaite schism over a succession dispute in the leadership of the Babylonian Jewish community (as well as questions of the calendar), all three of these sectarian conflicts were later reinterpreted as stemming from differing attitudes toward the Oral Torah.[182] This is all the more remarkable in view of the fact that the Oral Torah did not exist as such, or at least was not codified, at the time when the Samaritans and the Sadducees first arose.

The ultimate straitening of the gate (and charging with punishments of the scroll) of rabbinic orthodoxy came in the seventeenth-century reaction to the apocalyptic Sabbatian movement that proclaimed Sabbatai Zvi as the long-expected messiah. As the authentic interpreters of God's word, the rabbis, like established authorities in most religious traditions, could hardly tolerate those "sudden outbreaks of prophetic spirit and apocalyptic vision" that threatened to undermine the order of things.[183] Rabbinic opposition to Sabbatianism, which divided and traumatized Jewish communities throughout Europe and the Middle East, was further heightened by its antinomian fringe as well as by Sabbatai's subsequent apostasy and conversion to Islam. In reacting to this heresy, Moses Hagiz (1671–1751) went so far as to claim that "anyone who rejected any rabbinic teaching, no matter how minute, must be considered a Jewish heretic."[184] In time, the rabbinic battle against Sabbatianism, "the most vile and subversive Jewish messianism and heresy since the birth of Christianity," evolved into "an effort to suppress all forms of religious renewal."[185] Thus, rabbinic stalwarts met the next great movement to arise within Judaism, eighteenth-century Hasidism, with the most serious charge possible from a rabbinic perspective, that the Hasidim "make an abomination of Torah study and of those engaged in it" and that they "despised the Oral Law."[186]

Rabbinic or normative Judaism, which had developed in the years following the destruction of the Temple in A.D. 70, reached the end of the line a little more than a century after the Sabbatian movement erupted. Its end was precursed by the open disparagement of the

Talmud by leaders in the eighteenth-century Haskalah (Jewish Enlightenment) movement. Jacob Neusner has dated the demise of this "normative" form of Judaism to the year 1787, though he also notes that rabbinic Judaism did not pass from the scene without spawning seven successor Judaisms of the last two centuries.[187] Although one of these successors claims the title of "Orthodox Judaism," its orthodoxy takes on meaning only in contrast to the reform Judaism that preceded it and to which it "owes its life."[188]

Neo-Confucianism

Although modern scholars have seldom treated the problem of heresy in the Neo-Confucian tradition very systematically, they have recognized the importance of the issue of Neo-Confucian orthodoxy. More than historians of the other religious traditions surveyed, however, students of Neo-Confucianism have interpreted orthodoxy as a many-splendored thing, a "rich and diverse phenomenon" with several types or aspects.[189]

As Benjamin Elman has pointed out, types (or prototypes) of Confucian orthodoxy existed in China even before the rise of Neo-Confucianism in the eleventh and twelfth centuries. As early as the Former Han era (202 B.C.—A.D. 9), a form of Confucianism based on the "New-Text" versions of the classics became the state orthodoxy, while under the T'ang dynasty (618–906), the "Old-Text" classics and classicists held sway. By far the most durable and influential state orthodoxy in the history of imperial China, however, was that based on the Neo-Confucian teachings of Ch'eng I (1033–1107) and Chu Hsi (1130–1200), which were first officially recognized in 1241, and then "enshrined in the civil service examinations of the Ming (1368–1644) and Ch'ing (1644–1911) dynasties as the orthodox curriculum."[190]

But state orthodoxies were not the only aspect of Neo-Confucian orthodoxy current in late-traditional China. There existed intellectual orthodoxies as well, which were formed by the consensus of scholars. In late-traditional China, these intellectual orthodoxies were also generally associated with the Ch'eng-Chu philosophy, though they might be designated by any one of several different names.[191] Of these, the term *Tao-hsüeh* (Learning of the Way or "Tao Learning") is the one that seems to refer most specifically to the intellectual school or tradition that adhered to the teachings of Ch'eng I and Chu Hsi, though even this concept changed over time. Many who considered themselves to be followers of the Confucian sages were not part of this Tao Learning group or tradition, either by their own choice or through their being excluded as heretics. In the interest of truth, justice, and the liberal American way, it might be tempting to redefine 'Neo-Confucian orthodoxy' in such a way as to retroactively enfranchise or empower the unjustly marginalized, as some modern historians have attempted to do for ancient Christian heretics. But while such an approach might make the dead feel somewhat better, it would obscure our comprehension of Ch'eng-Chu orthodoxy as it was understood in late-traditional China. As Thomas Wilson has pointed out, the term "Tao Learning" was itself used as an ideological code word in late-imperial China "to exclude many Confucians from the orthodox tradition of the Way."[192]

Admittedly, this orthodoxy is even more difficult to circumscribe than are those that prevailed in the early Christian, Islamic, and Jewish traditions outlined above. If an intellectual orthodoxy is defined as the "consensus on a doctrinal minimum beyond which one could not go without danger of exclusion,"[193] then where is this doctrine expressed in the Ch'eng-Chu philosophy? As far as I know, there are no Neo-Confucian creeds or formal statements of the articles of belief such as those found in early Christianity, Islam, and even rabbinic Judaism. In the words of William T. de Bary, "the orthodox tradition, even more than a set moral code or philosophical system, was a life-style, an attitude of mind, a type of character formation, and a spiritual ideal that eluded precise definition."[194]

But this should not cause us to despair of ever identifying a set of beliefs or ideas that set the orthodox Ch'eng-Chu school apart from other Neo-Confucian schools and tendencies. In the absence of creeds and formal statements of belief in Neo-Confucianism, the most likely source for the expression of doctrinal boundaries is Neo-Confucian heresiographical writing, which is primarily concerned with distinguishing between orthodox beliefs and heretical notions on such touchstone issues as the nature of human nature (*jen-hsing*). More than any other genre of Neo-Confucian literature, heresiographical works indicate that doctrines and beliefs were matters of serious if not ultimate concern in the orthodox Ch'eng-Chu school, that there was in this school some modicum of a "doctrinal minimum beyond which one could not go without danger of exclusion" (though this minimum might vary over time).

As is the case with orthodoxies in the other major traditions considered here, the Ch'eng-Chu school was only one strand of a much broader movement. This broader intellectual and cultural movement, to which some Western scholars have applied the name 'Neo-Confucianism' and others 'Sung learning,' arose in the eleventh century as a revival of classical Confucianism after a long period in which heterodox teachings, particularly forms of Buddhism and Taoism, had been dominant. As was the case with early Christianity and Islam, the orthodox form of this new religious movement did not emerge until more than a century after the movement's inception.

As recent studies by Peter Bol, Hoyt Tillman, and others have pointed out, the eleventh-century initiators of the Confucian revival in the Sung "did not constitute a single, self-conscious school" gathered around a single figure. Ch'eng I, the founder of the orthodox movement in its narrower form, "was in his own day one of several men with persuasive ideas," and not the dominant philosopher of his era.[195] Even through most of the twelfth century, the Neo-Confucian movement retained a broad and fluid nature. It included such diverse figures as Chu Hsi, Lu Hsiang-shan (1139–1192), Chang Shih (1133–1180), Lü Tsu-ch'ien (1137–1180), Ch'en Liang (1143–1194), and Yeh Shih (1150–1223), many of whom "had drastically variant temperaments and strongly divergent ideas."[196] The narrowing of this broad Neo-Confucian fellowship into a rather exclusive orthodox school focused on the thought of Ch'eng I and Chu Hsi, occurred in the late twelfth and early thirteenth centuries.

Although Chu Hsi himself made the greatest contribution to this narrowing of Neo-Confucianism, he was precursed in this as in much else by Ch'eng I, who once observed that "scholars of the empire split into three groups, specializing respectively in the study of the classics, moral principles, and belles-lettres; only those who concentrate on moral principles are true Confucians."[197] However, even Ch'eng I's antiheretical strictures were not enough to prevent most of his disciples from falling away into Ch'an Buddhism.[198] With most of Ch'eng's immediate disciples thus out of the picture, Chu Hsi asserted his claim to have fallen heir to the orthodox line of transmission (*Tao-t'ung*), which he proceeded to narrow in the course of intellectually disinheriting his rivals, particularly in his later years after the removal of Lü Tsuch'ien's moderating influence. Chu even excluded earlier Neo-Confucian figures whom the Ch'engs had included, such as Ssu-ma Kuang (1019–1086) and Shao Yung (1011–1077), from the Tao Learning lineage.[199] He recognized only the "four Northern Sung masters," Chou Tun-i (1017–1073), Chang Tsai (1020–1077), Ch'eng I, and Ch'eng Hao (1032–1086), as truly orthodox.

The aura and authority of Chu Hsi, however awe-inspiring in later centuries, was not in itself sufficient to ensure the triumph of his version of Tao Learning as both the state orthodoxy and the preferred intellectual orthodoxy of much of the upper class. On the contrary, the government officially branded the Ch'eng-Chu mode of Tao Learning as "false learning" (*wei-hsüeh*), and proscribed it from 1195 to 1202.[200] Even though Chu's funeral in 1200 was well attended, "all those who went were regarded as heretics, mourning the death of the 'heresiarch.'"[201] Even after the proscription against the Ch'eng-Chu teachings was lifted, their official status remained unsettled for decades.[202]

Chu Hsi and his school attracted not only official condemnation but the disapproval of other Confucian scholars as well, many of whom "resented its claim to exclusive insight into the Confucian Tao."[203] This claim particularly rankled Ch'en Liang, the leading "utilitarian Confucian" of the day, who compared Chu Hsi's Tao Learning to an exclusive heterodox sect: "They demark and establish boundaries between themselves and others like ties at the sacrificial altar of a secret society. They completely exclude a generation of men as outside their school."[204] In fact, even the term "Tao Learning" was "originally a derisive title, implying a pretentious manner and obsessive behavior" that deviated from the mainstream.[205]

Nor did Chu's Tao Learning eventually triumph because of an absence of active opposition or credible alternatives. Throughout much of the Northern Sung era (960–1126), the court officially supported the new Confucianism of the reformer Wang An-shih (1021–1086) and widely disseminated it through the school system while suppressing the teachings of the Ch'eng brothers.[206] And even after the fall of the Northern Sung dynasty in 1126, the Juchen rulers in the North patronized followers of Su Shih (1036–1101) and Ou-yang Hsiu (1007–1072), while Wang An-shih continued to command some official support in the South under the Southern Sung. If political backing for Chu Hsi's emerging Tao Learning was not a foregone conclusion, neither did it sweep the field necessarily because of sheer intellectual superiority or greater fidelity to the classical Confucians whose teachings it set out to restore. Although Chu Hsi's writings are certainly more voluminous than are those of his major competitors, their intellectual brilliance and philosophical acuity did not so far outshine that of his opponents as to be sufficient to eclipse his rivals. Even Chu Hsi's main claim to orthodoxy, that his philosophy, building on that of his Tao Learning predecessors, restored the Way of the classical Confucians, particularly of Confucius and Mencius, is open to question. According to Shu-hsien Liu, the thought of Chu's most celebrated philosophical rival, Lu Hsiang-shan, "stands much closer to Mencius" than does that of Chu Hsi.[207]

In sum, the triumph of the Ch'eng-Chu school as the orthodoxy of both state and scholars in late-traditional China was by no means inevitable. Indeed, at the time of Chu Hsi's death in the year 1200, even its survival was open to question. How, then, did a "side branch" or "peripheral current" of Neo-Confucianism rise to such a position of dominance which it maintained through most of the next five or six centuries?[208] Chu Hsi's personal qualities, "his great scholarship, his indefatigable hard work, and his unquestionable integrity" certainly played a role,[209] as did the synthetic grandeur of his intellectual system. The fact that Chu Hsi, like Teng Hsiao-p'ing, outlived his principal competitors or rivals, such as Lu Hsiang-shan, also accrued to his advantage. Yet the greatest leap forward in the direction of winning orthodox standing for the Ch'eng-Chu school was taken not by Chu himself or by any of his followers but by the state, which in 1202 lifted the ban against Tao Learning, in 1208 granted posthumous honors to Chu Hsi, in 1227 gave official sanction to Chu's commmentaries on the Confucian Four Books, and finally in 1241 "formally proclaimed the *Tao-hsüeh* interpretations to be the state orthodoxy."[210] The court also affirmed Chu Hsi's version of the orthodox line of transmission (*Tao-t'ung*), which Chu held had been interrupted after Mencius and then resumed by the Northern Sung masters, the predecessors of Chu Hsi.

According to James T. C. Liu, the prime mover in this accession of Tao Learning to the status of state orthodoxy was the political situation of the time, particularly court politics and the mounting international crisis. Threatened ever more seriously by rising Mongol power and claims to political legitimacy, "the southern empire tried to boost its political prestige by cultural propaganda."[211] By accepting and publicizing Tao Learning claims to have inherited the orthodox line of transmission from antiquity, the tottering Southern Sung dynasty could enhance its political legitimacy by presenting itself as the locus of orthodoxy. However, since the court had so recently banned Tao Learning, it saved face for this awkward change of heart by rechristening "*Tao-hsüeh*" as "*Li-hsüeh*," the Learning of Principle.[212] This official recognition and rehabilitation of Tao Learning under the Southern Sung was, however, little more than a political gesture at the time, since it translated into neither political power for Tao Learning scholars nor the application of Tao Learning theories to the actual conduct of government.

This deathbed conversion of the Southern Sung rulers to Tao Learning was no more effective in preserving the dynasty than Constantine's conversion was in saving the Roman Empire from dismemberment. But just as the Germanic tribes that conquered the Western empire embraced Christianity, so did the Mongol conquerors

of China officially adopt Ch'eng-Chu Confucianism, though not quite
so unreservedly as did their European counterparts. In 1313, the Yüan
dynasty (1279–1368) founded by the Mongols decreed that the Tao
Learning masters of the Northern Sung be honored with religious sac-
rifices, and the next year stipulated that the Confucian classics with
their Ch'eng-Chu commentaries be the standard texts for the presti-
gious imperial civil service examinations.[213] This led to Tao Learning
domination of the educational curricula in schools throughout China,
though there were few career opportunities in officialdom for ethnic
Chinese, especially southerners, under the Yüan dynasty. But whatever its effect on education at the time, this move did help the Yüan
dynasty to enhance *its* claim to political legitimacy by posing as defenders of the Confucian faith.

The native and nativist Ming dynasty that succeeded the Mongols in 1368 reacted harshly against many aspects of the Yüan, yet
embraced Tao Learning orthodoxy more fervently than had any of its
predecessors. The Ming widely promulgated the Ch'eng-Chu interpretations of the classics, particularly through an expanded examination
system, and did not just officially endorse them. In 1415, it established
Tao Learning texts as the basis of the state curriculum to be "studied
and mastered by millions of examination candidates for the civil
service."[214]

Early Ming rulers and their house intellectuals were drawn to Tao
Learning not just by its nativist pedigree, but also by the facility with
which its precepts and principles might be adapted to promote civic
virtue—Ming-Chinese style. For example, "Chu Hsi's view on the priority of public values over private interests dovetailed neatly in
theoretical terms with [Ming autocracy's] negative view of factional
alignments in politics," as Benjamin Elman has remarked.[215] But Ming
imperial ideologists did not simply replicate Chu Hsi's philosophy in
the political realm. While "state ideology may have had many 'elective
affinities' with Confucian moral philosophy, . . . the political purposes
to which those affinities were applied were determined by the needs of
the state rather than the integrity of the philosophy."[216]

The close adherence to the Ch'eng-Chu school that marked the
early Ming gave way in the sixteenth century to the teaching of Wang
Yang-ming (1472–1529), which was later branded as heretical by Tao
Learning heresiographers of the seventeenth century. The Ming imperial state, however, continued to sponsor and support Ch'eng-Chu. In
1642, only two years before the fall of the dynasty, the last Ming emper-
or further elevated the place of the Sung masters of Tao Learning in the
Confucian Temple.[217] Like the Southern Sung before it, the Ming expe-

rienced a sort of deathbed conversion (or reconversion) to Ch'eng-Chu. The first emperors of the Ch'ing dynasty, which succeeded the Ming in 1644, raised official support for the Ch'eng-Chu school to new heights, renewing its perennial domination of the imperial civil service examination system, reprinting the works of the orthodox Sung philosophers, and elevating Chu Hsi's position in the Confucian temple.[218] Although new intellectual trends in the middle and late Ch'ing gradually displaced the Ch'eng-Chu teaching from the center of high-cultural gravity, this orthodox form of Neo-Confucianism continued to dominate the all-important examination system until the latter was officially abolished in 1905.

The making of Neo-Confucian orthodoxy after Chu Hsi was not, however, just an affair of state. It was also an intellectual and cultural process, though this does not necessarily mean that there were two distinct orthodoxies, the political and the intellectual. Indeed, these two aspects of Ch'eng-Chu orthodoxy were related to one another in intricate and subtle ways; both were "continually reconstructed" through their interaction.[219] Generally speaking, however, Ch'eng-Chu as state orthodoxy or imperial ideology was more "extracted from" than "reflective of" the intellectual orthodoxy.[220]

Considered as an intellectual and social phenomenon, Chu Hsi's version of Neo-Confucianism had certain advantages over its rivals that helped to bring about its initial triumph in the waning years of the Southern Sung. First, Tao Learning's emphasis on moral conduct and example provided a justification for the elite status of righteous scholars who faced diminished prospects of securing elite positions in government.[221] The moralistic focus of Tao Learning also suggested an attractively simple solution for China's pressing political and military problems: moral rearmament. This would presumably make China "less vulnerable to outside attack, either from 'barbarian' peoples or 'heterodox' religions."[222] Third, the comparatively exclusivist ethos of the Tao Learning adherents, based on the idea that they alone were the true transmitters of the Tao, gave them a greater degree of cohesion which actually seemed to increase under pressure. This facilitated the formation of networks, as well as the long-term survival of the group as a whole.[223] Fourth, Chu's heresiographical rhetoric, especially his presentation of Tao Learning as the orthodox mean between two heretical extremes, helped to discredit his rivals intellectually, as well as to establish his own preeminence. In sum, even if Chu Hsi's thought was not necessarily superior to its rivals as an intellectual or philosophical system, it was more definitely superior in the social (and in some cases anti-social) advantages it gave to its adherents. It was, in a word, the

Neo-Confucian school best suited to guide politics and society in an age of cultural despair.

The superior cohesiveness, commitment, and self-confidence of the Tao Learning group under Chu's influence also contributed to its spreading the faith through various cultural and educational activities, particularly "the many academies founded by Chu Hsi's pupils."[224] Ch'eng-Chu teachings in the Yüan and later even permeated popular culture, especially through vernacular literature and the performing arts.[225] George Orwell's remark that "Only the educated are completely orthodox" may be as applicable to premodern China as to most traditional societies.[226] But the extent of uneducated orthodoxy should not be underestimated.

While the Ch'eng-Chu version of Neo-Confucianism remained the state orthodoxy under the two imperial dynasties, the Ming and the Ch'ing, that succeeded the Yüan, Ch'eng-Chu's career as an intellectual orthodoxy was more checquered. In the first place, Ch'eng-Chu orthodoxy was not a monolith; not every later scholar in the tradition simply replicated the ideas of his illustrious orthodox predecessors. As is well known, even Chu Hsi diverged from the Ch'engs on such significant points as the interpretation of the *Changes Classic*. The noted fifteenth-century Ch'eng-Chu scholar, Hsüeh Hsüan (1392–1464), departed from Chu Hsi on the important cosmological issue of whether or not moral principle (*li*) is prior or superior to material force (*ch'i*). Even Lo Ch'in-shun (1465–1547), the most prominent Ch'eng-Chu philosopher of the Ming era, was impelled "to revise substantially a number of the primary metaphysical formulations of Ch'eng I . . . and Chu Hsi, as well as their views on human nature and the goals of cultivation."[227]

Not only did the Ch'eng-Chu scholars of the Yüan and Ming eras not maintain as strict a doctrinal or philosophical orthodoxy as was common in Western religious traditions, but the Ch'eng-Chu school itself did not dominate the intellectual world of late-traditional China to as great an extent as Catholicism dominated that of the medieval West. First, despite expressions of official support and sponsorship for Ch'eng-Chu during the Yüan and Ming eras, various forms of syncretism were in vogue during those periods. Almost as soon as the Southern Sung officially recognized the orthodoxy of Tao Learning in the middle of the thirteenth century, a syncretic movement to reconcile the Ch'eng-Chu teaching with that of its most celebrated philosophical rival, Lu Hsiang-shan, sprang up. The movement gathered such force that by the early fourteenth century, Wu Ch'eng (1249–1333), the most prominent Ch'eng-Chu scholar of the early Yüan era, "found it necessary to involve Lu's idea of 'honoring the moral nature' as a corrective to Chu's intellectual approach to the Confucian way."[228] Orthodox scholars of the early Ming era, such as Sung Lien (1310–1381), also adopted a conciliatory attitude toward Lu Hsiang-shan and his ilk, leading de Bary to remark on the liberality and catholicity of early-Ming Neo-Confucian orthodoxy.[229]

The widening or loosening of Neo-Confucian orthodoxy in the Ming reached a sort of culmination in the early sixteenth century with the teaching of the greatest Confucian thinker of the era, Wang Yang-ming. Unlike Chu Hsi, the grand heresiographer in the Neo-Confucian tradition, Wang had a rather low regard for polemics. He went so far as to criticize Mencius as "pitiable" for the tirelessness of his tirades against the ancient philosophers Mo Ti and Yang Chu, the principal heretics of his day.[230] Despite his being categorized by later historians as the principal successor of Lu Hsiang-shan and a major opponent of Chu Hsi, Wang expressed great respect for Chu, even where he disagreed with him: "All my life Chu Hsi's doctrine has been a revelation to me, as though from the gods."[231] There is some evidence that Wang's expression of admiration for Chu was not merely a polite formality, for Wang drew on Chu Hsi for the development of his own philosophy.[232] If some of Wang's more popular writings and statements exalt Lu Hsiang-shan over Chu, that was principally to rescue Lu from a state of relative neglect.[233]

Wang, however, was concerned not only with restoring the proper balance between Chu and Lu, but also with synthesizing the two. Although his harmonization of Chu and Lu was not the first work of that genre, it is by far the most notorious; it "left behind a legacy of controversy that continued long after his death."[234] This controversy centered principally on Wang's contention, expressed by a disciple, that Chu Hsi "when he reached old age . . . began to regret the mistakes of his previous effort toward self-cultivation in the spirit of genuine and personal concern" that brought him much closer to Lu Hsiang-shan (and to Wang Yang-ming).[235] As later critics pointed out, Wang's thesis in his *Chu Hsi's Final Conclusions of His Later Years* is undermined if not invalidated by his having mistaken some of Chu's earlier works for his later works. Wang himself all but admitted this, but protested that "my chief idea was that it was important to compromise as much as possible."[236]

Wang's compromising hand was extended not only to fellow Confucians, but also to Buddhists and Taoists. While he himself was a Confucian, Wang remarked that "the excellence of the two systems [Buddhism and Taoism] differs from that of the Sage only in infinitesimal amount."[237] Although the question of the extent of Buddhist and Taoist influence on Wang's teaching remains open to debate, it is at least clear that Wang opposed making polemical attacks against Buddhism and Taoism.[238] This opened the way for some of Wang's students to actively attempt to synthesize Confucianism with Buddhism and Taoism.

If Wang Yang-ming was so tolerant of even the maximum heterodoxies of his day, Buddhism and Taoism, did he have any standard of orthodoxy or heresy at all? Wang did, in fact, pronounce such a standard, though it was so ambiguous, subjective, and unrelated to matters of doctrine and belief that it could hardly have passed heresiographical muster in most traditions:

> Someone asked about heresy. The Teacher said, "What can be understood and practiced by men and women of simple intelligence is called universal virtue. What cannot be understood and practiced by men and women of simple intelligence is called a heresy."[239]

Wang Yang-ming's populist characterization of heresy perhaps contributed to the popularization of his teachings in the sixteenth century to the point that they seemed to eclipse, for a time, those of Ch'eng-Chu.[240]

By some accounts, the teachings of Wang and his school became so popular in the sixteenth century as to virtually displace Ch'eng-Chu orthodoxy in the intellectual life of China, if not in the official examination system, for more than a hundred years. The orthodox sixteenth-century heresiographer, Ch'en Chien, lamented that "in today's world, everyone reveres and believes in the school of Lu [Hsiang-shan]; and I alone reject it."[241] The early-Ch'ing philosopher, Chang Li-hsiang (1611–1674), complained that "the works of Ch'eng and Chu are not current in the world, while every household has the works of Lu and Wang."[242] From the perspective of T'ung Neng-ling (1683–1745), from the *Cheng-te* [1506–1522] through the *Ch'ung-chen* [1628–1644] periods, the teachings of Lu and Wang flourished while "Master Chu's school was virtually eclipsed."[243] Modern scholars have echoed these late-Ming and early-Ch'ing accounts of the Wang school's sixteenth-century apotheosis, Chu Wei-cheng remarking that "for a little over a hundred years it held a central place in Chinese intellectual and cultural circles," and de Bary commenting that it almost "replaced the 'Ch'eng-Chu' teaching as the official orthodoxy in the late sixteenth century."[244]

On the other hand, there are a couple of reasons for suspecting that such accounts of the Lu-Wang school's eclipse of Ch'eng-Chu in the sixteenth century may be a little overdrawn. First, the early-Ch'ing statements to this effect propound a heresiographical motif or *idée fixe* that goes back to Mencius: the presentation of self as a member of a tiny, embattled orthodox minority struggling to preserve or revive orthodoxy against the legions of error. Just as Mencius no doubt exaggerated in claiming that all the people of his time gravitated to one or the other of the two heresiarchs, Yang or Mo (*Mencius* 3B. 9), so seventeenth-century Ch'eng-Chu scholars may be suspected of having indulged in a little heresiographical hyperbole. In doing so, they were not only appropriating a common heresiographical trope but also buttressing their extravagant claim that the influence of Wang and his school was responsible for the decline and fall of the Ming dynasty. Unless the Wang school had been a major and even dominant cultural force in the late Ming era, it could not easily have caused such a monumental political catastrophe. Unfortunately, some modern scholars have overlooked both the heresiographical motif and the political circumstances that influenced early-Ch'ing scholars' accounts of the Wang school's domination of the late Ming intellectual scene, and have accepted their statements regarding the sixteenth-century displacement of Ch'eng-Chu orthodoxy a little too uncritically.

Some of these scholars have also cited the imperial decree of 1584, which honored Wang Yang-ming by enshrining his tablet in the Confucian temple, as further evidence of the Wang's school's displacement of Ch'eng-Chu orthodoxy. However, this recognition came more from Wang's political achievements than from his intellectual ones, and, moreover, was not won easily. Further, the publication of Wang's collected works, which took place at about the same time as he achieved official recognition, was accomplished by "a man of questionable conduct who compiled and published Wang's works for purely selfish reasons," and not by a band of devoted followers, indicating that "Wang Yang-ming's true followers must have been few or inattentive."[245] This, again, should lead us to question early-Ch'ing scholars' hyperbolic characterizations of the Wang school as a mighty force that swept all before it.

But the teachings and influence of Wang Yang-ming and his "school" were not the only major challenges to Ch'eng-Chu orthodoxy in the late Ming. Another, more pervasive and diffuse intellectual phenomenon was religious syncretism, which flourished in the Ming as never before in Chinese history at both the high intellectual and the popular levels.[246] Syncretic trends in the late Ming manifested themselves in at least two major forms, both of which were anticipated by Wang Yang-ming as well as earlier Tao Learning figures. The more

moderate of these forms sought to reconcile or harmonize the teachings of the major Confucian schools, such as those associated with
Ch'eng-Chu and Lu-Wang. Prominent among the advocates of this
form of Confucian syncretism were the leading members of the politi-
cal-intellectual party known as the Tung-lin school, particularly Ku
Hsien-ch'eng (1550–1612) and Kao P'an-lung (1562–1626), as well as
more independent philosophers such as Liu Tsung-chou (1578–1646)
and Sun Ch'i-feng (1584–1675). All of these figures, however, attempted to quarantine the more extremist and riotous outgrowths of the
Wang school which they stigmatized as "wild Ch'an."

Ironically, those whom these rather moderate Confucian syncretists most fervently condemned were also syncretists, though of a
different color. That is, many of the "wild Ch'anists" advanced the syncretist idea of the unitary nature of truth to a higher power, seeking to
harmonize the "three religions," Confucianism, Taoism, and Buddhism, and not just the Ch'eng-Chu and Lu-Wang schools. The most
prominent and notorious of these greater syncretists were associated
with the T'ai-chou school, sometimes characterized as "left-wing Wang
Yang-ming." They include the founder of the school, Wang Chi (1498–
1583), who wrote that "what the Buddha taught is fundamentally the
great path of us Confucians," Chou Ju-teng (1547–1629), who "argued
that Confucianism and Buddhism needed each other," Yüan Tsung-tao
(1560–1600), who claimed "that Buddhism was necessary for a proper
understanding of Confucianism," and Chiao Hung (c. 1540–1620), who
"used the Taoist concept of the transcendent Way to reconcile Confucianism and Buddhism."[247] Although seventeenth-century scholars'
testimonies to the strength of this "Unity of the Three Teachings"
movement in the late Ming may be open to question, this movement
was significant enough to elicit a vigorous response from more orthodox and purist Confucian scholars such as those associated with the
Tung-lin fellowship, cited above. As is often the case in intellectual history, these scholars concocted a lesser syncretism, that of properly
reformed Confucian schools, to combat a great syncretism, that which
sought to harmonize all of the major religious traditions known to the
sixteenth-century Chinese.

In sum, the degree to which the established Ch'eng-Chu orthodoxy was unmade in the late Ming is rather difficult to gauge,
particularly in view of the fact that the heresiographical histrionics of
seventeenth-century Tao Learning scholars can hardly be taken as objective accounts of the situation of orthodoxy under the Ming. A more
objective source on this issue might be the rigidly orthodox Korean vis-
itors to sixteenth-century China who noted "alarming trends . . . in

China's intellectual life," particularly "the adulteration of the Ch'eng-Chu legacy."[248] But even these accounts might be suspected of stretching a point in order to claim for Korea recognition as the new abode of the orthodox Way, a sort of Neo-Confucian Third Rome.

Whatever the state of orthodoxy in the late Ming, it was revived in the early Ch'ing with a vengeance and narrowness of conception that went beyond Chu Hsi. A major motive, or at least justification, for this revival among Confucian scholars and intellectuals of the day was the political catastrophe and social dislocation of the late-Ming era, culminating in the Manchu conquest of 1644. In view of the close association in Confucian thought between the state of culture and scholarship on the one hand, and that of politics and society on the other, it was both easy and natural to attribute the political collapse and social upheaval of the late Ming to the new intellectual fashions of that era associated with Wang and his followers. As it had in the late Southern Sung when it first arose to a position of orthodoxy, the rigorist, moralist Ch'eng-Chu teaching seemed to offer a means of moral rearmament in the face of political and social disasters. Like rabbinic Judaism, which attained a position of dominance in the years after the destruction of Jerusalem in A.D. 70, as well as Catholic Christianity, which defeated its heretical rivals in the fourth century just as imperial Rome itself was heading toward its final defeat, Tao Learning in both the Southern Sung and the early Ch'ing (as well as the late Ming) rode the wave of political catastrophe and cultural despair to a place of preeminence. In doing so, it accused its rivals, especially Wang Yangming's followers, of having promoted moral laxity and libertinism through their doctrine that the individual's own mind, and not the classics or the patterns of the world, was the primary locus of moral principle (li), truth, and value. In a world which believed that "the streets are full of sages," each acknowledging no authority higher than his own heart/mind, true sages, it seemed, could no longer be recognized; nor could traditional values and institutions easily be upheld or justified.

The neo-orthodox revival of the early Ch'ing had antecedents in the late Ming, particularly among the scholars of the revisionist Tung-lin fellowship, mentioned above, who sought to "ameliorate the excesses of the Yang-ming schoolmen and to reintegrate Wang's contributions into the orthodox mainstream."[249] But the Tung-lin partisans, conservative moralists though they were, were not rigorist or purist enough for their early-Ch'ing successors. Rather than admitting a lesser syncretism, that of the Ch'eng-Chu with a sanitized Lu-Wang, as a means of combatting a greater syncretism, the doctrine of the unity of the three teachings, the early-Ch'ing Ch'eng-Chu scholars rejected all forms of syncretism to an extent unprecedented in the Confucian intellectual tradition up to that time.

The most stalwart and prolific early-Ch'ing advocates of Ch'eng-Chu were probably Lu Lung-ch'i and Lü Liu-liang (1629–1683), both of whom saw little merit in any of their Neo-Confucian predecessors besides Chu Hsi. Lü, indeed, went so far as to remark that the Confucian Way had been in eclipse for about five hundred years, that is, ever since Chu's death.[250] Even the most celebrated Ming-era supporters of Chu Hsi's philosophy, Lo Ch'in-shun and Ch'en Chien (1497–1567), did not quite measure up to Lü's exacting standards.[251] Lü took a hard line on heresy, proclaiming that "If Mencius is right, then Yang and Mo are wrong. Thus, one cannot take a middle (or neutral) position."[252] He also rejected the argument that Wang Yang-ming should be excused on the grounds of extenuating historical circumstances, insisting that "there only exist the two words 'right' and 'wrong.'"[253] Lü was not only the most "hardline exponent of Ch'eng-Chu doctrine" in his day, but also one of the most influential. His views on orthodoxy and heresy were widely disseminated through his published lectures and discussions on the Four Books and through the collections of model examination essays that he edited, as de Bary has noted.[254]

While Lu Lung-chi's Ch'eng-Chu affiliation was not quite so pure and uncompromising as was Lü's, he too criticized his Ming predecessors, such as the Tung-lin scholars Ku Hsien-ch'eng and Kao P'an-lung, as not quite orthodox: "It is all right to say that they honored Master Chu, but not to say that they were of Master Chu's orthodox line."[255] While generally praising Lo Ch'in-shun, he also criticized him for having set aside Chu's cosmological teachings.[256] Even the relatively less rigorist Chang Li-hsiang (1611–1672) identified only two true exponents of the Confucian Way in the entire Ming dynasty, the early Ming scholars Hsüeh Hsüan and Hu Chü-jen (1434–1484).[257] For all three of these seventeenth-century scholars, moreover, Ch'eng-Chu orthodoxy had narrowed to the point of becoming Chu orthodoxy, as they seldom spoke of Ch'eng I or of Chu Hsi's other Neo-Confucian predecessors.

While one may lament this early-Ch'ing "tendency to define orthodoxy in narrower terms,"[258] it is certainly not a rare phenomenon in the history of orthodox traditions. It appears not only in the history of Western religious orthodoxies and in Hinduism,[259] but also in earlier Neo-Confucianism, as mentioned above. As several recent scholars have pointed out, Confucianism in the T'ang and early Sung eras was much more latitudinarian and pluralistic than in subsequent peri-

ods.[260] During the Southern Sung era, particularly the last two decades
of the twelfth century, Tao Learning developed under Chu Hsi's aegis
"from diversity to orthodoxy," or "from a loose association of individual intellectuals with divergent ideas into a school of thought
recognized as state orthodoxy."[261] Even Chu Hsi, however, was broader and more inclusive than were some of his later followers in drawing
the boundaries of Tao Learning orthodoxy.[262] Throughout this narrowing process, Tao Learning scholars, according to Hoyt Tillman,
"generated a mode of discourse involving terms of inclusion and exclusion: 'our Confucians,' 'this *Tao* of ours,' 'this culture of ours,' and
by the 1170s, even 'our faction.'"[263] This narrowing of Neo-Confucianism, moreover, was recapitulated not only in early Ch'ing China, as
outlined above, but also in Yi dynasty Korea, where Martina Deuchler
has noted "a growing intolerance of the guardians of orthodoxy to intellectual diversity."[264]

   The rising rigorism of Ch'eng-Chu orthodoxy in China, Korea,
and even eighteenth-century Japan, contrasts rather sharply with the
antisectarian sentiments expressed by its main philosophical rivals, Lu
Hsiang-shan and Wang Yang-ming.[265] Judging from these Neo-Confucian cases, as well as those in Western religious traditions, at least in
their later phases, it almost seems as though one of the patterns of later
religious evolution is the survival of the most exclusionary.

   Just as the narrowing of Neo-Confucianism in the late twelfth
century was followed within a few decades by its adoption as state orthodoxy, so the narrowing of neo-orthodox Neo-Confucianism in the
seventeenth century was a prelude to its official re-apotheosis in the
Ch'ing dynasty. At the behest of the K'ang-hsi emperor, Chu Hsi's
works were re-edited, a new Neo-Confucian anthology compiled, and
Chu Hsi's tablet in the Confucian temple moved up next to those of
Confucius' twelve classical disciples. "All this was a sign that the emperor favored the 'Back to Ch'eng-Chu' movement."[266] The Ch'ing
dynasty had ample reason for this patronage and reaffirmation of
Ch'eng-Chu orthodoxy. First, as the long-established orthodoxy of the
Chinese imperial state and cultural elite, it offered special attractions to
a dynasty of non-Chinese (Manchu) origin in search of political and
cultural legitimacy. Second, its emphasis on the maintenance of authority relations must have been particularly alluring to an
authoritarian regime. Third, by supporting Ch'eng-Chu, the dynasty
coopted a leading symbolic refuge of former Ming loyalists who had
initially opposed the Manchu conquest of China in 1644.[267] Finally, several staunch Ch'eng-Chu scholars of the early Ch'ing, particularly
Hsiung Tz'u-li (1635–1709), Li Kuang-ti (1642–1718) and Chang Po-

hsing (1651–1725), won imperial patronage and positions as house intellectuals. As On-cho Ng has noted, "Kuang-ti, in essence, assumed
the illustrious role of the imperial interpreter of orthodoxy."[268]

While the Ch'ing dynasty's official embrace might have heightened Ch'eng-Chu orthodoxy's appeal in some quarters, it may have
been the kiss of death in others. As Tu Wei-ming has noted, Li Kuang-
ti's "effort to promote Chu Hsi's teaching under imperial sponsorship
actually prompted a powerful yet subtle reaction against the official
line of interpreting the classics, or 'official learning.'"[269] But the decline
of Ch'eng-Chu orthodoxy in China from the middle of the eighteenth
century has its own internal dynamic in addition to the probable political cause just stated. This intellectual dynamic arose primarily from
the further extension of the purist attack on syncretism initiated by the
Tung-lin movement in the late Ming and continued by the Ch'eng-Chu
scholars of the early Ch'ing. Just as early-Ch'ing commentators faulted
their Tung-lin predecessors for not proceeding far enough in their de-
syncretization of the Confucian tradition, specifically for their
inclusion of a purified Wang Yang-ming, so mid-Ch'ing scholars criticized their earlier Ch'ing predecessors for their admission even of Chu
Hsi into that tradition. Suspecting that not just Wang Yang-ming but
even Chu Hsi and the Sung Neo-Confucians were tainted with Buddhist and Taoist heterodoxies, they sought to restore the allegedly
purer Confucianism of the Han dynasty that was closer to the classical
sources and relatively free of heterodox influences. In a sense, the early
Ch'ing Ch'eng-Chu scholars were eventually hoisted on their own pe-
tard of purism, a purism that ended by rejecting virtually the entire
Neo-Confucian tradition.[270] So powerful was the heresiographical impulse in this case that it ended by undermining the tradition it had set
out to defend.

Having recounted the historical processes by which orthodoxies
were made (and in some cases unmade) in four traditions, we are now
in a position to describe the self-definition of orthodoxy in these traditions. Rather than treating each tradition separately, as we did in this
chapter, we have organized the following more comparatively, by the
major points in orthodoxy's composite self-portrait. This accentuates
the similarities in the ways that orthodoxies, even those in widely separated traditions, conceive and present themselves.

3

THE CONSTRUCTION OF ORTHODOXY

While the historical development of the orthodoxies discussed in the previous chapter may differ widely from one religious tradition to another, their self-definitions show remarkable similarities. All of the orthodox traditions surveyed here attributed to themselves certain qualities, particularly *primacy* (or originality), *a true transmission* from the founder to the present day, *unity, catholicity,* and a conception of orthodoxy as a *middle way* between heretical extremes. Since these imagined attributes were in some cases rather far removed from reality, as the discussion in Chapter Two should make clear, the possibility arises that they had a generalized polemical value, which would help to explain their ubiquity. The party that convincingly portrayed itself in these terms could enhance its claim to the mantle of orthodoxy, however much or little this portrayal corresponded to reality. Thus, alongside the political and social factors that contributed to the making of orthodoxy in various religious traditions, the self-definition of orthodoxy might also have played a role in its triumph over other would-be orthodoxies that may have lacked such a winsome self-portrait. However, this self-portrait of orthodoxy is not entirely uniform from one tradition to another: orthodox traditions differed in the degree to which they accentuated as well as in the way they defined particular points in their self-definitions.

Primacy

It was in early Christianity that the idea of the primacy or originality of orthodoxy received the most emphasis. The classical expression of the view "that orthodoxy is primary and heresies are deviations, corruptions of a previously pure, virgin orthodoxy,"[1] appears prominently in the *Ecclesiastical History* of Eusebius (263–339), bishop of Caesarea in Palestine at about the time of the conversion of the Emperor Constantine:

. . . [U]ntil then [the early second century] the church had remained a virgin, pure and uncorrupted, since those who were
trying to corrupt the wholesome standard of the saving message,
if such there were, lurked somewhere under cover of darkness.
But when the sacred band of the apostles had in various ways
reached the end of their life, and the generation of those privi-
leged to listen with their own ears to the divine wisdom had
passed on, then godless error began to take shape, through the
deceit of false teachers, who now that none of the apostles was
left threw off the mask and attempted to counter the preaching
of the truth by knowledge falsely so called.[2]

This classical statement of the primacy of orthodoxy is based ultimately on a description by the early Christian heresiographer, Hegesippus, of the Church of Jerusalem, which Eusebius presents as
follows: "They used to call the church a virgin for this reason, that she
had not yet been seduced by listening to nonsense. But Thebuthis, because he had not been made bishop began to seduce her by means of
the seven sects."[3] Eusebius applied Hegesippus' metaphorical description of the primitive church at Jerusalem as a virgin unsullied to
the early Church in general. But he also presented Christian history as
"the record of the triumph of an unchanging orthodoxy over the attempts by heretics to introduce change and novelty,"[4] thus mitigating
the effects of the loss of primitive purity lamented by Hegesippus. Eusebius went on to condemn later heretics and heresies for their alleged innovations, calling the Montanists "newfangled," Paul of
Samosata (d. c. 268) an "innovator," and the heresy of Artemon a "recent novelty."[5]

    Although Eusebius was probably the most noted and influential
expositor of the notion of the primacy of orthodoxy and the novelty of
heresy, other Fathers of the early Church expressed similar opinions.
Irenaeus (c. 130–c. 200), for example, remarked that heretics "rose up
in their apostasy much later, in the middle of the Church's history."
Firmilian claimed that they "afterward introduced their wicked sects
and perverse inventions as each one was led by error." Clement of Alexandria (d. c. 215) said that heresies were much younger than the
Catholic Church, and Tertullian (c. 155–c. 222) that "Our teaching is
not later; it is earlier than them all." Gregory the Great (d. 604) argued
that "The Church is older than heresy, in every way its senior."[6] The
master heresiographer Epiphanius (315–402) went so far as to date the
primacy of orthodoxy from "the beginning of everything," not just
from Jesus and the apostles. In the beginning, he says:

There was no Judaism or Hellenism or any other sect, but so to speak the faith which now holds sway in the holy Catholic church of God, so recently founded, a faith which was in the beginning and which later was revealed again. For those who wish [to investigate?] the matter from love of truth, [it is possible?] to see, from the bearing of the history, [that] the beginning of everything is the holy Catholic church.[7]

Among the major patristic writers, only Origen (d. c. 254), it seems, showed an awareness that divergent doctrinal traditions might be "rooted not in later corruption but in primitive apostolic tradition."[8] But Origen was, of course, later himself condemned as heretical by the Church.

Less scrupulous Patristic writers not only proclaimed the primacy and originality of the orthodox faith but even went so far as to skew historical chronology so as to portray heresy as a later development. Hegesippus, for example, "manifests a tendency to move churchmen as close as possible to the generation of the apostles . . . while he obscures the chronology of the heretics so that they appear to be more recent."[9] And Tertullian, in the course of trying to establish the comparative lateness of heresies, placed Marcion's breach with the Church at a later date than when it actually occurred.[10]

The self-portrait of orthodoxy as "a virgin unsullied" was a major feature of Christian historiography through the seventeenth century. However, few historians nowadays accept this version of Christian history in its pure form, as noted above in Chapter Two. Some even affirm that heretics are often the more conservative party inasmuch as they refuse to accept new doctrinal formulations.[11] But in a society and culture that associated antiquity with truth, orthodoxy could not afford to present itself as novel, especially when Roman authorities were more likely to give protection to established sects than to newcomers.[12]

Orthodox Sunnis in Islam were at least as inclined as their Christian counterparts to portray their faith as the pure and primary form that had remained unchanged from the beginning, "lacking any history of development."[13] All innovations were, by definition, heretical: the primary meaning of one of the major Arabic words for heresy, bid'a, is "innovation," as mentioned above in Chapter One. In the case of Sunni Islam, the association of innovation with heresy was prompted not only by polemical requirements, but also by a "dislike of change and novelty" that "goes back to pre-Islamic times when the accepted ideal was to follow exactly the time-honoured practice of the tribe or clan."[14] Small wonder, then, that many Sunni apologists' condemnations of religious innovations are so absolute and unqualified, particularly those of the fideist Hanbalites. According to Ibn Qudama (d. 1223), "every innovation is a heretical innovation, and every heretical innovation is an error."[15] Ibn Batta (d. 997) attributed to the Prophet the words: "whoever honors an innovator contributes to the destruction of Islam."[16] The Ash'arite apologist Ibn 'Asakir (1106–1176) also recognized no shades of gray where innovation was concerned: "There is no good superior to the Sunna, nor is there any evil worse than innovation."[17] Indeed, *sunna* (the beaten path or standard practice of the Prophet) and *bid'a* (innovation) were not only antithetical in a religious sense, but also antonyms in a linguistic sense.

Both Ash'arites and Hanbalites claimed that their own particular sect was not really a "sect" (*firqa*), much less an "innovative" one. Rather, it was "the continuation of the pristine condition of Islam."[18] But partisans of other "sects," including Shi'ites, also claimed that their views "existed from the beginning and never changed in essence."[19] Indeed, the Shi'ites' tracing of their line of imams back to the Prophet was conceived as a proof of the primordiality of Shi'ism.

Although Sunni orthodoxy did not emerge as such before the latter half of the ninth century, this could hardly have been admitted by orthodox apologists and polemicists. For such an admission would have decisively undermined the legitimacy of orthodoxy. The defenders of even such an innovative figure as the theologian al-Ash'ari endeavored to minimize his originality and novelty to the greatest extent possible.[20] For the revelation was complete and final with Muhammad, the Seal of the Prophets, who defined once and for all the bounds of both orthodoxy and orthopraxy. But ironically, even the doctrine that Muhammad was the Seal of the Prophets was a later innovation in orthodox Sunni theology.

Like the Fathers of the Church who were their near contemporaries, the early rabbis held that their tradition was primordially an "uncorrupted virgin," and more generally and less metaphorically that "truth precedes error, that heresy is a corruption of the one, holy, and true."[21] But as with orthodox Christians and Sunnite Muslims, there is evidence that the rabbis were more innovative than were some of their rivals.[22] In any case, the rabbis' rather questionable status vis a vis earlier Jewish tradition made it all the more important for them to appropriate this tradition for themselves through such techniques as the anachronistic rabbinization of scriptural heroes such as Moses and David.

Neo-Confucian scholars of the Ch'eng-Chu persuasion also occasionally affirmed the primacy of Confucianism in the world, and the

relative lateness of heterodoxy. The early Ch'ing scholar, Hsiung Tz'u-
li (1635–1709), for example, declared that "from the beginning of the
world through [the legendary sage kings of high antiquity] Fu Hsi and
Shen Nung until the Yellow Emperor and Confucius, the universe contained only Confucians. With the coming forth of Lao-tzu, heretical
learning originated."[23] The early Ming scholar, Hsüeh Hsüan (1392–
1464), also attested to the historical priority of the Confucian Way and
the relative lateness of Taoist heterodoxy:

> Confucius transmitted but did not create, studying the Way of the
> sages and worthies. To *not* transmit the words of the sages and
> worthies and to establish one's own new-fangled theories is to
> distance oneself from the Way. Thus Lao-tzu and Chuang-tzu did
> not transmit the words of the former sages but concocted their
> own new-fangled theories, thereby inventing heresies.[24]

As de Bary points out, later Ch'eng-Chu opponents of Wang Yang-ming
similarly condemned the latter for his "new learning" and "new interpretations."[25]

True Transmission

Ch'eng-Chu scholars' accounts of the primacy of Tao Learning
were commonly expressed more indirectly. Rather than emphasize the
primordiality of their form of Confucianism, the Neo-Confucians of
the Ch'eng-Chu school were more inclined to insist that they were the
legitimate heirs of the Way transmitted from classical times. In other
words, most Ch'eng-Chu scholars concentrated less on the point that
orthodoxy was established from the beginning and more on the argument that its basic principles had been authentically transmitted, albeit
interruptedly, from the classical sages to themselves. In this Neo-Confucian schema, heresy was not so much a corruption of an originally
pure orthodoxy as it was a position (or positions) outside of the orthodox line of transmission. The major concern of Ch'eng-Chu
heresiographers was to distinguish those of their predecessors and
contemporaries who fell into this line of transmission from those who
did not.[26]

The germ of the idea of the transmission of the Way in China has
been traced back to the classical Confucian philosophers. According to
the modern scholar, Hsiao Kung-ch'üan, Confucius himself alluded to
such a transmission in remarking, in a moment of peril, that "Since
heaven does not wish to forfeit this culture [which had been passed

down to him from King Wen], then what can the people of K'uang do to me?" (Analects 9.5).[27] The early-Ch'ing stalwart of Tao Learning, Chang Po-hsing (1652–1725), identified the famous final passage in the *Mencius* (7B. 38) which posits (and predicts) the appearance of a sage every five hundred years as the *locus classicus* for the transmission of the Way through a succession of sages.[28] In postclassical times, the idea of a lineage of sages was further developed in the arrangement of Han masters of classical exegesis as well as Taoist hierarchs in lines of descent, and later in the Ch'an doctrine of patriarchal transmission.[29] But the more immediate predecessor of the Neo-Confucian version of the transmission of the Way was the T'ang scholar and literatus, Han Yü (768–824), who delineated a Confucian genealogy of the Way in his famous essay "On the Origins of the Way" (*Yüan-tao lun*):

> Yao transmitted this [Way] to Shun [who] transmitted this to Yü [who] transmitted this to T'ang [who] transmitted this to Wen, Wu, and the Duke of Chou [who] transmitted this to Confucius [who] transmitted this to Mencius. When Mencius died no one received the transmission.[30]

Unlike the Ch'an transmission of the lamp, which depended upon direct face-to-face encounters between master and disciple, Han's genealogy of the Way was interrupted between the Duke of Chou and Confucius as well as after the death of Mencius, to be revived several hundred years later, presumably by Han Yü himself. This Confucian Way did not have to be transmitted by physical contact or by word of mouth, but could be mediated through texts, specifically by the classical texts that contained the words of the sages. Unencumbered by the classical Taoist and Ch'an distrust of words and language, Confucians and Neo-Confucians held that a proper comprehension of these words could resume the interrupted transmission of the Way, even after a hiatus of more than a thousand years.

Just when and by whom this transmission was resumed was not settled in the Tao Learning tradition until Chu Hsi. Although Han Yü's general idea of the genealogy of the Way (as well as his exaltation of Mencius) was apparently shared by several of his contemporaries, it did not achieve wide intellectual currency until the rise of Tao Learning in the late eleventh century.[31] Later Tao-Learning genealogists generally excluded Han himself from the main line of the orthodox transmission of the Way, complaining that he was not pure enough to meet their high standards. According to Chu Chen (1072–1138), the transmission of the Way, broken off after Mencius, was "rediscovered and taken up by the Ch'eng brothers . . . during the Northern Sung. Henceforth their school was the champion of true orthodoxy."[32] Ch'eng I (1033–1107) made a similar claim on behalf of his elder brother, Ch'eng Hao (1032–1085), who "had recovered the learning of the sages" that no one since Mencius had understood.[33]

But it was Chu Hsi himself who established the transmission of the Way as the core concept of Tao Learning and gave it its standard name: *Tao-t'ung*. His first extant use of the term is in his preface to his commentary on the *Doctrine of the Mean* (Chung-yang chang-chü) (1189), one of the newly canonized Four Books.[34] In this preface, Chu not only relates how the Way was transmitted from the ancient sage kings to Confucius and his classical successors, but he also identifies the core or essence of that Way as the famous "sixteen-character transmission" from the "Counsels of the Great Yü" chapter of the *Documents Classic*: "What they transmitted among themselves was nothing more than this carefully repeated admonishment [i.e., the sixteen-character transmission]" distinguishing the "human mind" from the "mind of the Way."[35]

Chu Hsi's rearticulation and specification of the "transmission of the Way" was a major factor in establishing the orthodoxy of Tao Learning in the Sung and later eras. For it elevated a rather loose and unrepresentative collection of Sung thinkers into the position of being the orthodox successors of the ancient sages, while excluding their rivals. It was also a mainstay of Tao Learning's self-definition or self-conceptualization, as manifested in the intellectual genealogies composed by Chu and his Tao Learning successors.[36] By the end of the Sung era, the idea of the *Tao-t'ung* had become so strongly entrenched that the Tao Learning scholar Wang Po (1197–1274) went so far as to elevate it to the status of a cosmic principle that was immanent in heaven-and-earth even before the appearance of the sages.[37]

After Chu Hsi, a perennial theme in Neo-Confucian discourse was the identification of those who deserved to be included in the orthodox transmission of the Way, which presents a significant contrast to Western theologians' emphasis on the identification of heretics. On the one hand, some Ming and Ch'ing scholars simply reaffirmed Chu Hsi's version of the transmission of the Way without altering or adding to it.[38] On the other, the question of "through whom the succession ran, after Chu Hsi and his immediate disciples" became a pressing and divisive issue in Ming and Ch'ing times.[39] Orthodox anthologists of the Ch'ing era, such as Chang Po-hsing, T'ang Chien (1778–1861), and Fang Tung-shu (1772–1851), identified the early Ming scholars Hsüeh Hsüan and Hu Chü-jen (1434–1484) and the early Ch'ing scholars

Chang Li-hsiang (1611–1674) and Lu Lung-ch'i (1630–1692) as the orthodox continuators of Ch'eng-Chu in their respective eras.[40] Other
Ch'ing scholars, particularly Lü Liu-liang (1629–1683), rearticulated
the old Confucian theme of the degeneration of the Tao following the
demise of a great sage. According to Lü, the Tao had been in eclipse for
the five hundred years between the death of Chu Hsi and his own
time,[41] thus providing an opportunity for Lü's own brilliance to shine
forth to end the demi-millennial dark.

So popular and pervasive did the notion of the transmission of
the Way become in Ming and Ch'ing times that other schools of Confucian thought, apart from the Ch'eng-Chu, propounded their own
versions. Wang Yang-ming (1472–1528) devised an alternative *Tao-
t'ung* that resembled the Ch'eng-Chu version insofar as it broke off after Mencius and was revived by the Northern Sung masters. But
Wang's line of succession replaced the tradition of Ch'eng I and Chu
Hsi with Ch'eng Hao, Lu Hsiang-shan (1139–1192), and himself.[42] The
statecraft-oriented Ming scholar, Huang Wan (1477–1551), also rejected
the Ch'eng-Chu version of the transmission of the Way and devised his
own statecraft-oriented *Tao-t'ung*.[43] Han Learning scholars of the
Ch'ing era, such as Chiang Fan (1761–1831), likewise replaced the Tao
Learning lineage with their own transmission.[44] In modern times, the
paramount Neo-Confucian philosopher, Mou Tsung-san, devised yet
another version of the Confucian *Tao-t'ung*. As John Berthrong has remarked, Mou's "concern for the definition of orthodoxy and the
proper understanding of the 'transmission of the Way' is highly traditional. Nothing could be more Confucian than worrying about lineage
and teachings."[45]

In early Christianity, a rough analogue of the Neo-Confucian
"transmission of the Way" appears in the doctrine of apostolic succession. But the standard version of this Christian idea, propounded by
Ireneaus, has more in common with the Ch'an Buddhist transmission
of the lamp in that it apparently depended upon direct contact between master and disciple: "the apostles had been instructed by Christ;
they appointed elders as their successors, who, in their turn, appointed
their successors, and so on in a continuous line."[46] Unlike the Ch'an
transmission, however, that of early orthodox Christianity was made
visible and public in order "to refute the esoteric, unverifiable oral traditions of the Gnostics."[47]

Although this early Christian apostolic succession may have had
little basis in historical reality, it was nevertheless an effective polemical weapon against both the Gnostics and later heretics. But however
polemically effective, the idea of the apostolic succession was not quite

so essential to the defense of early Christian orthodoxy as the "transmission of the Way" was to that of Tao Learning. It was actually more useful in the consolidation of ecclesiastical authority than of orthodox doctrine. Indeed, Eusebius' version of the apostolic succession, propounded in his *Ecclesiastical History*, "laid no emphasis on the transmission of correct doctrine," but focused instead on episcopal succession.[48]

Given the Rabbanites' emphasis on their role as custodians of an Oral Torah, allegedly revealed to Moses on Sinai but not recorded as part of the Pentateuch, the rabbis were more constrained than were their early Christian counterparts to produce a chain of transmission to legitimize this central feature of their faith. Lacking such a chain, the canonicity of the Oral Law, adherence to which was the touchstone of rabbinic orthodoxy, could hardly be validated. A statement of a chain of transmission does appear in the Mishnah Abot, which records that "Moses received Torah at Sinai and handed it on to Joshua, Joshua to elders, and elders to prophets. And prophets handed it on to the men of the great assembly," and so on.[49] The "Torah" in this passage was generally understood as referring to the Oral Law as well as the Written,[50] the first extant redaction of which is the Mishnah itself.

This rabbinic "chain of tradition" was later reaffirmed and elaborated in response to the Karaite rebellion against the authority of the Talmud in the eighth century.[51] In later medieval times, such noted authorities as Rabad of Posquières (b. c. 1120), Abraham ibn Daud (c. 1110–1180), and Moses Maimonides (1135–1204) further extended it.[52] Maimonides, for example, presents "a chain of rabbinic authority that reaches from Sinai down to the point of composition of the *Mishneh-Torah* in the year 4937 A.M. (1177 C.E.)."[53] By thus validating the canonicity of the Oral Torah, these rabbinic authorities simultaneously bolstered the legitimacy of rabbinic institutions that were based on a general belief in that Torah. They also retroactively presented all of their predecessors in the "chain," back to and including Moses, as rabbis.

There is a notable resemblance between this rabbinic chain of tradition and the apostolic succession of the early Christian church, as well as the Neo-Platonic "golden chain" that linked Plato with the later Neo-Platonists.[54] Indeed, "The notion of succession was widespread in Hellenistic philosophy" in general.[55] That this idea of a chain of succession occurs so widely in various religious and philosophical traditions should not be too surprising, even when their mutual influences are removed from consideration. For the formulation of a chain of tradition is one of two major ways by which later adherents of a religion can demonstrate fidelity to the founder and his teachings, the other way being interpretation of the words of the sacred text of that religion. But despite its resemblance to the orthodox Christian idea of apostolic succession, the rabbinic chain of tradition was less open and public, in this respect more similar to that of the heretical Gnostics. It, indeed, had to be somewhat less open; if it were not, the relatively esoteric quality of the Oral Torah, and even its orality, might be hard to account for.

The general idea of a chain of tradition was also integral to Sunnite Islam, which was based on the *sunna*, the standard practice or "beaten path" of the Prophet. Being so widely and unquestioningly accepted, it did not have to be reaffirmed so frequently or stridently as did the "transmission of the Way" in Ch'eng-Chu Neo-Confucianism. It became an issue only in a sort of negative way, as a counterpoint against the extravagant imamologies of the Shi'ites that threatened to deroutinize charisma by establishing a chain of charismatic imams who did not simply transmit revelation but embodied it. So widely and firmly established was the notion of a chain of tradition in the Islamic world that rabbinic commentators even used it to argue by analogy for the validity of the Oral Torah and its transmissions.[56]

In Sunnite Islam, there seems to have been an even greater emphasis than in the other religious traditions surveyed here on the tradition's having been transmitted in its pristine state without any alteration or elaboration. Thus later Islamic commentators tried to fit those of their predecessors who played some role in the transmission of Islam into one monolithic mold, neglecting their individual differences or distinctive views.[57] Such commentators also expended much effort in authenticating the chains of transmission (*isnad*) of the *hadith*, which purportedly recorded the anecdotes and actions of Muhammad, even developing their method into a science. They insisted that the authentic "*hadith* or Traditions about Muhammad had been handed on with complete verbal accuracy from the Companions to later generations of Muslims."[58]

The general idea of a chain of tradition for the transmission of truth is not limited to religious or philosophical traditions of the past, but appears in modern ideologies and even in the history of science. In the latter field, in particular, "It places disparate individuals in an imagined community of like-minded searchers after truth."[59] For example, it creates such fictions as that Newton simply took up where Galileo and Kepler left off in the development of a modern physics and astronomy. In the history of science, in contrast to the history of religion, the various links in the genealogical chain are supposed to develop truth, not simply transmit it. But in either case, the production of a scholastic genealogy entails "the loss of the differences" between its various members.[60]

Unity

Apart from primacy and fidelity to the teaching of Christ as transmitted through the apostolic tradition, a third major feature of the self-portrait of early Christian orthodoxy was its unity and consistency. Heretics, in contrast, were supposedly "marked by inconsistency, multiplicity, and novelty." "The truth is one, while 'the sects' . . . form a multitude."[61] This notion of the unity of orthodoxy may be traced as far back as the New Testament Book of Acts which maintains that "The apostolic churches stand in complete harmony with one another."[62] In Acts, "Paul is made to look as Petrine as possible and Peter as Pauline as possible."[63]

Having been adumbrated in Acts, the idea of orthodox unity was definitively expressed by the Church Fathers. Irenaeus wrote that the Church "believes these points [of doctrine] just as if she had but one soul, and one and the same heart, and she proclaims them, and teaches them, and hands them down, with perfect harmony, as if she possessed only one mouth."[64] According to Epiphanius, heretics are just the opposite, "with each one saying something different, in a different way, at a different time."[65] Heretical parties "did nothing but stutter while they sang their rival songs and, each in its own way, they completely missed the truth of the matter."[66] Cyprian (d. 258) devoted an entire treatise to the subject of the unity of the Church and its doctrine, in which he proclaimed that "That unity cannot be broken; that one body cannot be divided by any cleavage of its structure, nor cut up in fragments with its vitals torn out."[67] This, Cyprian illustrated by the metaphor of the cloak of the crucified Christ:

> This holy mystery of oneness, this unbreakable bond of closeknit harmony is portrayed in the Gospel by our Lord Jesus Christ's coat, which was not divided or cut at all, but when they drew lots for the vesture of Christ to see which of them should put on Christ, it was the whole coat that was won, the garment was acquired unspoiled and undivided.[68]

So enamored were the Church Fathers with the idea of unity that they applied it not only to the teaching and organization of the Church as a whole, but also to particular points of doctrine: they affirmed "that there is one God, one canon of Scripture, one church, and one Jesus

Christ."[69] And so compelling was the picture of orthodox unity (and heretical multiplicity) presented by the Fathers that it continues to influence modern scholars' accounts of the early Church, even that of the iconoclastic Walter Bauer, who questions the priority of orthodoxy, but not its unity.[70] In none of the orthodox traditions surveyed here has the mystique of unity exerted such a powerful attraction through the ages as in Christianity.

Yet this highly touted unity of Christian orthodoxy is questionable. As Basil (d. 379) pointed out as early as the fourth century, "Not only is heresy divided against orthodoxy, but even right doctrine against itself."[71] Basil thus anticipated Chairman Mao's epoch-making discovery of contradictions among the people. However, when differences did appear in the orthodox camp in post-Nicene Christianity, the belief in orthodox unity tended to become a self-fulfilling prophecy that helped to bring about the narrowing of orthodoxy through the exclusion of those who threatened to disrupt this unity.

Since Sunni orthodoxy harbored several distinct theological and legal schools, the idea of orthodox unity was a little harder to maintain in Islam than in post-Nicene Christianity. But Sunni apologists and heresiographers were at least able to plausibly project this unity back upon the early years of Islam when "a unified theocratic community" had supposedly existed.[72] The breakup of this community ushered in the "fragmentation of an earlier and absolutely monolithic unity."[73] Still, later Sunni heresiographers who operated in a consensual mode sometimes chose to downplay this fragmentation, at least among parties with some claim to orthodoxy. Both al-Baghdadi (d. 1037) and al-Shahrastani (1086–1153), for example, passed over the differences between the emerging Ash'arite and Maturidite theological schools, the two most orthodox Sunni schools.[74] Even the great Hanbalite polemicist, Ibn Taymiyya (1263–1368), asserted that the more orthodox were the more unified and the more heretical the more fragmented:

[T]he people who follow the Messenger most closely disagree among themselves less than all other groups who claim to adhere to the Sunna. All those who are close to the Sunna disagree among themselves less than those who are far from it, such as the Mu'tazilis and the Rafidis, whom we find to be in disagreement amongst themselves more than any other group.[75]

Shahrastani concurred that the Shi'a Imamites among the Rafidites ("Rejectors") were the most fractious of all: "Their differences, indeed, are more numerous than those of all other sects put together."

So lost and scattered were the various Imamite sub-sects that "Even God did not seem to care in what *wadi* he destroyed them."[76]

Of all the orthodox traditions surveyed here, that of rabbinic Judaism put the least polemical emphasis on its unity. As an ethnic religion, Judaism's unity was in a sense inborn or implicit, and thus did not have to be asserted so vigorously or maintained so carefully as in those multi-ethnic and multi-cultural religions, Christianity and Islam. Nevertheless, at least one important figure in medieval Judaism, Maimonides, did assert that orthodoxy "united its believers and held them together," while "heresy was primarily characterized by quarrelsomeness and divisiveness."[77] The great medieval Jewish apologist, Judah Halevi (c. 1086–1145), applied such a dichotomy to the criticism of a particular Jewish heresy, remarking that "The Sages are in accord, the Karaites in discord."[78] On the other hand, the Karaite heresiographer, al-Qirqisani (fl. 930–940), asserted that the gap between the Rabbanites of Syria and those of Iraq was greater than that between either of them and the Karaites. This, he said, "discredits their claim to represent tradition and to derive their practices from the prophets."[79] Like other heresiographers, al-Qirqisani seems to have assumed that truth is unified while error is diverse. A memorable image illustrating this principle appears in the Theravada Buddhist tradition:

> Altogether there were eighteen sects: seventeen schismatic traditions and one orthodoxy. The most excellent Theravada is like a great banyan tree: it represents the complete teaching of the Buddha with nothing added to it and nothing taken away. The other sects grew from it like thorns on a tree.[80]

Expressions of the idea that orthodoxy is united and heresy multifarious also appear occasionally in the writings of Ch'eng-Chu Neo-Confucians. The Ch'ing scholar, Tang Ch'eng, for example, remarked that "the orthodox Way is one road while depraved paths are myriad."[81] Hsüeh Hsüan maintained that the orthodox were really unified, despite appearances, while the heterodox philosophers were just the opposite:

> Although the words of the sages have fragmentary sayings, by juxtaposing them they can all be strung together. The books of the [heterodox] philosophers are not lacking in fine words. But if one tries to combine them one by one to produce a unity, there will be some intractable points.[82]

In those areas where Ch'eng-Chu anthologists saw variations among more recent Tao Learning philosophers, they tried to gloss over these disparities in the interest of presenting the impression of a greater coherence.[83] In fact, the manufacture of such a coherence among those philosophers who "transmitted the Way" was one of the major aims of these anthologists.

Catholicity

Just as early Christianity developed the mystique of orthodox unity more fully than did the other religious orthodoxies surveyed here, so did it also develop the related idea of the catholicity of orthodoxy. According to the very famous and widely cited rule propounded by Vincent of Lérins (fl. c. 434), catholicity was indeed the primary standard of orthodoxy: "in the catholic church itself especial care must be taken that we hold to that which has been believed everywhere, always, and by all men. For that is truly and rightly 'catholic,' as the very etymology of the word shows, which includes almost all universally."[84] Writing two centuries later, the great early medieval encyclopedist, Isidore of Seville (d. 636), gave a particular geographical spin to the idea of the catholicity of orthodoxy. Whereas the Catholic church was universal, "The conventicles of the heretics are not like this, but are drawn together tightly in each region, not scattered and diffused throughout the whole world."[85]

To Christian writers of the second and third centuries, however, orthodoxy was catholic not so much in its demographical and geographical preponderance (which it could not yet justifiably claim) as in its openness, as opposed to the secret traditions of the Gnostics. According to Tertullian, "The Lord spoke openly without any hint of any hidden mystery. He had himself commanded them to preach in the light and on the house-tops whatever they had heard in secret."[86] The earliest extant Christian heresiography, that by Irenaeus, also contrasted the secret traditions of the Gnostics and the esoteric prophecies of the Montanists, transmitted to only a chosen few, with the open proclamation of the orthodox apostolic tradition to all.[87] Hippolytus also "makes much of the secret character of heretical doctrines and his program consists in breaking that secret."[88] With the progressive narrowing of doctrinal orthodoxy in the centuries between Irenaeus and Chalcedon, however, the Church's catholicity came to rest less in its openness and inclusiveness, and more in its claim to represent the preponderant view of Christians everywhere. But so strait and subtle was the gate of Trinitarian and Christological orthodoxy erected at Nicea, Constantinople, and Chalcedon that one wonders how this catholic majority could have successfully negotiated it without help from above. Even the saintly Hilary of Poitiers (d. 367) admitted that he was "always in danger, ever fearful of going aside from the narrow paths, or of falling into the ditches, or of being ensnared by the traps."[89] John Henry Cardinal Newman was not the first to have noted "the 'straitness' of the true faith, and the difficulty of finding and keeping it, in the case of thinking and speculative minds."[90]

While early Christian writers frequently used the idea of the catholicity of orthodoxy as a polemical weapon to condemn heretics whom they claimed had only local followings, their counterparts in Sunnite Islam were more inclined to use catholicity to conciliate rather than to condemn. Indeed, the Ash'arite school, reputedly the most orthodox of Muslim theological schools, was also one of the most conciliatory and harmonizing, at least in its early phases. "Al-Ash'ari [himself] was a genuine eclectic whose wish it was to reconcile all the established Sunni tendencies: at times he would take a Shafi'ite position; at others, he would express himself as a Malikite or even, occasionally, as a Hanbalite."[91] Small wonder that the theology of the Ash'arite school in general took on a multiformed dimension: "sometimes more rational, sometimes more faithful to the texts, particularly the *hadith*; sometimes more concerned with discovering the true face of God, sometimes more inclined toward the logic and coherence of His language."[92] Al-Ghazali, probably the greatest Ash'arite thinker after Ash'ari himself, pushed Ash'arite eclecticism to the extreme of declaring that the non-eclectic were heretical: "whoever makes truth the preserve of any one theologian is himself nearest to heresy . . . because he gives his master a rank that belongs only to the Prophet."[93] Only by combining the views of several later theologians could one hope to approach the catholicity of the Prophet.

Although the early Ash'arites carried doctrinal catholicity to its greatest extent, Sunni Islam in general was founded on the notion of consensus (*ijma'*) which "came to be accepted as the central pillar of orthodoxy."[94] In contrast to the Shi'ites, who gloried in the memory of their martyrs, Sunni theologians and heresiographers had a marked tendency to gloss over sectarian controversies in the early history of Islam, and even to glorify the actors on both sides: "An attempt is made to forget that they had fought one another so bitterly, and to hold to the fact only that they were brother Muslims."[95] So powerful was the "catholic instinct" in Sunni Islam that some of its adherents changed the famous saying attributed to the Prophet, that only one of the proverbial seventy-three sects of Islam would be saved, to say that only one of the seventy-three would *not* be saved.[96]

With respect to the four orthodox Sunni schools of law, as opposed to those of theology, later Sunni orthodoxy was also quite latitudinarian and accommodationist. Despite the doctrinal diversity of these schools, as well as their mutual hostility during their formative period, they "are seen as different but inseparable aspects of the same unity."[97] The idea of the "mutual orthodoxy" of these schools of law was most highly developed by the sixteenth-century legal philosopher, ash-Sha'rani (fl. 1530), who "rationalises and minimises the existing differences between them."[98] Indeed, so wide was the catholic embrace of Sunnism that it accommodated some of the more moderate of its archenemies, the Shi'ites. However, the catholicity of the Sunnites did not preclude their engaging in spirited polemics, particularly against those esoteric or extremist sects that they regarded as uncatholic. To those who place such a high premium on catholicity as a means of Islamic self-preservation, any who resisted harmonization and conciliation were all the more despicable and dangerous.

While the early Christians claimed to be catholic in a social, geographical, or demographical sense, rabbinic Judaism was more concerned with a catholicity of the intellect. The intellectual catholicity of early rabbinic orthodoxy was set at the convocation of the protorabbis at Yavneh around A.D. 90, which sought to end Jewish sectarianism and to create a society that accommodated and even encouraged disputes among its members.[99] The rabbis at Yavneh supposedly even celebrated their accomodationism. As R. Elazar ben Azaria is reported to have said at Yavneh, the words of two disputing parties were both correct, both the words of the Living God, even when they contradicted one another: "So you too shall fill your heart with chambers and make room for the words of Beit Shammai and the words of Beit Hillel, the words of those who declare unclean and those who declare clean."[100]

But the catholicity of early rabbinic Judaism was not confined to accommodating rabbinic disputants. According to Jacob Neusner, this form of Judaism was "unique in its catholic definition of 'Israel'," in "its insistence that all Israel be holy and be made holy."[101] While Rabbanites through the ages were no strangers to polemics, this conciliatory stance of early rabbinic Judaism retained enough influence to foster occasional compromise with later sectarian movements. In the early nineteenth century, for example, Rabbanites reached an accommodation with the Hasidim, after decades of strife and polemics between the two groups.[102]

The mystique of catholicity may have been most pronounced in early Christianity, and accommodationist sentiment strongest in Sunni Islam and rabbinic Judaism. But the contrast between orthodox catholicity and heretical partiality was most frequently drawn in Neo-Confucianism. This may stem in part from the fact that the Chinese character for "orthodox" or "correct" (cheng) may mean "to achieve completeness, as distinguished from partiality."[103] It might also be traced to a famous saying by Confucius recorded in the Analects: "The gentleman is catholic and not partisan; the inferior man is partisan and not catholic" (Analects 2.14). Mencius, the second sage of Confucianism, attributed to Confucius himself this gentlemanly quality, contrasting Confucius' complete and perfect virtue with the partial virtues of earlier legendary sages, Po-i, I-yin, and Liu-hsia Hui.[104] The great synthesizer of Sung Neo-Confucianism, Chu Hsi, borrowed Mencius's characterization of Confucius as "a complete concert" (chi ta-ch'eng) to describe his own illustrious predecessor, Ch'eng I, and to contrast him with the "partial" Neo-Confucian, Chang Tsai (1020–1077).[105]

Ch'eng-Chu scholars of the Ming and Ch'ing eras repeated this litany of orthodox catholicity vs. heterodox partiality, though they increasingly referred to orthodox and heterodox traditions as a whole rather than to specific sages. Hu Chü-jen, for example, contrasted the narrowness, rigidity, and specialization of Buddhism with Confucianism's encompassing the myriad things.[106] Lo Ch'in-shun remarked more metaphorically that "When one looks at heretical doctrines and heterodox theories, they are really like rivulets in comparison with the vast ocean."[107] In the early Ch'ing era, Lu Shih-i (1611–1672) posited the nonsectarianism of Confucianism; and Li Kuang-ti (1642–1718) contrasted Confucianism's comprehensiveness with the narrow focus of Buddhism and Taoism.[108] Finally, the eighteenth-century Japanese Neo-Confucian scholar, Rai Shunsui, characterized Ch'eng-Chu Confucianism as "a synthesis of the fundamental and the derivative," while charging that "Heterodoxy, by contrast, focuses on one or another aspect of the Way but cannot integrate them."[109]

The above examples point to a significant difference between Neo-Confucian notions of catholicity and those of the post-Nicene Christians. Whereas the latter commonly referred more to the geographical reach and demographical preponderance of the orthodox church and faith, the former was confined more to the realm of ideas. The catholicity of Neo-Confucianism arose from its alleged synthesis of ideals and values into a grand syncretic whole to form "a complete concert." For example, the Neo-Confucians claimed to have recognized both the "mind of the Way" and the "human mind" mentioned in the famous "sixteen-character transmission" from the *Documents Classic*. They thus avoided the errors of both the Buddhists and the heterodox philosophers of ancient times who ignored either one or the other.[110] On the other hand, Ch'eng-Chu Confucians were often reluctant to claim for their school the sort of geographical or demographical preponderance so favored by Western ecclesiastics such as Vincent of Lérins. On the contrary, they sometimes took delight in posing as a righteous remnant "alone in a Philistine wilderness,"[111] somewhat akin to Confucius himself. As broad as the Confucian Way supposedly was, this righteous remnant often acted as though they preferred to keep the right-of-way to themselves.

The idea of the catholicity of orthodoxy was not just a matter of the self-definitions of the four orthodox traditions discussed above. It may even have some basis in social reality. In the opinion of the sociologist Lewis Coser, "Whereas the church-type group strengthens its inner cohesion by allowing various conflicting tendencies to exist within its ranks, the political or religious sect must continuously expel dissenters to maintain or increase cohesion among the remaining 'worthy' participants."[112] To the extent that orthodoxy is established or institutionalized, it is thus also catholic according to this assessment.

The Middle Way

A final feature in the self-portrait of orthodoxy in the four religious traditions surveyed, the idea of orthodoxy as a middle way between two heretical extremes, may seem to run a little contrary to the previous point, catholicity. Catholicity and the middle way might, however, be reconciled by considering the latter as broad enough to accommodate all but the outer fringes, and in some cases all *including* the outer fringes.[113] But even if some disjunctions do exist between the images of orthodoxy as catholic and orthodoxy as the middle way, we should not expect the self-portrait of orthodoxy to add up to a strictly logical or even self-consistent system, which it was not conceived to be.

Expressions of the mediality of orthodoxy are so ubiquitous in all of the religious traditions surveyed here, with the possible exception of rabbinic Judaism, that they might well be made the subject of a separate substantial study. The difficulty of dealing with this final feature in the self-portrait of orthodoxy is further increased by the issue of to what extent it corresponded with reality, and was not simply a polemical ploy or a rhetorical trope of orthodox writers. With regard to most of the other aspects of the orthodox self-definition, including primacy, true transmission, unity, and even catholicity, it is possible to do a sort of reality check, which in most cases reveals significant distortions in the orthodox self-portrait. But the problem of who or what represents the middle way is more a matter of opinion. Orthodox writers' assertions that their credo constituted such a middle way were thus more difficult to refute, which may help to explain why they made them so frequently.

So attractive and unreadily falsifiable is the proposition of orthodox mediality that even modern historians of Christianity often assert it, however much they might hesitate to affirm other features in the self-portrait of early Christian orthodoxy. Jaroslav Pelikan, for example, writes that "it was characteristic both of true doctrine and of rational moral philosophy to occupy a middle place between extremes."[114] H. E. W. Turner uses what is perhaps the most shopworn image in Western literature in asserting that "Orthodoxy must always steer a difficult course between the Scylla of archaism and the Charybdis of innovation."[115] Finally, Daniel Sahas, invoking a questionable etymology, contrasts orthodoxy with "anything that 'inclines to this way or the other' . . . , 'to either the right or the left.'"[116]

Early Christian writers, however, were more inclined to define the orthodox middle in relation to specific heresies or heretical doctrines, and were not so given to cosmic characterizations of the mediality of rectitude as are our modern historians. Gregory of Nyssa (d. c. 395), for example, located the true Christian doctrine of God at the midpoint between Jewish monotheism and pagan polytheism:

> Truth passes in the mean between these two conceptions, destroying each heresy, and yet accepting what is useful to it from each. The Jewish dogma is destroyed by the acceptance of the Logos and by the belief in the Spirit, while the polytheistic error of the Greek school is made to vanish by the unity of the [divine] nature abrogating this notion of plurality.[117]

Hilary of Poitiers's reassertion of the orthodox Christian conception of God as a mean between absolute monotheism and polytheism is formulated in a paradoxical way characteristic of later Christian statements on this subject: "We have adopted a middle course between these two positions. We do not deny the one God, but teach that there is God and God on the testimony of the very man who proclaimed that there is one God."[118] John of Damascus (d. c. 749), however, restored a modicum of clarity to the doctrine of the mediumship of the orthodox

God, declaring that "the truth keeps up in the middle of the road, utterly denying these absurdities and teaching us to confess one God who is one nature and three persons: Father, Son and Holy Spirit."[119] But the problem of finding a happy orthodox medium on trinitarian questions was not easily resolved: "Cyril of Alexandria (d. 444) devoted a lifetime to the task but it would be a bold man who asserted his success."[120]

What are we to make of this extreme mediatropism of early Christian orthodoxy? In some usages, it was primarily a polemical ploy employed to refute one's theological opponents. This was apparently the case with the iconophile Epiphanius the Deacon, who condemned the iconoclasts of eighth-century Byzantium in the following terms: "Having walked far from the royal way which does not incline either to the right or to the left, they deviated from the teaching of the Apostles and of the Fathers."[121] In other cases, orthodox writers' temperaments may have inclined them to mediumship. A modern historian has remarked of Ireneaus, for example, that "His strength lay in his moderation. All excess and fantasy were alien to his practical disposition."[122]

But on crucial doctrinal matters, particularly Trinitarian and Christological questions, a kind of dialectic appears to have been at work to produce an orthodox compromise or synthesis that could readily be presented or conceived as a middle way. The main motive force for this compromise or synthesis was the rejection of unacceptable alternatives, which were usually paired as a duality. In the case of the Christological issue, the unacceptable alternatives, which apparently antedated the orthodox formulation, were to regard Christ as primarily either God (the docetist position) or man (the adoptionist position), as either "the eternal, preexistent Son," or as "the historic, individual man."[123] Falling into either of these two extremes mortally threatened the economy of salvation. As Gregory of Nazianzus (d. 389) put it, "In order that we may live, we need a God who was incarnate and suffered death."[124] But formulating and even maintaining the correct balance between the two was not easy, particularly because the two extremes corresponded to more natural, or commonsensical categories. Even after orthodox Christology was finally crystallized at Chalcedon, its defenders continued to labor against "those who seemed to make too little of the union between the divine and human [in Christ] as well as those who seemed to make too much of it."[125]

The related Trinitarian question concerning the doctrine of God also presented two unacceptable extremes, tritheism and modalism, which could hardly be embraced without rejecting either monotheism or Christ's distinctiveness and mission of salvation. But the Trinitarian "middle way" between these two positions was so paradoxical and precarious that even such a great theologian as Augustine had trouble maintaining it.[126] In fact, about the only aspect of the orthodox doctrine of the Trinity that is really clear is the unorthodox alternatives it was formulated to avoid. Thus the middle way, which one might normally think of as the path of reason, nature, or common sense, became in the orthodox Christian context a virtually incomprehensible mystery defined more by what it was not than by what it was. Attempts to express the mystery more directly often resorted to, and even revelled in, paradox and illogic, as in the following statement by Vincent of Lérins on the Trinity:

> In God is one substance but three persons; in Christ two substances, but one person. In the Trinity, different substances, not different persons. How in the Trinity are there different persons, not different substances?

and on Christology:

> [B]ut one and the same Christ is God and man, the same not created and created; . . . the same both equal to and inferior to the Father; the same begotten of the Father before the ages began, the same born of the mother in time, perfect God, perfect man.[127]

According to modern historians, early orthodox Christians took a middle position on a rather broad range of issues, not just on the primary Trinitarian and Christological questions. J. D. G. Dunn, for example, argues that the Gospel of Matthew "seems to be steering a middle course between a more conservative (Ebionite-like?) Jewish Christianity and a more liberal Hellenistic Jewish Christianity."[128] E. Earle Ellis posits that Paul, too, "stands between the two fronts: he fights for freedom but against licentiousness, for obedience but against legalism."[129] Harold Brown credits the orthodox definition of the canon of scripture formulated in the second century with having made certain "that nothing was properly excluded" on the one hand, and "that biblical revelation was not diluted by the addition of spurious private revelations" on the other.[130] According to Joan O'Grady, the orthodox position on grace, "as in so many previous instances, was formulated in a moderate statement, avoiding extremes."[131] Finally, Jaroslav Pelikan holds that the orthodox teaching in the iconoclastic controversies in eighth- and ninth-century Byzantium "was a via media between the false spiritualism of the iconoclasts and the false materialism of the idolaters."[132] In sum, the mystique of the orthodox middle way seems to have mystified modern historians as much as early Christian writers, though those historians generally apply the concept more loosely and broadly than did the early Christians. Insofar as the other traditional criteria of orthodoxy, such as primacy, true transmission, unity, and catholicity, have been more seriously undermined by modern critical scholarship, the mark of the middle way has had to bear more of the responsibility for establishing that 'orthodoxy' was not merely the propaganda of the victorious but was the correct doctrine after all. But if there ever was an arbitrary conception in religious or philosophical discourse, the doctrine of the middle way is it, as "heretics" illustrated by delineating their own way as the mean.[133]

In view of the popular association of Islam with extremism of various sorts, it may come as a surprise that Islamic orthodoxy surpasses even Christian orthodoxy in the multitude and multifariousness of its expressions of the middle way. So ubiquitous and inventive are these expressions that Sunni Islam has as great a claim to being identified as the religion of the middle way as do the Eastern traditions that are more commonly celebrated for their middle ways, Buddhism and Confucianism. Indeed, both Islamic writers and Western historians have characterized Islam as a whole as a sort of "just middle" (*wasat*) between Christianity and Judaism. According to the great Hanbalite theologian, Ibn Taymiyya (d. 1328), "The Jews, then, are those who fall short of the truth and the Christians, who go beyond the bounds."[134] The noted historian al-Tabari (b. 839) elaborated on this point, remarking that Muslims "are neither people of excess like the Christians who went to extremes in their monastic practices as well as in what they said concerning Jesus, nor are they people of deficiency like the Jews, who altered the Book of God, killed their prophets, gave the lie to their Lord, and rejected faith in Him. Rather they are people of the middle path and of balance in their religion."[135] The modern Islamic scholar Maulana Azad maintains that Islam found a just balance on the question of the attributes of God, between the "wrathful and majestic aspects" emphasized by Judaism and "the attributes of kindness and love" emphasized by Christianity "which left no room for justice and retribution."[136] A Western Islamicist, Julian Baldick, presents Islam as "a religion which tries to steer a middle course between Christian spirituality and Jewish legalism,"[137] invoking yet another pair of extremes in relation to which Islam constitutes a mediating middle. Baldick's version of the Islamic middle is apparently similar to that of many Muslims who "believe that Jewish theology has an exclusively worldly conception of life, while the Christian vision is purely spiritual; only Islam combines the spiritual and the secular."[138]

Declarations of Islamic mediation between Judaism and Christianity are apparently meant to assert the distinctiveness of Islam in relation to its main rivals, and more particularly to establish its place as the most advanced stage or expression of divine revelation, as a sort of final synthesis to Jewish thesis and Christian antithesis. But Sunni statements of the mediumship of their way *within* Islam are probably intended more to mediate between Islam's fractious sects than to divide and conquer. These sects threatened to splinter the Islamic community, thus making it more vulnerable to attacks from the outside, while bringing ruin upon themselves. According to a Tradition, the Prophet himself remarked to his son-in-law and nephew, 'Ali, the godfather of the Shi'ites: "Because of thee, two parties will come to ruin: thy overzealous admirers and thy passionate haters."[139] Later Sunnis thus sought to avoid extremes on the question of 'Ali, as well as on other issues, while mapping out a middle way broad enough to include or at least accommodate all but the most incorrigible. For example, the great heresiographer al-Baghdadi "proposes a rather broad set of doctrinal principles to which these Sunnis are supposed to adhere: a theology which stops short of Mu'tazilism, and a traditionalism which stops short of *hashw*."[140] Even the relatively uncompromising Hanbalite theologian, Ibn Taymiyya, referred to the Sunnis as a whole as the people within Islam who occupied the "just middle (*wasat*)," just as Islam as a whole "occupies the position of just middle between the two other great scriptural religions, Judaism and Christianity."[141]

But if the Sunnis made up the broad middle within Islam as a whole (which in turn constituted an even broader middle with respect to Judaism and Christianity), it was the Ash'arites who claimed most convincingly and extensively the position of the narrower middle within Sunnism. In fact, leading Ash'arites regarded their primary religious vocation as mediation between several groups or extremes. This mediatory attitude, in turn, promoted Ash'arite influence, "and contributed to mak[ing] it the official representative of orthodox Islam."[142] It might not be too much to say that Ash'arism's primary claim to doctrinal orthodoxy was its adoption of the middle way, an inclination that it shared with the other major ultra-orthodox school, the Maturidite.[143]

In view of their sharp inclination toward the just middle, which formed the very *raison d'être* of their school, it is hardly surprising that Ash'arite (and Maturidite) positions on most doctrinal issues were presented as mediatory ones. This is particularly true of the key theological issue of the attributes of God. In an essay on "The Middle Position of al-Ash'ari," the later Ash'arite apologist Ibn 'Asakir (1106–1176) expounds thirteen points on which al-Ash'ari allegedly struck the golden mean. The first point spoke of al-Ash'ari's mean on the question of the divine attributes:

> He studied the books of the Mu'tazila, the Jahmiyya, and the Rafida, and saw that they stripped and cancelled and held that God has no knowledge, no power, no hearing, no sight, no life, no perdurance, and no will. On the other hand, the Hashwiyya and the Mujassima and the Mukayyifa al-Muhaddida held that God has a knowledge like other knowledges, and a power like other powers, and a hearing like other hearings, and a sight like other sights. But al-Ash'ari followed a course between them and held that God has a knowledge which is not like other knowledges, and a power which is not like other powers, and a hearing which is not like other hearings, and a sight which is not like other sights.[144]

A more philosophical Ash'arite solution to the problem of the attributes of God, reported by Shahrastani, bears some resemblance to the famous fourfold negation of the Madhyamika school of Mahayana Buddhism: "These attributes, Ash'ari says, are eternal and subsist in the essence of God. It cannot be said that they are he or other than he; nor can it be said that they are not he, nor that they are not other than he."[145]

Both of the above statements were designed to avoid the extremes of anthropomorphically attributing to God all sorts of gross physical attributes unworthy of His majesty and divinity on the one hand, and denying to Him all manner of attributes in blatant contradiction to both the text of the Qur'an and the psychological needs of believers on the other. In some cases, Ash'ari accomplished this judicious mediation between extremes with respect to *particular* divine attributes or acts, as opposed to considering them in the aggregate. For example, regarding the Qur'anic representation of God as seated on a throne, Ash'ari held that "Everything above us is called the 'sky'; as for the word 'throne,' that signifies the culminating point of the skies."[146] Ash'ari's interpretation of the throne verse is thus neither dismissive nor anthropomorphic.

On other theological issues as well, the Ash'arites posited a middle position. Regarding the question of the use of reason in religion,
they stood between the "two extremes of either the rejection of reason
[= the Hanbalites] or its acceptance as the absolute, unique criterion [=
the Mu'tazilites]."[147] The Ash'arites also mediated between the Hanbalites and the Mu'tazilites on the issue of the createdness of the
Qur'an, holding "that the Qur'an is God's speech, eternal, immutable,
uncreated, unbegun, and unoriginated; but the separate letters, the
bodies, the colors, the sounds, things limited, and all the qualified
things of the world are created, originated, produced."[148] On the vexed
question of free will (or free agency), the Ash'arites navigated an even
more torturous middle way which sought to reconcile divine justice
with divine omnipotence by "teaching that actions are from God in one
sense and from man in another":[149] As al-Baghdadi put it, "man ac-
quires his acts," and thus could be held responsible for his deeds, "yet
God is the creator of the acquired act."[150]

By this point, alas, the broad middle way blazed by the early con-
sensually-oriented Sunnis narrows almost to a razor's edge. This is
particularly apparent in the great theologian al-Ghazali's statement on
the straitness of the middle gate on the question of allegorism: "The
true middle path between a complete allegorism [in interpreting the
Qur'an] and rigid Hanbalism is narrow and obscure. It is found only
by those who enjoy divine help and who reach the heart of things by
divine light, not by hearsay."[151] Ghazali did, however, go on to characterize rather matter-of-factly the Ash'arite middle way on the question
of allegorical interpretation of the attributes of God as follows:

> One of the parties, trying to follow a middle way, opens the door
> of allegorical interpretation regarding all that is related to the
> qualities of Allah; whereas they take in the literal sense the de-
> scriptions of the last things, which they do not allow to be inter-
> preted allegorically. These are the Ash'arites.[152]

A final major doctrinal issue on which the Ash'arites engineered
a middle way is the question of the imamate or leadership of the Islamic community, the most contentious issue in Islamic history. One of the
two extremes on this issue was represented by the Shi'ites, who "ultimately came to maintain that leadership was a matter of divine right,
the ruler deriving his authority from the hereditary transmission of divine inspiration along the line of the Prophet's descendants" through
'Ali. The other was that of the Kharijites who "held that the ruler was
to be elected—and, if necessary, deposed—by the votes of the entire

community."[153] Further, while the Shi'ites apotheosized 'Ali and his descendants, the Kharijites were the only Muslim sect that cursed and abhorred 'Ali. Indeed, "in A.D. 661, 'Ali fell by the dagger of a Kharijite."[154] The Ash'arites and their orthodox Sunni allies steered a middle course between the two by revering 'Ali and his family while rejecting their more divine pretentions.

The Ash'arite middle way was not confined to the major theological questions in the history of Islam. It mediated between sectarian opinions on minor issues as well, such as the legitimacy of visits to the tombs of saints, the propriety of religious retreats, the status of those Muslims guilty of great sins, and the efficacy of the Prophet's intercession.[155] The middle way in Ash'arism thus seems to obey a sort of Parkinsonian law: it always extends to bisect any doctrinal issue.

But the Ash'arite was not the only Islamic sect or school to stake a claim to the middle way. As Keith Lewinstein has remarked, the "striving for the center is of course a feature of all claimants to orthodoxy."[156] This was even true of the Hanbalites, who had themselves been consigned to the margins of Sunni orthodoxy by Ash'arite heresiographers. However, Ibn Hanbal's (780–855) "middle position" was a rather curious one, somewhat analogous to "don't ask—don't tell": "This position consisted in an honest effort to cling to Qur'an and *sunna* without asking further questions, approximately in the same way the pious ancestors had done."[157]

Later Hanbalites, particularly the enormously influential Ibn Taymiyya, fleshed out this rather minimalist middle way of the Hanbalite founder. In so doing, they attributed extreme positions to the Ash'arites, purportedly the masters of the mediatory middle. Ibn Taymiyya, for example, accused the followers of al-Ash'ari of adhering to the extreme of determinism (as opposed to Mu'tazilite voluntarism) and of soulless legalism (as opposed to antinomianism).[158] He proceeded to characterize the Hanbalite traditionists as occupying the position of the just middle on practically every major theological issue, and with respect to practically every major sect:

> On the question of the divine attributes, they occupy the position of the just middle between the Jahmite partisans of negation and the anthropomorphist partisans of comparing God with his creatures.
>
> On the question of the divine acts, they occupy the position of the just middle between the Qadarites and the Jabrites.

Similarly, on the question of the divine promise, they occupy the position of the just middle between the Murjites and the Au'idiya

. . . .

Similarly on the question of the definition of faith and religion, they are in the just middle between the Haruriya and the Mu'tazilites on the one hand, and the Murjites and the Jahmites on the other.

Finally, on the question of the companions [of the Prophet], they occupy the position of the just middle between the Rawafid and the Kharijites.[159]

Ibn Taymiyya was not the only Hanbalite apologist or theologian to have elaborated a Hanbalite version of the middle way. Ibn Qudama (d. 1223), in particular, sought to refute the Ash'arite criticism that Hanbalism veered to the extreme of anthropomorphism on the question of the divine attributes by relating an anthropomorphism that was even more extreme, namely *tasbih-* and *tagsim-*anthropomorphism:

Now, *tashib-* and *tagsim-*anthropomorphism result only from him who makes the attributes of God accord in meaning with the attributes of created beings. But we do not believe this, nor do we follow it as our religion; on the contrary, we know that so far as God is concerned, "There is nothing anything like Him."[160]

How rhetorically convenient it is to have a greater extreme to make a lesser extreme look moderate! However disastrous two-front wars are in the sphere of military conflict, they are often desirable in verbal warfare where the ideal position is to be flanked by two extremes.

Even the Mu'tazilites, whom the orthodox Ash'arite heresiographers depicted as being at the opposite extreme from the Hanbalites on the key question of the divine attributes, presented themselves as masters of the middle way on this issue. While maintaining that God is not like other things, most Mu'tazilites were prepared to admit that "God is a thing" and even that "he is knowing, powerful, and living."[161] In other words, "there is a certain relation of God to things or creatures which enables us to employ mundane and creaturely predicates of Him." That the Mu'tazilites succumbed to the mystique of the middle way is evident from some of their own characterizations of their position vis-a-vis other sects:

We do not go so far as the Haruriya, yet do not hold back so much as the Murjites; thus the religion of God lies between reserve and exaggeration. And this is the etymology (for the Mu'ta-zila), namely the middle position and sticking to the middle of the road.[162]

On the question of the imamate in particular, the Mu'tazilites were engaged in a "two-front war" against both the proponents and the opponents of the party of 'Ali.[163] According to the Shi'ite heresiographer, al-Nawbakhti, "they declared that 'it is not proper to either fight with 'Ali or fight against him.'"[164]

Even the Shi'ites, who have been known in both medieval and modern times as extremists *par excellence*, sometimes present themselves as middle-of-the-roaders. This is particularly true of modern Shi'ite authors. One such author, for example, writes of the issue of the divine attributes that "Islam has commanded its followers to preserve a just balance between affirmation and negation."[165] Another argues that "The Qur'an itself strikes a middle course between the stagnant and narrow-minded attitude of the Akhbaris and the unwarranted and deviate interpretations of the Batinis."[166] Mystics in most religious traditions are not obvious candidates for middle-of-the-roaders. Yet even Sufis sometimes succumbed to the mystique of the middle way, or at least got caught up in its rhetoric: "Thus one Sufi observes that Syriac (as the language of eastern Christians) represents what is highest and most hidden, whereas Hebrew (as the language of Judaism) represents what is lowest and most obvious, and Arabic (as the language of Islam) unites the two extremes."[167]

In sum, affirmations of the middle way are fairly widespread in Islamic sectarian writings, and not limited to the works of the Ash'arites. However, the apparent ubiquity of this protestation of mediation in Islamic sectarian literature may be in part an indication of Ash'arite success in establishing the orthodoxy of their school through claims to the "just middle." These claims were particularly appealing to rulers who, "for obvious reasons, tended to avoid religious extremes."[168] Desiring to project a similar appeal, other sects adopted this Ash'arite tactic with mixed results.

While claims to the middle way are common in Islamic sectarian literature, they are relatively rare in rabbinical writings. However, a characterization of the middle way as the proper approach to the Torah does appear in the Talmud: "The teaching," it is said there, "is like two paths, one of fire and one of snow. If one inclines to this side, one dies by fire; to that side, and one dies by snow. What should one do? Walk in the middle."[169] The most influential purveyor of middle way ideology in the history of rabbinic Judaism was probably Maimonides, who applied the ideal to such varied issues as manners of worship "in which there is no burden or excess" and personal dispositions which "shall occupy the exact middle between the extremes."[170] Maimonides did not often use the idea of a mediatory middle in a theological or sectarian context. But one of his commentators did, in a rather curious way, arguing against any alteration to the Torah on the grounds that it might skew this "ultimate in balance": "if one were to add or subtract, the Torah would be out of balance and would tend toward one of the two extremes [of exaggeration and negligence], which would be blameworthy."[171] Since the Torah was the primal expression of Aristotle's perfectly poised Golden Mean, tampering with it was taboo.

If ancient and medieval references to Rabbinism as the middle way are relatively rare, those of modern historians are a little more abundant. According to Ralph Marcus' whimsical classification of ancient Jewish sects, the Pharisees (or protoRabbis) constituted the "Center," with the Sadducees on the "Extreme Right," the Essenes and Gnostics "Left of Center," and the Zealots on the "Extreme Left."[172] Another modern scholar, Reuben Kaufman, maintains that the Pharisees occupied the middle position on a basic doctrinal matter: "The Essenes believed that everything is determined by destiny; the Pharisees believed in destiny but also in the freedom of the will . . . ; and the Sadducees believed that there is no destiny at all."[173] This echoes the ancient historian Josephus' characterization of the Pharisaic middle position on the question of fate, their belief that "some actions, but not all, are the work of fate, and some of them are in our own power, and that they are liable to fate, but are not caused by fate."[174]

Moving to a later period in the history of Judaism, Kaufman credits the Kabbalah with being "instrumental in steering Judaism into the straight channel, avoiding the reef of speculative philosophy on the one side and the rocks of *pipulistic* legalism on the other."[175] He also celebrates those eighteenth-century rabbis who followed the *derech hamemutza*, "the middle course," in attempting to achieve reconciliation with both the Hasidim and the Maskilim.[176] Finally, a contemporary Jewish philosopher, Louis Jacobs, speaks of conservative Judaism as a "middle way" between orthodox and reform Judaism.[177] This version of the middle way does not, however, seek so much to conciliate those on either extreme as to appropriate for one's own sect the best features from other sects, to create the best of all possible worlds while leaving other worlds to shift for themselves.

Of all the major scriptural traditions surveyed here, the conception of orthodoxy as the middle way had the firmest canonical grounding in the Confucian tradition. Confucius himself criticized some of his disciples for going to extremes and missing the middle way, remarking that while Tzu-chang exceeds the proper standard, Tzu-hsia falls short of it (Analects 11.15). In a more abstract formulation of the ideality of mediality, "Confucius said: 'When native substance exceeds refinement, crudeness results; when refinement exceeds native substance, pedantry results. When refinement and native substance are in balance, gentlemanliness prevails" (Analects 6.16). Mencius, the second sage of Confucianism, elaborated on this Confucian theme:

> Confucius [said], "If one fails to find those who follow the middle way as associates, one can only fall back on the wild and the squeamish. The wild rush forward, while the squeamish find certain things beneath them." Of course Confucius wanted those who followed the middle way, but he could not be sure of finding such men.[178]

In this passage, the middle way appears to be the absolute opposite of what is middling and mediocre. Far from being normal, it is very precarious and difficult to attain.[179] In this sense it is reminiscent of the orthodox middle way characterized by later Christian and Islamic theologians.

Mencius not only recommended the mean in matters of personal conduct, but also steered a more polemical middle way between his primary philosophical opponents, the alleged egotist Yang Chu and the ultra-altruist Mo Ti (*Mencius* 3B. 9). In this case, Mencius's middle way looks a little contrived, since Yang Chu, in contrast to Mo Ti, apparently enjoyed little support in the intellectual world of his time.[180] However, the appeal to centrality was such a good rhetorical strategy that Mencius evidently resorted to exaggerating the significance of one of the extremes in order to stake a more convincing claim to the coveted middle ground.

The mania for the middle and avoidance of extremes in classical Chinese thought was not limited to Confucius and Mencius. It appears prominently in the influential "Great Norm" chapter of the *Documents Classic*, in the celebrated "sixteen-character transmission" from the "Counsels of the Great Yü" chapter of the same classic, and in the *Changes Classic* and the *Hsün-tzu*, among other places. It even figures in non-Confucian works of classical philosophy, such as the *Chuang-tzu*, which advises one to "Shrink from fame when you do good; shrink from punishment when you do evil; pursue always the middle course."[181] Finally, one of the Confucian Four Books, the *Doctrine of the*

Mean (Chung-yung), is centrally concerned with the value of centrality. So pivotal was this value in Confucianism that "From the *Lun yü* [Analects] onward it has dominated the behavior of the ideal Confucian gentleman. . . . It means, for him, that going too far is quite as undesirable as falling short. Hence he should be neither too ceremonial nor too spontaneous, neither too pedantic nor too imaginative, and so on."[182] The mean in the Confucian tradition was thus a standard of conduct in everyday life, not just a standard of orthodoxy. In modern times, the principle of the mean has even been interpreted as a kind of national wisdom of China. According to Liang Ch'i-ch'ao, the main reason why Confucianism was so successful was that "it represented this characteristic trait of the Chinese people."[183]

The classical Confucian inclination toward the mean was further exaggerated by the Sung Neo-Confucians. Among the Tao Learning scholars, Chu Hsi was the most prolific and influential advocate of centrality and mediality. Indeed, "Chu generally saw himself as the Mean between what he regarded as the more extreme alternatives of his day." Moreover, he "often appears to have striven for what he regarded as the Mean,"[184] such as that between Buddhism and Taoism on the one hand and Legalism and utilitarianism on the other. Hence his later reputation as the "great middleman" (*chung-hsing-che*) among the sages.[185]

But Chu was not the only major Neo-Confucian thinker to have cultivated and celebrated the orthodox mean. The theme is so pervasive in Neo-Confucian thought that a substantial study would be required to do it justice. Here, we can only touch on a few of the middle way's high points in the history of Neo-Confucian discourse.

Among Ch'eng-Chu scholars of the Ming, Hsüeh Hsüan identified the transmission of the Way of the Sages with the virtue of centrality (*chung*); while Lo Ch'in-shun specified the heretical extremes to be avoided: "To drown in the external and neglect the internal is vulgar learning. To be confined to the internal and neglectful of the external is the learning of Ch'an."[186] In the early Ch'ing era, Chang Li-hsiang warned that if one is "humane and does not hold to centrality and orthodoxy, then the humaneness will perhaps stray into universal love [like the Mohists]; and rightness will perhaps stray into egotism [like Yang Chu]; and the ultimate of man will not be established."[187] And Hsiung Tz'u-li (1635–1709) contrasted the principle of great centrality (*ta-chung*) with the extremes of loftiness which enters into Buddhism and Taoism and lowliness which strays into Legalism.[188] Finally, the Neo-Confucian middle way was extensive enough to span the Straits of Tsushima and to enter into Japanese Confucianism with

Fujiwara Seika (1561–1619). Like his Chinese Neo-Confucian predecessors, Fujiwara held that an essential mark of Confucian orthodoxy was its hold on the proper balance between the unity of principle and the diversity of its particularizations (*li-i fen-shu*).[189]

Neo-Confucians of the Ch'eng-Chu persuasion did not monopolize the middle way. Like their Ash'arite counterparts in Islam, they were constrained to share their claims with rivals. In Sung times, for example, Su Shih (1037–1101) described his fellow literatus, Ou-yang Hsiu (1007–1072), as "the modern Mencius, defending the Confucian way from the extremes of Yang and Mo"; and the "utilitarian Confucian" Ch'en Liang (1143–1194) sought to achieve a synthetic middle way between moralistic Confucians and pragmatic Legalists that would reintegrate the fragmented Tao.[190] The positing of the middle way as a balance or synthesis between extremist sects or extreme viewpoints was also taken up by later Confucian scholars not strictly identified with Ch'eng-Chu, such as the Tung-lin scholars of the late Ming and Ku Yen-wu (1613–1681) and Wang Fu-chih (1619–1692) in the early Ch'ing.

In comparison with the rather monolithic middle ways of Western monotheisms, Confucian means were markedly more flexible. This flexibility sprang in part from a sort of compensatory strategy which legitimized mid-course corrections that overshot the mean. According to Liu Feng-lu (1776–1829), "the gentleman relieves refinement by means of rusticity, thus honoring centrality. This is only to accentuate what is biased in order to mend the deficiencies [caused by going to the opposite extreme]."[191] Chang Li-hsiang cited the moral philosophy of the Neo-Confucian cosmologist Chou Tun-i (1017–1073) as an instance of legitimate overcorrection that restored the mean, remarking that Chou stressed the practice of quiescence in order to eliminate selfish desires.[192] On the other hand, if one mistakenly took such a biased viewpoint resulting from a compensatory strategy to be a fixed principle, serious misapprehensions might result, as Ch'en Chien claimed was the case with Wang Yang-ming: "Wang Yang-ming took Master Chu's words [which Chu intended] to relieve one-sidedness and to medicate maladies to be a fixed theory."[193] This led to Wang's mistakenly conflating Chu's thought with that of his rival, Lu Hsiang-shan.

The Confucian and Neo-Confucian mean was flexible not only in the sense that it accommodated timely leanings to one side or the other. It was also less fixed in general. Mencius, in fact, went so far as to condemn fixation on the middle as being almost as objectionable as the extremes represented by Yang Chu and Mo Ti:

Mencius said, "Yang Chu chooses egoism. Even if he could benefit the Empire by pulling out one hair he would not do it. Mo Tzu
advocates love without discrimination. If by shaving his head
and showing his heels he could benefit the Empire, he would do
it. Tzu-mo holds on to the middle, half way between the two extremes. Holding on to the middle is closer to being right, but to
do this without the proper measure is no different from holding
to one extreme.[194]

In his commentary on this passage from the *Mencius*, Chu Hsi remarked
that "this chapter says that what is precious about the Way is its centrality, and what is precious about centrality is its weighing of circumstances."[195] The late-Ch'ing scholar Chiao Hsün (1763–1820) proceeded to
criticize Tzu-mo for adhering to a rigid standard of centrality and not
recognizing that there are times and circumstances in which one or the
other of the two extremes of reclusive egotism and indiscriminate altruism might be appropriate.[196] He even went so far as to redefine heresy
as that which adheres inflexibly to one principle.[197]

   In the course of characterizing orthodoxy according to the terms
discussed in this chapter, orthodox heresiographers were implicitly
characterizing heresy as well. For example, in representing orthodoxy
as a mean, they naturally consigned heresies to the extremes centered
on this mean. And in portraying orthodoxy as unified, they depicted
heresy as divided against itself. However, heresiographers' constructions of heresy were not confined to being simply a series of negations
of their constructions of orthodoxy. Heresiographers also mounted a
rather independent representation of the Other that was not merely the
obverse of the Same. The terms of this representation are explored in
the next chapter, "The Construction of Heresy."

4

The Construction of Heresy

That orthodox characterizations of heresy are historically inaccurate is not a very surprising or controversial assertion. In some cases, the degree of heresiographical distortion is so great that the modern historian has trouble matching heresiographers' accounts of a heresy with the surviving literature emanating from the refuted group.[1] Moreover, the extent of distortion tended to increase over time, as later heresiographers compounded the inaccuracies they inherited from earlier orthodox accounts of heresies.[2]

Modern historians of heresy have expended great efforts in attempting to recover the heretical thing-in-itself from the welter of heresiographical distortions and contortions. They are prone to lamenting the "widespread fate common to minorities, dissidents and fringe groups, whether religious or political, whose writings have been scattered or destroyed by their conquerors and whose image is thus filtered through, or distorted by, the eye of the opposition." And they labor mightily "to overcome this obstacle—the voice of the heresiologist, the prosecutor in a witch hunt, the conquistador describing the colonized tribes—which stands between the historian and the actual reality of the protagonists."[3] In so doing, they sometimes forget that the obstacles themselves, the heresiographical distortions, reveal significant patterns. In fact, these patterns of the ways by which orthodoxy constructs heresy may be of even broader and greater significance than the actual historical character of the heresies. For they may illustrate universal tendencies or templates in human culture and even psychology for representing a hostile or threatening other, particularly an internal enemy. While such a general heresiographical template might be difficult to identify or verify by focusing on one particular heresiographical tradition, such as that of early Christianity, it is more readily discernible in a comparative study that incorporates several such traditions. In this case, Niels Bohr's observation that clarity is achieved through breadth seems to hold true.

Schematization of Heresy

Heresiographical modes of schematizing heresy run the gamut from the numerological, to the binary, to the reductionist, to the inventive. In early Christian heresiology, the most prominent numerological image of heresy is that of the eighty concubines which Epiphanius drew from the following passage in the Song of Solomon (Canticles 6:8): "There are sixty queens and eighty concubines, and young women without number. My dove, my perfect one, is only one, the darling of her mother, a chosen one to her that bore her." As Epiphanius explains in the concluding essay to his heresiological treatise, the *Panarion* ("Medicine Chest"), the one dove is the true Church, the sixty queens represent the generations of the faithful before Christ, and the eighty concubines are the heresies, groups which illegitimately use the name of Christ as the concubine uses the name of her master.[4] Epiphanius did not, however, take the number eighty as simply a ballpark figure for the number of heresies or as a cipher denoting multiplicity in general, but as an exact enumeration of heresies that would arise before the end of time. Convinced that the end was indeed near and that all of the prophesized heresies had come to pass, Epiphanius organized his heresiology, the *Panarion*, into eighty divisions, one for each of the canonically fixed number of heresies. To arrive at this number, however, he was forced to compress artificially many heresies and subdivide others.[5]

Numerology was only one of the means by which early Christian heresiologists schematized heresies. Another proto-arithmetical method widely used in Christian heresiological schematization was the arrangement of major heresies into neat binary oppositions or antitheses symmetrically centered on an orthodox middle way. Since this form of heresiological schematization generally depended upon rather subtle systematizations and statements of orthodox doctrine, it did not develop until comparatively late in the heresiological tradition. But it appears prominently in the work on *The Trinity* by Hilary of Poitiers (d. 367), particularly in his account of the equal and opposite errors of the Arians and the Sabellians: "This one, [Arius] will introduce the Son as working, and this one [Sabellius] will contend that God is present in the works. The latter [Sabellius] will speak of the one God, the former [Arius] will deny the one God."[6] Hilary held that such a binary opposition of two heresies was actually advantageous to the true faith, since they cancelled out one another: "Let them conquer, as they will, because they are conquered by mutually conquering one another."[7] A little later in the Greek East, John Chrysostom (d. 407) similarly symmetrically dichotomized the Manicheans and the Jews:

The Manicheans and those who are sick with their disease seem to accept the Christ who was foretold but they dishonor the prophets and patriarchs who foretold him. On the other hand, we see that the Jews accept and revere those who foretold Christ, I mean the prophets and the lawgiver, but they dishonor him whom they foretold.[8]

The later defenders of the orthodox Christological doctrine affirmed at Chalcedon also presented their heretical opponents as representing "two perfectly opposed views" or "antithetical errors" on the question of the nature of Christ.[9] However, one of these heretical extremes, Nestorianism, appears to have been "prefabricated for the purpose of opposing it symmetrically to the antithetical monophysite heresy."[10] According to orthodox accounts, the iconoclasts of eighth- and ninth-century Byzantium also fell into either one or the other of two symmetrically opposing Christological errors, that Christ was a mere man and that Christ was God and not man.[11] The Byzantine heresiologist, John Cassian (b. c. 360), argued that the symmetry of opposing heresies resulted from later heresies arising in reaction to earlier ones, and going to the opposite extreme by way of compensation. For example, the Sabellian heresy, which held that there was "no distinction between the Father, Son, and Holy Ghost," was a reaction to the Ebionite heresy which denied Jesus' union with divinity. "And so one after another out of reaction against heresies they give rise to heresies."[12]

The schematic arrangement of heresies into binary oppositions did not end with the demise of the Byzantines. It appears occasionally in modern ideological polemics as well, particularly in the Marxist tradition. According to Lenin, "Right doctrinairism persisted in recognising only the old forms," while "Left doctrinairism persists in the unconditional repudiation of certain old forms."[13] Mao Tse-tung's characterization of right and left deviations is a little different in content, though it expresses a similar symmetry of binary opposites: "struggle without unity is a 'Left' deviationist mistake and unity without struggle is a Right deviationist mistake."[14]

Among other twentieth-century ideologies, Freudian psychoanalysis also exhibits an almost obsessive propensity to pair perversions (in lieu of heresies) as complementary opposites. In Freud's own words, "certain among the impulses to perversion occur regularly as pairs of opposites."[15] Such binary oppositions may exist not only between two different perversions, such as sadism and masochism, but also within a single aberration, particularly hysteria.

According to Freud, psychoanalysis exposes the "pair of opposites by which it [=hysteria] is characterized—exaggerated sexual need and excessive aversion to sexuality."[16] By revealing the dualistic inner structure of various forms of perversion and suggesting how they might be cured, Freud's essay on "The Sexual Aberrations" plays the role of a modern heresiological treatise, somewhat akin to Epiphanius' *Panarion* ("Medicine Chest").

Early Christian heresiologists also schematized various heresies by unifying them or reducing them to one another. Somewhat inconsistently (or maybe just paradoxically), orthodox heresiologists "found in heresy a contrivance of the devil that was at the same time diverse and homogeneous."[17] As Hippolytus of Rome (d. c. 236), one of the earliest Christian heresiologists, remarked, "error is many and diversified, resembling, in truth, the hydra." But it is also unified in a sense, "having a mutual connection through (the same) spirit of error."[18] Later Christian heresiologists presumed to identify more specifically those points supposedly held in common by diverse heretics. According to Firmillian of Caesarea, though heretics "disagree in certain minor points, nevertheless in that which is most important they have a unanimity that is one and the same: to blaspheme the Creator."[19] Vincent of Lérins (fl. c. 434) enumerated several points to which heretics of diverse stripes adhered. While positing that all heresies bubble up "under a definite name, in a definite place, at a definite time," he averred that "there is a sort of established and legal rule that they always take delight in godless innovations, loathe the decisions of antiquity, and through contradictions of knowledge, falsely so named, suffer shipwreck from the faith."[20]

The heresiographical tendency to present all heresies as a single enemy, as the multiple heads of one monster, seems to have increased over time. In medieval Europe, "there was an increasing probability as time passed that each manifestation of religious dissent would be assimilated by those who encountered it into the general pattern which already existed in the minds of the observers."[21] But the "theory of the secret correspondence and basic unity of heresies of widely different provenance and theological content" received its most sophisticated expression from the great nineteenth-century apologist, John Henry Newman.[22] Newman maintained that "All heresies seem connected together and to run into each other. When the mind has embraced one, it is almost certain to run into others, apparently the most opposite, it is quite uncertain which."[23] As an example of a heresy running into its apparent opposite, Newman cited the Arian which "denied that our Lord was God" and the Monophysite which denied that he was man.

"But their agreement lay in this compromise, that strictly speaking He was neither God nor man."[24] One notable consequence of Newman's reduction of all heresies to one another is that it does not matter much which heresy one falls into initially, since all heresies are of a piece.[25]

However historically inaccurate was the heresiological reduction of all heresies to a single state, it tended in time to become a self-fulfilling prophecy. Once heretics were identified and condemned as such by the authorities, their common pariahship gave them a basis for solidarity.[26] "The label therefore creates a new reality"[27] both socially and intellectually.

The idea of the underlying unity of all heresies, like the pairing of two heresies in the form of a binary opposition, has some possible progeny in recent times. Some of the most potent of these are conspiracy theories, which are so ubiquitous in modern political discourse that one might be led to suspect the existence of a conspiracy behind all of these conspiracy theories. Such theories often link various and sundry persons, groups, and trends together in an unholy alliance which supposedly seeks to corrupt or dominate. While a direct line of descent between medieval heresiology and modern conspiracy theories might be difficult to draw, nineteenth-century Catholic conservatives' condemnation of "modern thought, scientific criticism, and democracy, lumping them together into one unified, systematic heresy," might well represent a transitional state between the two.[28]

A more rational, or at least academic, mode of unifying one's enemies are modern social psychologists' theories on the nature of prejudice, notably Gordon Allport's idea that "people who reject one out-group will tend to reject other out-groups. If a person is anti-Jewish, he is likely to be anti-Catholic, anti-Negro, anti any out-group."[29] According to Allport, "any differences of form a prejudice may assume over time or in different milieus are unimportant in comparison to prejudice's essence or nature."[30]

The heresiological schematization of heresy took the form of constructing and even inventing individual heresies as well as linking these heresies with one another. Indeed, before heresies could be organized into any sort of system, or even reduced to one another, they had first to be constructed or invented from an elusive and unstable congeries of heresoidal phenomena. These heresiological constitutions of individual heresies were more homogeneous and simplified than were their historical prototypes.[31] For example, most early Christian heresiologists, beginning with Irenaeus (c. 130–c. 200), construed the Jewish Christians as a monolithic entity, the "Ebionite heresy." But "the simplistic, dogmatically determined classification of Jewish Christianity as a heresy which confronts the 'great church' as a homogeneous unit does not do justice to the complex situation existing within legalistic Jewish Christianity."[32] Another early Christian heresy that heresiologists constituted from rather diverse strands was Gnosticism. As with the Ebionite heresy, a theological common demominator was found to underpin the diverse forms of "Gnosticism," namely a heretical distinction between the immoral Demiurge of the Old Testament and the good God of the New.[33] By this artifice, Origen was able to amalgamate the Marcionites, Valentinians, and Basilidites into one heretical group, blurring or effacing their differences. A later Christian theologian and heresiologist, Augustine, was also partly responsible for the construction and condensation of a heresy, Pelagianism. As Frank Kermode has written, Augustine "systematised Pelagianism in order to suppress it."[34] Indeed, "Pelagianism as an 'ism came into existence in the mind of Augustine."[35] Even modern historians have advanced the schematization and simplification of historical heresies, such as 'adoptionism,' "a word without a fixed historical reference."[36] They have labelled as "adoptionist" a wide range of historically unrelated figures, doctrines and sects ranging from the second century through the early middle ages, which are all supposedly linked by a common belief that Jesus was the adopted, not the begotten, Son of God. In this case, as in others, heresiologists and historians have abstracted and simplified heresies by reducing them to a few condemned theological propositions, sometimes as few as one.

After heresies had been duly constituted and constructed by early orthodox writers, a natural tendency was to reduce later heresies to the earlier ones that were already properly catalogued and refuted, if for no other reason than to save intellectual and scribal labor employed in the business of refutation. A good example of this form of heresiological schematization appears in the works of the Byzantine polemicist, John Cassian. Cassian discredited the Nestorians of his day, and incidentally saved himself the trouble of refuting them point by point, by accusing them of "belching out the poison of Pelagianism, and hissing with the very spirit of Pelagianism. Whence it comes that you seem to have been already judged . . . since your error is one and the same."[37] A few centuries later in the Latin West, Alcuin (d. 804) and other Carolingian authorities in turn assimilated a new form of "adoptionism" that arose in eighth-century Spain to fifth-century Nestorianism. Alcuin was so confident of his identification of the adoptionism he confronted in his own day as a species of Nestorianism that "he mocks the very idea that it could be anything essentially new or indigenous to the West."[38]

While heresiographers constructed some heresies from building blocks of diverse provenance, they wove others almost out of whole cloth. Among the heresies invented by early Christian heresiologists is the Cainite, "a figment of their imagination, an artificial construct," and the Symmachian, also "a product of the imagination of early Christian authors."[39] Other early Christian sects, while not entirely fictive, "are simply persons who take a particular position."[40]

At first glance, early Islamic sects present rather unpromising raw material for heresiographical schematization. In the eighth century, the lines of division between the sects were so imprecise and uncertain that one sectarian figure "was called both Kharijite and Mu'tazilite, and also Qadarite . . . and even Murji'ite."[41] But like their Christian counterparts, Islamic heresiographers were more than equal to the challenge of schematization, and at least as adept in "imposing their formal categories with scant regard for historical reality."[42] In time, some of these formal categories did assume an historical and even social reality, as heresiographical schemas began to infiltrate the consciousness of sectarians. "History does not happen like heresiography. But sometimes it does,"[43] particularly when heresiography is mistaken for history.

As in early Christianity, the most general and abstract Islamic heresiographical schematizations were numerological. In fact, the leitmotif of the heresiographical genre as a whole is the famous Tradition or *hadith* in which the Prophet predicts a division of the Islamic community into seventy-three sects, seventy-two of which are destined for Hell and only one for salvation.[44] As the pioneering Western Islamicist, Ignaz Goldziher, remarked, this *hadith* "formed the basis for the history of religion and of sects in Muhammadan literature."[45] Most of the great Sunni heresiographers, including al-Shahrastani (1086–1153) and al-Baghdadi (d. 1037), deployed the seventy-three-sect schema in their heresiographical works. The Ash'arite theologian 'Adud al-Din al-Iji (c. 1281–1355) went so far as to identify the one "salvation-giving sect" as the Ash'arite.[46] This schema, however, appears not only in Ash'arite literature, but also in Hanbalite creeds and professions of faith, such as that of Ibn Batta (d. 997).[47]

Having declared their allegiance to the seventy-three-sect enumeration revealed by the Prophet, the heresiographers were left with the daunting task of dividing the world of Islamic heresy into precisely seventy-two units. In some cases, they made "convulsive endeavors to squeeze out the required number," particularly by "cutting, inserting, and combining, till they reach the number of 73."[48] Among the more curious devices used by Baghdadi for arriving at the canonical number is "regarding each of the more important Mu'tazilites as head of a sect and, when he had too many sects, stating that some were so heretical that they had ceased to be Muslims. The procedure of ash-Shahrastani is somewhat similar."[49] The noted Hanbalite traditionist and theologian, al-Jili (d. 1166), adopted the more economical strategy of simply counting some sects twice, under two different rubrics, in order to produce the canonical seventy-two.[50] Such heresiographical manipulations were facilitated, and even perhaps partly justified, by the fact that some Islamic sects were neither very discrete nor stable. In fact, the Arabic term *'firqa'* "is used to refer not only to a sect proper, but to doctrinal tendencies within sects and even to lone individuals."[51]

Having divided the world of Islam into seventy-three sectarian units, Shahrastani and other Islamic heresiographers related these sects to one another by their positions on major doctrinal issues, not according to their historical connections. Shahrastani identified four such issues, which provided the rubric for his classification of the Islamic sects. The noted non-Ash'arite heresiographer, Ibn Hazm (994–1064), devised a similar schema in which he distinguished four mother-sects or master heresies by their doctrinal positions on as many issues.[52] In this advanced form of schematization, not only are the historical connections among the sects rendered irrelevant, but so are their tenets and teachings, apart from one master doctrine which supposedly determines the character of the group. For example, Ibn Hazm remarked summarily of the Shi'ites that "the pillar of their speculation is the question of the Imamate and the Degrees of excellence of the Companions of the Prophet. Outside of this they differ as much as the others. . . . He who agrees with the Shi'ites that 'Ali is the most excellent of men after the Prophet and that he and his descendants after him are worthier of the Imamate than anyone, is a Shi'ite, though he differ from them in all other matters regarding which the Muslims are divided in their opinions."[53] This propensity "to isolate one concept . . . rather than to describe the range of ideas in a given group" is not limited to Ibn Hazm, but appears in other Islamic heresiographical works as well.[54]

The artificiality of the theological clusters into which later Sunni heresiographers arranged the sects may be confirmed by the existence in Eastern Muslim sources of traces of "pre-cluster heresiographers" who present the sects as independent of one another, not as embedded in a network structure.[55] Eventually, however, even Eastern heresiographers succumbed to a schematizing impulse, though they assembled the sects in rather different ways from those used in the Ash'arite standard tradition. Specifically, they "adopt a neat 6 X 12 plan: the Community is divided into six major sectarian groupings, each of which in turn splits into twelve sub-sects, producing seventy-two errant sects."[56]

Medieval Islamic heresiographers also constructed binary arrangements for schematizing heresies. "By organizing the major heterodox groups into mutually opposed pairs," they were able "to stake out the coveted middle ground" for their own sect,[57] as indicated above in Chapter Three. For example, Shahrastani implicitly claimed for orthodox Sunnis the middle way between denying God's attributes with the heretical Mu'tazilites and ascribing to God bodily attributes with the equally heretical anthropomorphists.[58] He went on to propound the binary opposition of heresies as a general rule:

> The sects of the Mu'tazilites and Sifatiya are utterly opposed to each other. The same may be said of the Qadarites and Jabrites, the Murji'a and Wa'idiya, the Shi'ites and Kharijites. This opposition between one group and another has at all times manifested itself.[59]

In the course of schematizing Islamic sects in various arrays, binary or otherwise, the heresiographers often found it necessary not only to construct artificial networks between the sects with scant basis in historical reality, but also to reconfigure particular sects to meet the demands of the schema. One type of such reconfiguring involves the fleshing out of a bare-bones "sect," which might consist of little more than a name, so that it could bear the weight placed on it in a binary schema. For example, Shahrastani beefed up the elusive Jabrite "sect," which supposedly taught that man acts under the compulsion (*jabr*) of God, in order to create a foil for the far more substantial Qadarites, who taught that man controls his own actions. He did so primarily "to maintain that the Ash'arite view is a mean between those of the Jabriyya and Qadariyya," to avoid placing the Ash'arites in the polemically precarious position of seeming to adhere to an extreme position on an important issue.[60] This maneuver did not, however, prevent the later Hanbalite apologist and theologian, Ibn Taymiyya (1263–1368), from assimilating the Ash'arite position on this question to that of the heretical "Jahmites" (supposedly a sect of the Jabrites).[61] Since the supposed founder of this allegedly predestinarian sect, Jahm ibn Safwan (d. 745), left no writings or recognizable group of disciples, it was not possible to either confirm or disprove this accusation. Indeed, the word 'Jahmite' was less the name of an identifiable sect than it was a vituperative term taken over by heresiographers to facilitate their classifications.[62]

Another early Islamic "sect" whose remains were far too meager to fill the substantial slot allotted it in heresiographical schemas was that of the Sufrites. As Keith Lewinstein remarks, "The main problem confronting heresiographers was the lack of characteristically Sufrite doctrines with which the niche so carefully carved out for the group could be filled." However, "Heresiographers got better at disguising the problem as time went on."[63] They apparently attempted to "flesh out the sect" by equipping it with several satellite subsects. They even provided the sect with an eponymous founder, Ibn Saffar, whose historical existence is highly questionable.[64]

If the heresiographers filled out or beefed up some sects in the course of constructing their schemas, they also seem to have scaled back other sects because highlighting them did not serve their polemical purposes or systematic design. According to Montgomery Watt, this was the case with the Murji'ites: "In the historical development of Islamic thought, the Murji'ite trend was of great importance, but in the hands of the heresiographers Murji'ism dwindles away to almost nothing. The reason for this is doubtless that Murji'ism presented no clear heretical idea, since to a great extent it was a predecessor of Sunnism."[65] Because Sunnism, from the viewpoint of the Sunni heresiographers, was orthodox and therefore eternal, or at least fully present at the creation, it could not have undergone any significant historical development. Since designating the Murji'ite or any other sect as its predecessor would have been to admit as much, Murji'ism had to be downplayed lest its historical existence call into question the primacy and originality of Sunni orthodoxy.

Sunni heresiographers generally tended to view heresy as well as orthodoxy as historically inert. They "could not conceive of a development of doctrine but thought that it remained static and unchanging."[66] Hence their practice of reading contemporary heresies back into the past and interpreting heresies of their own day as reappearances of more ancient ones, in effect reducing past and present heresies to one another. This impression of the timelessness of particular heresies in Islamic heresiography is strengthened by the tendency, noted above, of characterizing individual heresies not as historical or social entities, or even as complexes of ideas, but as embodiments of a particular point. Thus Shahrastani's definition of the Kharijites as those who "rebelled against the legitimate imam accepted by the people" might be and was reductively applied to rebels of any time and place, irrespective of historical or social context. It did not matter "whether this rebellion took place at the time of the Companions against the rightfully guided imams, or against their worthy successors, or against the imams of any time."[67] Thus was the astonishing diversity of Islamic sectarianism schematically reduced to a few standard positions on key issues.

The diversity of Jewish sects during the period of rabbinic domination was somewhat less astonishing. Partly for this reason, the schemas constructed by rabbinic heresiographers for dealing with Jewish heresies were less elaborate than were their counterparts in either early Christianity or Islam. However, varieties of the same schematizing strategies used in the latter two religious traditions can be seen operating in rabbinic Judaism, if only in a reduced form. One of these is the numerological.

According to a famous saying by Rabbi Johanan recorded in the Tractate Sanhedrin 10 of the Talmud, "Israel did not go into exile until it had turned into twenty-four parties of heretics."[68] That is, "there were 24 different kinds of *minim* at the [time of the] destruction of the Temple" in A.D. 70.[69] This mythical number of twenty-four did not, however, loom nearly so large in rabbinic writings as did the number seventy-two in Islamic heresiography. Few if any rabbinic authors actually attempted to count Jewish sects by this numerological schema. To do so would have required a very fine appreciation of sectarian subtleties. A fifteenth-century author, al-Maqrizi, was constrained to include such obscure "splinter groups like the Jalutiyites who overstressed biblical anthropomorphism, Fayyumites who excessively applied the *notarion* (treatment of words as abbreviations) in their biblical exegesis, and even the Shahrashtanites who claimed that eighty verses had dropped out of the masoretic Pentateuch" even to reach the more modest number of ten Jewish sects plus the Rabbanites and Karaites.[70]

However, even Jewish writers who did not order their descriptions of heresies by a numerological standard show the almost universal heresiographical tendency to inventively multiply "hardly distinguishable confessional groups."[71] The great tenth-century Karaite heresiographer, al-Qirqisani, for example, treated as sects "small groups which clustered around the peculiar opinions of a certain teacher."[72] In other cases rabbis seem to have invented sects by simply adducing theoretical possibilities of denying orthodox doctrine, with little or no regard for historical reality.

A similar lack of regard for historical relationships informs the schemas by which rabbinic writers grouped Jewish heresies. Probably the most famous example of such a schema is Maimonides' classification of kinds of heretics by which of his celebrated "thirteen principles" they deny.[73] As with the similar schemas propounded by such Islamic heresiographers as Shahrastani, heresiography made for strange bedfellows: it associated "sects" that were not only mutually hostile to one another, but which might not have even recognized one another's existence.

If the grander heresiographical schemas, such as those propounded by Qirqisani, tended to multiply heresies to either fill out a classificatory schema or to score polemical points, Jewish writers more commonly operated in a reductionist mode, placing diverse sectarian tendencies under a single rubric. The prime example of such reductionist heresiography from late antique Judaism is that focused on the elusive "two powers in heaven" heresy. It is not certain that this term ever referred to a single group. But is is evident that its usage was eventually expanded to cover many different groups, including Christians, Gnostics, and Jews, most of whom regarded themselves as monotheistic.[74] By subsuming these various groups under one master doctrinal deviation, the claim that there were "two powers in heaven," which violated the most basic tenet of Judaism, rabbinic writers relieved themselves of the necessity of recognizing the nuances of sectarian shadings. Like their orthodox counterparts in other traditions, they realized the polemical advantage of tagging diverse groups of heretics by the tenets of the most radical, the extreme Gnostics who really *did* believe in "two powers in heaven."[75]

The master-heretical successor to the "two powers" heresy of antiquity, under which lesser heresies were subsumed in medieval Judaism, was the Karaite heresy. Karaism, like the two powers heresy, "was not a single movement but a constellation of movements, frequently in vigorous opposition to one another."[76] Nevertheless, it was commonly represented as rather monolithic in most rabbinic sources.

Finally, rabbinic writers operated in a similar reductionist mode, albeit on a smaller scale, in their polemical attacks on the most prominent heretical movement in early modern Judaism, Sabbatianism. In general, such polemicists as Moses Hagiz (1671–1751) ignored the complex distinctions between Sabbatian sub-groups, and portrayed it as a one-dimensional heresy. As Elisheva Carlebach has pointed out, "Hagiz was thoroughly acquainted with the spectrum of ideologies which made up eighteenth century Sabbatianism." But "it was easier and more dramatic to simplify the welter of different voices into one starkly drawn adversary."[77] This simplifying strategy also made it possible to project the most extremely aberrant behavior of a few individuals in the group, broadly defined, onto everyone associated with Sabbatianism.[78] In sum, rabbinic heresiographers, like their counterparts in other orthodox traditions, were capable of making the most subtle of distinctions between sectarian tendencies, as well as of collapsing all such distinctions into one grand heretical category, each as the polemical (or pedagogical) occasion demanded.

Unlike the three Western orthodox traditions surveyed, Neo-Confucianism lacked a canonical numerological basis for counting and ordering heresies. Even so, Neo-Confucian writers were as inclined toward schematizing heresies as were their counterparts in Western traditions.

Perhaps the most venerable of all the schematizing devices used by Neo-Confucian heresiographers was their binary pairing of heresies as complementary opposites centered on an orthodox middle way. As noted above in Chapter Three, the *locus classicus* for this sort of arrangement is Mencius's coupling of Yang Chu's alleged egotism with Mo Ti's indiscriminate altruism, which was cited by such major Neo-Confucian authorities as the Ch'eng brothers.[79] But later Neo-Confucian writers applied this sort of binary pairing of heretical opposites to other heresies and heterodoxies as well. The prominent Ming heresiographer, Ch'en Chien (1497–1567), for example, remarked that of those who reject Ch'eng-Chu orthodoxy, "the lofty enter into Buddhism and Taoism while the lowly incline toward utilitarianism."[80] A scholar of the Ch'ing era, Yang Ming-shih (1661–1736), posed a similar dichotomy, accusing Han and T'ang Confucians of "stagnating in [their concern with] the external while forgetting the internal," and Taoists and Buddhists of "concentrating on the internal while ignoring the external."[81]

Another prominent means by which Neo-Confucian writers schematically related heresies to one another and to orthodoxy was by arranging them in hierarchical networks. Ch'eng-Chu writers keyed these hierarchies to various scales, one of which was according to the degree to which the various heresies harmed the orthodox Way. According to Ch'eng Hao (1035–1085),

> The harm of Yang [Chu] and Mo [Ti] is greater than that of Shen-tzu and Han-tzu [two ancient Legalist philosophers], and the harm of the Buddha and Lao-tzu is greater than that of Yang and Mo . . . . Since the shallowness and crudeness of Shen-tzu and Han-tzu is obvious, Mencius only refuted Yang and Mo because of their deluding the world to a greater extent. The words of the Buddha are near to the truth, and thus cannot be matched by Yang and Mo. That is why they are so harmful.[82]

Later Neo-Confucians developed this hierarchy of heretical harmfulness in various ways. Chu Hsi, for example, distinguished the toxicity of different forms of Buddhism. He differentiated ordinary Buddhism, which merely damaged human morality, from Ch'an, which "wiped out all moral principles with nothing left."[83] The prominent early-Ming orthodox scholar, Hu Chü-jen (1434–1484), also ranked Ch'an as the most harmful of all heresies, remarking that "Ch'an's annihilation of heavenly principles is most rapid and exhaustive; Lao-tzu ranks next; and the utilitarians next."[84] Hu also arrayed Lao-tzu, Chuang-tzu, and Buddhism, in a similar hierarchy of harmfulness, as follows:

> Although Lao-tzu goes against the Way of the Sages, he does not dare to insult the Sages. Chuang-tzu does insult the Sages. But although he insults the Sages, he does not dare to insult the cosmos. The Buddha, however, insults the cosmos.[85]

In addition to grading their degree of harmfulness to the orthodox Way, scholars of the Ch'eng-Chu school also ranked heresies and heretics by the order in which the wayward were apt to be converted either from or to them. A canonical adumbration of this second sort of hierarchy of heresy appears in *Mencius*: "Those who desert the Mohist school are sure to turn to that of Yang; those who desert the Yang school are sure to turn to the Confucianist. When they turn to us we simply accept them."[86] Later Ch'eng-Chu scholars, however, commonly reversed the direction of such conversion sequences, primarily to show how indulgence in relatively minor heresies might lead to entrapment in a major one. Thus Ch'en Chien warned that the road to Ch'an led through Chuang-tzu.[87]

One of the most common types of heresiographical schematization or simplification in the Neo-Confucian tradition, as in other traditions, did not distinguish between heresies, hierarchically or otherwise, but rather reduced them to a sort of common denominator of error. This heresiographical maneuver was perhaps even more common in Neo-Confucianism than in the other traditions surveyed here in which the contrast between the unity of orthodoxy and the multiplicity of heresy was a major theme. This form of heresiographical reductionism may also be traced back to the first great Confucian heresiographer, Mencius. Although Mencius criticized his two major opponents, Yang Chu and Mo Ti, for going to opposite extremes, he also criticized them together "because in his mind they had both made a similar kind of mistake," as P. J. Ivanhoe has pointed out: "they had argued for moral judgments based upon calculations of *li* (benefit)."[88] If Mencius provided a precedent for finding a common point of error behind diverse heresies, he also furnished a memorable reductionist trope, based on a parable in which Mencius asked a ruler whether or not soldiers who fled only fifty paces from the scene of a battle were more meritorious than those who fled a full hundred paces (*Mencius* 1A. 3). Later heresiographers such as Chu Hsi and Lu Lung-ch'i (1630–1692) cited this parable to argue that divergent heresies were really pretty much the same in order of merit (or demerit).[89]

Later Ch'eng-Chu scholars gave different accounts of just what was the common point on which supposedly divergent heresies converged. The most attractive possiblity was selfishness, cited by Chu Hsi and some of his successors as the common failing of both the utilitarians on the one hand and the Buddhists and Taoists on the other.[90] According to the Ming heresiographer, Ch'en Chien, the heretical schools "all negate the naturalness of heavenly principles. They are as one in proceeding from the machinations and manipulations of selfish knowledge."[91]

Besides reducing all heresies to a common doctrinal (or moral) point, Neo-Confucian heresiographers also reduced them to one another, as did their counterparts in Western heresiographical traditions. But in contrast to the standard practice in the West, Ch'eng-Chu heresiographers overwhelmingly identified later heresies and heretics with the canonical ur-heresies condemned by Mencius, those of Yang Chu, Mo Ti, and Kao-tzu. As in other matters heresiographical, Chu Hsi set the Neo-Confucian precedent for this identification by likening those he regarded as the major heretics of his own era, Wang An-shih (1021–1086) and Su Shih (1036–1101), to Mo and Yang, respectively.[92] But Chu also likened Mo Ti's teachings to those of the Buddhists,[93] indicating perhaps that Chu used Mo more as an all-purpose heretical trope than as the basis for an exercise in comparative philosophy.

In any case, Chu's identification of latter-day heretics with the primary ur-heretics, Yang and Mo, resonated down through the Neo-Confucian tradition. The Ming heresiographer, Feng K'o (1524–1601), accused Wang Yang-ming of promoting Mo,[94] while the seventeenth-century philosopher, Huang Tsung-hsi (1616–1686), remarked that Buddhism was nothing more than a deepening of Yang and Mo. Indeed, Huang went so far as to claim that "from ancient times to the present, all harm stemmed from Yang and Mo."[95]

But Yang and Mo were not the only Mencian prototypes for all later heretics. Kao-tzu, Mencius's famous antagonist on the key issue of the nature of human nature, was just as fabulous a figure in the Neo-

Confucian chamber of heretical horrors. Here again, Chu Hsi set the tone for the reductionist identification of later heretics with Kao-tzu, particularly in his remark celebrating the death of his philosophical rival, Lu Hsiang-shan: "It is regrettable that Kao Tzu has passed away."[96] But Chu also specifically identified Kao-tzu's interpretation of human nature with that of the Buddhists, as well as Hu Hung and Su Shih, somewhat erroneously according to a modern philosophical analysis.[97] Later Ch'eng-Chu scholars, including Ch'en Ch'un (1159–1223) and Feng K'o, repeated Chu's identification, with Ch'en Chien, Lu Lung-ch'i (1630–1693), Hsiung Tz'u-li (1635–1709), and Lo Tse-nan (1808–1856) adding Wang Yang-ming to the equation.[98] In all these cases, Ch'eng-Chu scholars saw fit to gloss over subtle (and some not so subtle) philosophical differences among the varieties of heretics. Like the infamous first emperor of the Ch'in dynasty who decreed the standardization of all axle lengths in the realm, they sought to force-fit all heretical ways into one rut, mainly that created by the heresiarchs condemned by Mencius.

In sum, Neo-Confucian heresiographers were particularly inclined to make the simplifying assumptions that later heresies were disguised versions of earlier ones and minor heresies of major ones. Far from exhibiting a monstrous diversity, heresy for them presented the appearance of a monolithic poverty.

Sources of Heresy

Heresiographers' schematization of heresies tended to present them as static entities that lacked a developmental aspect. But while individual heresies might be so lacking, heresy as a whole, as depicted by orthodox heresiographers, was diachronic in a sense: it originated from some source or sources, then was transmitted through a line of succession, and finally reached a point of culmination at a time close to the present. Naturally, some of the schematizing tendencies we have seen illustrated above also operated on a diachronic scale in the "history" of heresy as recounted by the heresiographers.

While Christian heresiologists often obtained polemical advantage by contrasting the multiplicity of error to the singularity of orthodoxy, they also undertook to trace all error back to a single source. Occasionally, this source was conceived in moral or doctrinal terms. Augustine, for example, held that all heresies originated from a lack of charity.[99] And the sixth-century Byzantine heresiologist, Leontius of Byzantium, declared that all of the four major heresies known to him, those of Sabellius, Arius, Nestorius, and the Monophysites, came from the same root, the confusion of the hypostases and natures of Christ.[100]

But early Christian heresiologists more frequently personified the cause or source of heretical error in the figure of a heresiarch. Heresiarchs, of whom there were several in early Christianity, were for the most part originally historical persons, though they were gradually enveloped in a mythical aura. While the Devil was increasingly recognized as the ultimate source or inspiration of error, with the eschatological false prophet rating at least a (dis)honorable mention,[101] the primary Christian heresiarchs were not of the demonic race save by adoption.

By far the most popular (or unpopular) candidate for heresiarch in early Christianity was Simon the Magician (Simon Magus), generally identified with the Simon who makes a brief appearance in the New Testament in Acts 8:9–24 where he offers St. Peter money in exchange for the gift of the Holy Spirit. Peter rebukes him for what became known as the sin of "simony." From this rather unpromising beginning, Simon's heresiarchal stature swelled to the point where he was recognized as the patriarch of heretics—not bad for a country boy from Samaria. According to Irenaeus, "all sorts of heresies derive their origin" from Simon.[102] The great church historian, Eusebius (d. c. 340), seconded this opinion, calling Simon "the prime author of every heresy."[103] Cyril of Jerusalem (d. 386) designated Simon as "the inventor of all heresy" and "the first dragon of wickedness" who spawned numerous heresies.[104] And Vincent of Lérins referred to him as "the one struck down by the apostle's reprimand, from whom that ancient torrent of vilenesses [Gnosticism] has, without interruption and in secret, continually flowed on."[105]

As the tale of Simon's manifold sins and wickedness grew with the telling, he increasingly took on a wider repertoire of demonic roles, as well as divine pretentions. Early Christian heresiologists condemned him primarily as the father of Gnosticism, the first great Christian heresy. But "As time went on, he was painted as a pseudo-Messiah and even as the Antichrist himself. More and more dreadful stories were told of the erstwhile magician," and "new features were ever being added until the portrait had achieved the desired degree of villainy. . . . Every conceivable heretical trait has been projected upon this one figure until he serves as the personification of heresy itself."[106] Simon thus provided a "solution" for the whole problem of heresy in the sense that "a single figure could be made accountable for the troublesome phenomenon."[107] So comprehensive and attractive (or unattractive) was this heresiographical portrait of Simon the heresiarch that even members of Gnostic sects, purportedly the first great heresy sparked by Simon, may have identified him as the Antichrist.[108] Although even Hitler and Stalin have their admirers, no one before modern times ventured to rehabilitate Simon, whose worst crime was apparently attempting to purchase the gift of the Holy Spirit. The ancient heresiologists were certainly among the most effective propagandists in world history, particularly over the long term.

To be sure, Simon was supposed to have been responsible for spawning a "demon-inspired succession of heretics," paralleling the apostolic succession headed by St. Peter.[109] But even the first link in this demonic succession, that between Simon and the Gnostics of the second century, is highly tendentious historically. As R. Mc L. Wilson had observed, "All attempts so far made have failed to bridge the gap between the Simon of Acts and the Simon of the heresiologists. It cannot be shown that the historical Simon already held the developed gnostic doctrines later attributed to him."[110]

On the other hand, the horror with which Christian heresiologists regarded this prince of heresiarchs, Simon the Magician, might well be explained as a projection of, or perhaps a way of exorcising, Christianity's own magical origins. If, indeed, "Christianity almost failed by virtue of its magical reputation," as Daniel O'Keefe has proposed, the need for such an exorcism, effected by the scapegoating of Simon, would have been all the greater.[111] At any rate, Simon's heresiarchal career has spanned almost the full extent of European history. In the early modern period, one of his epithets ("Faustus," or favored one) found its way into a distinguished line of literary works.

Although Simon was the premier heresiarch of early Christianity, the heresiarchal role was apparently too large for him to monopolize. As new heresies arose, their purported founders or leaders were sometimes inducted into the heresiarchal hall of infamy. But early Christian heresiologists did not necessarily embrace polyheresiarchism. Rather, they frequently referred to the particular heresiarch they were discussing at the moment in the most extravagant terms, as the supreme heresiarch, even though they might make similar statements about other heresiarchs in other contexts. In other words, a sort of serial heresiarchism appears in the works of early Christian heresiologists.

Although he could hardly match Simon's heresiarchal omnipresence, the second-century heretic Marcion (d. c. 160) perhaps even surpassed him in the degree of vitriol he evoked from heresiologists.[112] Polycarp called him the "Firstborn of Satan," and Irenaeus cursed him as "the devil's mouth piece." Tertullian likened him to a raging beast, and Cyril of Alexandria (d. 386) spoke of his "mouth of godlessness."

In brief, "No vituperation was too strong for the representatives of the Church to apply to Marcion."[113] But not all early Christian heresiologists who most strongly condemned Marcion necessarily gave him priority of place among heresiarchs. Irenaeus, for example, regarded him as the seal of the heresiarchs rather than as the founder of all heresy.[114]

Although Simon and Marcion were probably the most celebrated heresiarchs in Christian antiquity, there were a few others worthy of note. These include Valentinus, Origen, Mani, Arius, and even the Eve of the Book of Genesis.[115] As the list of heresiarchs grew, Christian heresiologists curiously conflated some of these to form a more fearfully composite figure consonant with their portrayal of heresy as a hydra-headed monster.[116] While this conflation may be thought of as a rational process that sought to reduce heresies and heresiarchs to their lowest common denominator, it may also be likened to a monstrous dream image whose various parts are pulled irrationally from hither and yon to form one misshapen monstrosity.

Although the figure of the heresiarch was ubiquitous in early Christian heresiology, heresiarchs were not the only heresiological explanation for the rise of Christian heresy. One explanation less amenable to mythological elaboration was the tracing of the origins of heresies to pagan or pre-Christian religion and philosophy. This mode of explanation is at least as old as the heresiarchal. It appears in the earliest Christian heresiology, that by Hegesippus, which is no longer extant save in fragments. Hegesippus related Christian heresies to seven Jewish ones, one of which was that supposedly advocated by Simon.[117] A somewhat similar schema appears in Hippolytus' *Refutation of All Heresies*. Hippolytus, however, traced heresies not to Jewish sects but to Greek philosophical schools and other pre-Christian systems of pagan thought.[118] According to Hippolytus, "from the philosophers the heresiarchs deriv[ed] starting points, (and) like cobblers patching together, according to their own particular interpretation, the blunders of the ancients, have advanced them as novelties to those that are capable of being deceived."[119] For example, "the opinions propounded by Valentinus . . . [are] not constructed out of the Scriptures, but out of the Platonic and Pythagorean tenets;" the Sethians "have patched together their own system out of shreds of opinion taken from Musaeus, and Linus, and Orpheus;" and the doctrines of Basilides "are the tenets of Aristotle the Stagyrite, not (those) of Christ."[120] But heretical appropriations of Greek philosophical ideas and doctrines were not simply plagiaristic, which alone would have discredited their pretentions to Christian truth, but degenerative as well. For "Greek philosophical ideas about the divine," however much they fall short of Christian revelation, "are more noble than the heretical notions."[121]

Hippolytus was not the only ancient Christian heresiologist who traced the origins of Christian heresy to pagan religion and philosophy. The celebrated Christian apologist, Tertullian, also systematically paired Greek philosophical schools with Christian heresies. He asserted, for example, that Valentinus "belonged to the school of Plato," and that "The god of Marcion came from the Stoics."[122] Irenaeus also accused heretics of having plagiarized the philosophers and poets, as did Origen who assimilated heresies to forms of paganism.[123]

Like Hippolytus, most early Christian heresiologists were not content with simply tracing the origins of various Christian heresies to forms of paganism, but sought to demote heresy to a level below that of the pagans, portraying it as the lowest form of religious life. God winked at the ignorance of the pagans, asserted St. Paul (Acts 17:30); but woe to him who brought any other gospel to Christian communities (Gal. 1:8). As the Latin proverb says, *Corruptio optimi pessimum est* ("The corruption of the best is the worst.")[124] Thus New Testament writers condemned those responsible for such corruption in the most extreme terms, as "agents of Satan," "seducers of men's minds," "those who make God a liar," and "representatives of anti-Christ abroad in the world."[125]

Later writers, as well, almost invariably ranked heretics below pagans. Irenaeus, for example, "showed himself to be much harder on the Gnostics than on the Jews and was altogether gentle with the pagans."[126] Hilary of Poitiers exclaimed with heretics in view: "how much greater is your godlessness than that of the Jew! He raises his stones against the body, you against the soul."[127] And Augustine proclaimed more pedantically that "it is worse to be a deserter from the faith and, by reason of desertion, an enemy of the faith than to be one who has never lost what he never had."[128]

In sum, a comparison of early Christian views of pagans and heretics seems to support "the general principle that in most contexts 'the closer the relationship, the more intense the conflict.'"[129] But perhaps this is not simply a case of a quasi-Darwinian contest for the same religious niche among various claimants to orthodoxy. For heresy presents the ominous spectacle of the loss of "the absolute truth that was already present, expressed in an historically unmistakeable manner."[130] Although the source of heretical ideas might lie with the pagan philosophers, these philosophers themselves could be judged rather benignly since they had no access to Christian truth, and did not therefore present the possibility of its denial in light of its full revelation.

The consideration of the *fullness* of the Christian revelation brings up the third, and most benign, general source of heresy as related by the heresiologists, one already adumbrated in the discussion in Chapter Three on the catholicity of orthodoxy. This is that the root of heresy lay not so much in the demonic machinations of heresiarchs, or in the appropriation and degeneration of pagan philosophical and religious ideas, but in a partial or one-sided apprehension of the truth. In other words, what most distinguished heresy was its taking the part for the whole: "Heresies are thus truth, but only partial truth which becomes error inasmuch as it takes itself to be the complete truth."[131] In the words of George Santayana, heresy is "due to exclusive interest and confidence in some province of orthodoxy. This chosen part—sometimes the part last discovered—is taken for the key to the whole."[132] John of Damascus (d. c. 749) found an appropriate biblical image for such heretical partiality: "Impious men," like the Roman soldiers at the crucifixion, "seek to rend asunder the seamless robe of Christ and to cut His Body to pieces."[133]

In the earliest Christian heresiologies, the partiality of heresy rests primarily on its alleged concentration on certain parts of the scriptural canon while ignoring or rejecting other parts. Irenaeus, in fact, classified heretics by which of the four gospels they isolated and elevated above the other three: the Ebionites accepted only the Gospel of Matthew, the Marcionites only the Gospel of Luke, certain other Gnostics preferred the Gospel of Mark, and the Valentinians relied on the Gospel of John.[134] Tertullian in the same vein declared that "Any given heresy rejects one or another book of the Bible. What it accepts, it perverts with both additions and subtractions to suit its own teaching."[135] Cyprian (d. 258) accused heretics of fixating on isolated passages of scripture taken out of context; and Epiphanius asserted that heresies rest on a partial reading of scripture.[136] So influential and pervasive was this view of heresy that it has been reasserted by a leading modern scholar of Patristics, G. L. Prestige: "It was the heretics that relied most on isolated texts, and the Catholics who paid more attention on the whole to scriptural principles."[137] In so saying, Prestige rather uncritically takes what was later recognized as the orthodox version of the canon as a given. In other words, he faults ancient heretics for not living up to an orthodox standard which they for the most part either opposed or did not anticipate.

With respect to doctrinal questions that arose after the scriptural canon was defined, the partiality of heresy often took the form of exaggerating a particular point of orthodoxy to the point of ignoring others, or disturbing the just balance of orthodoxy by going to an extreme. Here again, error arose not from the radically other, such as might be embodied by a heresiarch or a pagan philosopher, but from an incomplete version of the same. Orthodoxy and heresy in this view are distinguished not on the scale of truth–falsehood, but rather on that of wholeness–fragmentation or balance–disproportion. In fourth-century Christianity, the exaggeration of an orthodox tenet might lead so inevitably and patently to heresy that Julian the Apostate (d. 363), one of the most clever and articulate opponents of the new faith, routinely "embarrassed the orthodox by carrying some of their assertions to extreme logical conclusions."[138]

According to orthodox accounts, it was a one-sided exaggeration of one or another aspect of the orthodox Trinitarian and Christological syntheses that produced the major theological heresies of the fourth and fifth centuries. On the Trinity, specifically the question of how the three persons can be only one God, those who overemphasized the unity of the divine nature fell into varieties of modalism, while those who overstressed the deity of each person of the Trinity tumbled into tritheism. On the still stickier Christological issue, the Adoptionists accentuated the humanity of Jesus while the Docetists highlighted His divinity, both of which positions were heretical because they shortchanged their opposites.[139] While these rather simplified characterizations do not do justice to the full complexity of the debates on the key Trinitarian and Christological issues in fourth- and fifth-century Christianity, they do illustrate the orthodox heresiological viewpoint expressed by Cardinal Newman: "Heresies are partial views of the truth, starting from some truth which they exaggerate, and disowning and protesting against other truth, which they fancy inconstant with it."[140]

In general, the view of heresy as disproportion succeeded that of heresy as omission inasmuch as later polemicists disputed the right relation of elements within the Christian tradition rather than what did and did not belong in the tradition in the first place. The latter issue having been more or less settled with the closure of the New Testament canon around the end of the second century, theologians and heresiologists could concentrate on finer theological points within the tradition.

A final dimension or aspect of the partiality of heresy as interpreted by early Christian heresiologists is more social than intellectual. This is their characterization of heresies as parochial, in contrast to the universality of orthodoxy. Athanasius (d. 373), for example, accused heretics of displacing the universal Christ with some parochial figure:

"For with them in place of Christ is Arius, as with the Manichees Man-ichaeus."[141] Of course, it was the orthodox heresiologists, not their subjects, who applied parochial labels to various heresies, characteriz-ing them as mere personal followings opposed to the universal Church. As Brent Shaw has pointed out, by suggesting that heresies were simply aberrations "perpetuated by a solitary human individual to whom they could be attributed . . . , centralist orthodoxy achieved its tactical goal of marginalizing the prey."[142]

The proponents of orthodoxy localized as well as parochialized their heretical adversaries. Augustine, for example, asserted that though "the nets are stretched out over the whole world," those who break out "do so in certain places. The Donatists broke away in Africa, the Arians broke away in Egypt, the Photinians broke away in Pan-noia, the Cataphyrigians broke away in Phyrgia, and the Manichaeans in Persia."[143] Leander of Seville declared that heresies "arise either against a single corner of the earth or against one nation, but the Cath-olic Church extends throughout the whole earth and is composed of a society of many nations."[144]

In sum, early Christian heresiologists' accounts of the sources of heresy were dictated more by the polemical occasion or issue of the moment than by a concern for logical consistency. Although the major explanations for heresy that the heresiologists posed, the machinations of heresiarchs, the influence of pagan philosophy and religion, and a one-sided or disproportionate apprehension of truth are not necesssar-ily mutually contradictory, the totalizing language of the heresiologists tended to obscure this.

Islamic heresiographers identified as the sources of error the same unholy trinity, namely heresiarchs, paganism, and partiality, as did their Christian counterparts, though seldom if ever systematically. As in later Christian heresiology, so for Shahrastani and other Islamic heresiographers, it was ultimately the Devil who introduced error into the world and gave impetus to all future heresy.[145] But like their Chris-tian heresiological counterparts, Islamic heresiographers were seldom satisfied with a merely cosmic or demonic explanation of heresy. They sought to personify it in human form as well. This they did by con-structing a "more or less fabulous figure, of superlative malignity and perversity, who functions as a *diabolus ex machina* to explain dissension and heresy in the Islamic community."[146]

Like the early Christians, Islamic heresiographers ascribed here-siarchal status to several such figures. Probably the most infamous of them all was the ninth-century heresiarch, Ibn al-Rawandi, called "the pillar of heresy."[147] So notorious was Rawandi that news of his infamy spread even to Karaite Jewish writers who referred to him as a particularly dangerous and violent heretic.[148] The primary or "original" character of Rawandi's heresy is unclear. Like his Christian counterparts, he was later constructed into a sort of composite figure embodying quite a wide range of error. But Islamic heresiographers most frequently cited him as well as other heresiarchs not for any specific theological error, but rather for having "attacked the revealed religions in general and Islam in particular," for having "perpetuated an old and venerable tradition of polemic against the monotheistic revealed religions."[149] In particular, Rawandi supposedly cast doubt on the necessity and validity of prophecy, without which there would be no Islam, heretical or otherwise. He thus in some ways bears more resemblance to a pagan, rationalist, or materialist critic of revealed religion than to an Islamic heretic. But like Salman Rushdie in a later time, his association with Islam was deemed to be close enough to qualify him for heresiarchal status, by no means a mere technicality when the capital consequences of such a position are taken into consideration.

Islamic heresiographers sometimes imputed heresiarchal status to whole sects or schools, as opposed to individuals. For example, al-Taftazani (1322–1389) identified the rationalist Mu'tazilites as "the first sect which laid the foundation for . . . that which contradicts the plain teaching of the Approved Way."[150] Since "It was in refuting the positions of the Mu'tazilite party that orthodox Islam finally came into its own and arrived at a mature expression of its Belief,"[151] there may be some historical basis for the identification of the Mu'tazilites as the mother of all heresies (or at least of orthodoxy).

Inasmuch as some of its heresiarchs are associated with paganism, there is more of an overlap in Islamic heresiography between the first and second sources of heresy, heresiarchs and paganism, than there was in early Christianity. In fact, a common accusation against noted heretics in Islam is that they are engaged in a plot to undermine Islam from within in favor of some other faith or philosophy.[152] Sunni fundamentalists of both ancient and modern times have traced beliefs and policies of the extremist Shi'a to Jewish and even Christian sources.[153] The semi-legendary figure accused of starting the tendency to *ghuluww* or extremism, Ibn as-Sawda, was reputedly a Jew who converted to Islam.[154] According to Steven Wasserstrom, "It would be difficult to find a Muslim heresy that was not at one time or another traced back to a Jewish originator."[155]

The sect of Islam which heresiographers most unreservedly traced to the influence of other religions is the Isma'ili, the "seveners" within the broader Shi'ite category. According to the great Sunni heresiographer, al-Baghdadi, the Isma'ilis' main goal and strategy was to smuggle foreign religious goods (or evils) into Islam under the guise of devotion to the family of the Prophet.[156] After mentioning earlier heresiographers' views that the Isma'ilis were crypto-Zoroastrians or crypto-Sabeans, al-Baghdadi reports his own "discovery," that "the Isma'ilis are Darhites and Zindiqs, who believe in the eternity of the world and deny positive religious law and prophecy."[157] Modern scholars, however, have contested the conclusions of the heresiographers on this point. According to W. Madelung, "The assertion of the anti-Isma'ili polemicists and heresiographers that Isma'ilism was derived from various dualist religions, Zoroastrianism, Manichaeism, Bardesan, Mazdakism, and the Khurramdiniyya is not borne out by its early doctrine."[158]

Although heresiographers in all three of the Western religious traditions considered here generally condemned heretics more stridently and severely than they did adherents of other religions, this tendency is especially marked in Islam. Here, again, it is the extremist Shi'ites, particularly the Isma'ilis or Batiniyya ("those who give primacy to the inner, esoteric, or *batini* meaning behind the literal wording of all religious texts"[159]), who bear the brunt of the ultimate anathema. According to al-Baghdadi, "the damage caused by the Batiniyya to the Muslim sects is greater than the damage caused them by the Jews, Christians and Magians; nay, graver than the injury inflicted on them by the Materialists and other non-believing sects; nay, graver than the injury resulting to them from the Antichrist who will appear at the end of time."[160] Later Sunnite heresiographers reaffirmed al-Baghdadi's condemnation of the Batiniyya and their ilk. Al-Ghazali (d. 1111) called the Isma'ilis "the worst of God's creatures, whose unbelief is even more serious than that of the Pharoah."[161] Abu Muhammad al-Iraqi, a near contemporary of Ghazali, also frantically attacked the Isma'ilis, "labelling them as far more dangerous to Islam than were Christians and Jews," for they "made the Prophet superfluous, by giving all authority to the imam."[162] Even mainstream Shi'ites, those of the Twelver persuasion, condemned their extremist coreligionists as worse than heathens. According to Shaykh Abu Ja'far, such *ghulat* (extremists or exaggerators) are "more wicked than the Jews, the Christians, the Fire-Worshippers, the Qadarites or the Kharijites."[163] Another Twelver Shi'ite, Ibn Babawayh al-Qumm (d. 991), also denounced the *ghulat* as "infidels and worse than the Jews, Christians, and polytheists."[164]

In view of the severity of orthodox condemnation of extremist Shi'ite groups, it is hardly surprising that Islamic heresiographers were not as inclined as were their early Christian counterparts to interpret heresies as arising from a partial apprehension of true religion. For how could heresies so horrible have their source in a partial understanding of orthodoxy? Nevertheless, the very use of the term 'extremist' or 'exaggerator' (*ghulat*) to characterize the worst heresies seems to imply a point of departure in an orthodox tenet, such as "veneration for prophets and the righteous,"[165] carried to the immoderate end of imam-worship. On the other hand, the orthodox image of Islam as "the straight path" seems to signify a more absolute division between orthodoxy and heresy in which the deviant no longer has even one foot anchored in the Way.

While the evidence that Islamic heresiographers conceived heresies as partial apprehensions of orthodoxy is not overwhelming, some of them did characterize particular heresies as parochial or partial in another way, as socially selective or secretive. According to al-Baghdadi, the batiniyya, in particular, "keep their doctrines secret and communicate them only to initiates who are made to swear never to reveal them."[166] This secretiveness, which reflected their belief that the Qur'an itself had an allegorized, inner meaning that could be penetrated only by the initiates, served to isolate them somewhat from the great community of Islam.

Although Jewish heresiographical literature is not as extensive as that of either Christianity or Islam, it arguably offers up the most impressive array of heresiarchs. A few of these, particularly Satan, Cain, and Simon Magus, rabbinic Jews shared with the Christians. But the most commonly invoked heresiarch in later rabbinic literature, Menasseh, is unique to Judaism. The historical Menasseh, a priest in Jerusalem around the time of Ezra who was deposed from the priesthood, was supposedly responsible for the conversion of the Samaritans as well as for inducing the latter to accept only the Pentateuch as completely authoritative scripture.[167] This position implied that the Oral Torah, the canonical character of which was the main touchstone of rabbinic orthodoxy, was of lesser value and of less than divine origin. Small wonder that "In the opinion of the Rabbis, Menasseh was the most renegade and the greatest of all infidels."[168] The rabbinic viewpoint on the essence of Menasseh's archheresy was perhaps best expressed by Maimonides:

> Indeed, Menasseh became, in the eyes of the Sages, the person strongest in heresy and hypocrisy for he thought that the Torah was composed of kernels and husks and that these dates and these narratives had no value and that they were composed by Moses. This is the issue of 'the Torah is not from heaven.'[169]

The denial that the Torah came from heaven was also the key point in the archheresy of a second prominent heresiarch in the rabbinic tradition, Korah. Although Korah was known primarily for his rebellion against the leadership of Moses and Aaron at Sinai, the Talmud also charged him with having claimed that "The Torah does not come from Heaven."[170] Thus both Menasseh and Korah, in contrast with the premier heresiarchs in the early Christian and Islamic traditions, were specifically linked with the major touchstone of doctrinal orthodoxy in their tradition, the status of the Torah.

In early rabbinic Judaism, however, a heretic at least as redoubtable as Menasseh and Korah was the infamous Elisha ben Abuya (c. 110–134). So notorious was Elisha in the emerging rabbinic tradition that he "was disrespectfully named 'Aher' (Other), by the rabbis, as if he were too infamous to name directly."[171] He functioned "as the heretic *par excellence*" in early Rabbinism, "as Simon Magus does in Christian heresiological tracts."[172] While the historical Elisha is at least as inaccessible as the historical Simon, his near contemporary, both heresiarchs were associated with Gnosticism. Again like Simon, Elisha served as a convenient peg on which later heresiographers hung a variety of heretical views, not just those of Gnosticism.[173] The most seriously heretical of these ideas was Elisha's alleged denial of monotheism, his admission of "two powers in heaven." He was supposedly led into this error by a vision in which he saw the angel Metatron sitting in heaven. "Knowing that only God and not the angels sits," he jumped to the conclusion that there were "Two Powers in heaven."[174]

Even after the demise of the Two Powers heresy in ancient Judaism, the figure of Elisha ben Abuyah continued to fascinate Jewish intellectuals. Isaac Abravanel (1437–1508) singled him out as one whose heresy was "brought about by premeditated rebelliousness" and for whom "the gates of repentance were sealed."[175] When a nineteenth-century Jewish man of letters translated Goethe's *Faust I* into Hebrew, "he could think of no better title for it that 'Ben Abuyah.'" Since the roots of the Faust legend have been traced to Elisha's contemporary, the heresiarch Simon Magus with whom he was sometimes conflated, this Hebrew translation of 'Faust' is appropriate.[176]

While Elisha ben Abuya was probably the primary heresiarch of early Rabbinism, the rabbis also pinned heresiarchal labels on biblical figures, including the Adam and Cain of the Book of Genesis. Since there was a long tradition of exegesis linking Cain with later heretical groups, it was natural to trace contemporary heretics back to this biblical progenitor, and even to put sectarian debates between the Sadducees and the Pharisees of the first century into the mouths of

Cain and Abel.[177] Later heretics who, like the Sadducees, denied the immortality of the soul were also linked with Cain.[178] In sum, Cain, like other heresiarchal figures, was later molded into a sort of heretical microcosm which contained the seeds of all things heretical.

The rabbis did not, however, monopolize heresiarchal discourse in the medieval Jewish tradition. The great tenth-century Karaite heresiographer, Ya'qub al-Qirqisani, identified the primal heresiarch and schismatic in Judaism as King Jeroboam. According to Qirqisani, "The first to show dissension in the Jewish religion, to sow disobedience to the Law among the people of Israel, subsequent to the establishment of the monarchy, to alter the divine ordinances and to supplant them was Jeroboam."[179] To Jeroboam, Qirqisani traced the depraved practices of the Rabbanites as well as those of other Jewish sectarians such as the Samaritans and the Sadducees. Thus while the heretical Gnostics in early Christianity and the heretical Shi'ites in Islam generally recognized the same heresiarchs as did the orthodox Christians and Muslims, the "heretical" Karaite, al-Qirqisani, nominated one of his own who occupied only a minor place in rabbinic heresiography.[180]

Since Judaism was older than most if not all other religions within its purview, rabbinic heresiographers were not in a position to seek the origin of the earlier Jewish heresies in pre-existing religions and philosophies. They did, however, occasionally express the fear that heresies such as the seventeenth-century messianic movement, Sabbatianism, were stepping stones leading to conversion to Christianity or Islam.[181] On the other hand, some Rabbinites regarded their heretical brethren as a step below adherents of other faiths (and even nonfaiths). Maimonides, for example, characterized the Samaritans as "much inferior to heathens."[182] And the Karaite Qirqisani remarked of the Rabbanites that "They surpass in nonsense and lying even the Christians."[183]

Regarding the third major alleged source of heresy in most traditions, the partial or one-sided apprehension of orthodox truth, the Rabbinites had less to say than did their orthodox Christian counterparts. However, Saadiah Gaon (882–942) did disapprovingly characterize the medieval Hasid as one "who all his life devotes himself to one particular religious commandment to which he stays obedient under any circumstances, even though he may be inconsistent in fulfilling other commandments."[184] A recent account of Maimonides' critique of heresy attributes to him the view that the partiality of heretics was more cynical and calculated, that "The heretics would cunningly lay hold of the borders of the truth" in order to gain a tactical advantage.[185] Maimonides and other sages also spoke out against the partial view that gave too much prominence to the Ten Commandments "because this might give rise to the heretical opinion that only these were revealed by God and not the rest of the Torah."[186]

Although Neo-Confucian heresiography had little if any historical contact with that of early Christianity, Islam, or Judaism, its accounts of the roots of heresy are rather similar to those of Western traditions. As in the Western monotheistic religions, Neo-Confucian heresiography traced heresy to three main sources: heresiarchs, the influences of other religions, and a partial or one-sided apprehension of orthodoxy.

Perhaps owing to the lack of a developed demonology or eschatalogy, Neo-Confucian accounts of heresiarchs are a little more mundane than are those in Western religious traditions. There is no specter of a Prince of Darkness, an Antichrist, or an eschatalogical false prophet or false messiah lingering in the shadows of more historical heresiarchs. Nor do the heresiarchs in Neo-Confucian representation rely so heavily as do some of their Western counterparts on deception and intrigue, an attribute which makes the latter more mysterious and menacing.

Among the most notable archheretics in the Neo-Confucian tradition are those (en)countered by the archheresiographer in that tradition, Mencius. According to Mencius and some of his later Neo-Confucian interpreters, the two heresiarchs, Yang Chu, who supposedly espoused egotism, and Mo Ti, who favored indiscriminate altruism, almost exhausted the possibilities of heresy in their own time as well as gave rise to later ones.[187] Other Neo-Confucian authorities, however, traced heresy and heterodoxy back to what they regarded as a more remote source, the classical philosopher Lao-tzu. According to Chu Hsi, "Yang Chu was the disciple of Lao-tzu. To say that Mencius did not refute Lao-tzu is to not know Mencius. To refute Yang and Mo is to include Lao and Chuang [in the refutation]."[188] Hsiung Tz'u-li, in a similar vein, called Lao-tzu "the granduncle of the heresies of all times."[189] Thus, the major heresiarchs identified by the Neo-Confucians, unlike most of those in Western heresiographical traditions, were outside the tradition in the sense that they did not pretend to be followers of the Confucian sages.

One consequence of this was a degree of overlap between our first two major sources of heresy, that is, heresiarchs and the influence of other religions, in Neo-Confucian heresiography. However, when they discussed the filiation of ideas of contemporary heretics, as opposed to the origins of heresy in general, Neo-Confucian commentators were more inclined to trace heretical error to the latter-day Buddhists than to the heterodox philosophers of classical antiquity. The noted sixteenth-century heresiographer, Ch'en Chien, attributed the corruption of Confucianism from the Sung era to his own time primarily to "the virulent contagion from Buddhism."[190] His contemporary, Feng K'o, traced the errors of Wang Yang-ming to the influence of Ch'an Buddhism, sounding a theme later echoed by Ch'eng-Chu scholars in the seventeenth century, such as Lu Lung-ch'i.[191]

Unlike their counterparts in Western traditions, particularly Islam, Neo-Confucian heresiographers do not seem to have consistently ranked Confucian heretics lower than the followers of heterodox traditions such as Buddhism and Taoism. However, the stalwart seventeenth-century Ch'eng-Chu scholar, Lu Lung-ch'i, did remark that "in evaluating [degrees of] heresy in the Han and Sung eras, [we find] that the Huang-Lao [Taoists] are relatively minor and the [Confucian] textual scholars major. In evaluating [degrees of] heresy in the Chin, Sung, Ch'i, Liang, Ch'en, Sui, and T'ang eras, [we find] that the Buddhists are relatively light and the [Confucian] poetasters heavy."[192] But even this statement is more measured and moderate than Christian and Islamic characterizations of heretics in their respective traditions. Perhaps the Neo-Confucian view of the potential goodness of human nature inspired Neo-Confucian scholars to take a kinder, gentler view of heretical lapses and of the possibility of correcting them.

In any case, Neo-Confucian commentators by far preferred the most benign general type of heresiographical explanation for the rise of heresy, namely that it was a partial or one-sided expression of orthodoxy. The germ of this mode of explanation may be traced back to the classical philosophers, even to Confucius himself, who expostulated on the pitfalls of one-sidedness: "Study without thinking is in vain; thinking without study is perilous" (Analects 2.15). According to standard accounts of the development of classical Confucianism, the Confucian Way first fell into disrepair following the death of the Master when his disciples each absolutized or overemphasized one side or another of the implicit polarities in his teaching.[193] One of these later disciples, Hsün-tzu, accused other classical philosophers of having followed the model of the ancient kings in only a fragmentary way and of teaching doctrines that were one-sided.[194] But the most comprehensive and influential statement from ancient China of the partiality of heresy or of rival schools of philosophy appears in the syncretist "T'ien-hsia" chapter of the *Chuang-tzu*, which probably dates from the early Han era (202 B.C.–A.D. 9):

The world fell into great disorder. Worthies and sages did not show themselves. The Tao . . . was no longer unified and the world's people for the most part gained only a single glimpse of it, according to whatever they themselves most liked. They were like the ear, eye, nose and mouth, each with its own perceptive faculty, not communicating with any other. So it is with the many ramifications of the Hundred Schools, none of which, though each has its own strength and utility at a particular time, is wholly sufficient or universal.[195]

The author of this chapter goes on to contrast the comprehensive philosophy of the Way with the partial teachings of six groups of philosophers, each of which only grasped one corner of the complete Way. The noted imperial bibliographer, Liu Hsiang (77–6 B.C.), transposed this sort of assessment of the classical schools of philosophy into a Confucian key in an essay later incorporated into the bibliographical treatise of the dynastic history of the Former Han era.[196] So well-established did this concept of heresy as partiality become in later Chinese thought that the T'ang-era Buddhist philosopher, Tsung Mi (780–841), used it to criticize rival Ch'an traditions or schools.[197] In the Ch'eng-Chu Neo-Confucian tradition, the characterization of heresy and heterodoxy as partiality or one-sidedness first appears in the works of the Ch'eng brothers, who accuse the Buddhists of embracing one end of a polarity while ignoring the other end: "In Buddhists' studies there is reverence in order to direct the inner [life], but there is lacking rightness to square the outer [world]. . . . This is the reason why Buddhist teaching is narrow."[198]

Chu Hsi also criticized his contemporary philosophical rivals for having allegedly shown partiality to one half of a complementary duality while ignoring the other. For example, he accused Lu Hsiang-shan of trying to apprehend the inner while ignoring the outer and Su Shih of trying to attain the Tao while discarding its instruments.[199] According to Li Kuang-ti, Chu even went so far as to criticize Mencius for neglecting material force while discussing principle, even as he reproved Hsün-tzu and Yang Chu for the opposite error.[200] Thus even Mencius was not immune from the charge of one-sidedness.

Chu's followers in the Southern Sung and Yüan eras echoed the Master's condemnations of heretical partiality. For example, Shih Te-ts'ao charged that "Buddhist discussions of human nature illuminate substance [or principles] but do not illuminate function [or practice]."[201] And Hsü Ch'ien (1269–1337) accused Kao-tzu, Mencius's principal opponent on the vexed question of human nature, of "pointing solely to the inner dimension," while crediting Mencius with "making the inner and outer both be attained."[202]

The early-Ch'ing Ch'eng-Chu scholar, Chang Li-hsiang (1611–1674), criticized Lu Hsiang-shan for his alleged partiality, particularly his having apprehended only one end of a key Neo-Confucian polarity, that "principle is one, but its particularizations are diverse" (li-i fen-shu). According to Chang, Lu "understood principle's being one, but did not understand its particularizations being diverse. Thus he drifted into Buddhism and Taoism."[203] Chang also charged that latter-day Confucians divided "honoring the moral nature" from "following the path of inquiry and study."[204] In short, for Chang, the basic source of error in the Confucian tradition was the one-sided emphasis on only one end of a polarity. No matter what the particular content or orientation of the polarity, Chang followed the same polemical formula of contrasting orthodox balance and completeness with heterodox imbalance and partiality. Chang's contemporary, Tiao Pao, adhered to a similar formula, contrasting the Confucian sages' comprehensive apprehension of human nature with that of "the Buddha who took the heart/mind to be the nature, Lao-tzu who took material force to be the nature, and the common people who take emotions to be the nature, all of whom obtain what is partial and lose what is comprehensive."[205]

The idea of error as partiality or imbalance was not limited to the four heresiographical traditions discussed above. Classical Hindu authorities, for example, accused the heterodox Buddhists and Jains of having exaggerated and unjustifiably universalized the Vedic teaching of ahimsa (non-harming).[206] In a remarkable modern heresiographical tract, Left-Wing Communism, an Infantile Disorder, Lenin charged that the leaders of the Second International had been "'enchanted' by one definite form of growth of the working class movement and of Socialism" to the point that "they forgot all about the one-sidedness of this form."[207] In the field of pathology, the nineteenth-century "positivist" theory that attributed disease to "exaggeration, disproportion, [and] discordance of normal phenomena"[208] also bears some resemblance to the conception of heresy as one-sidedness. So does Freud's characterization of psychosexual perversions, such as sadism, which "would correspond to an aggressive component of the sexual instinct which has become independent and exaggerated and, by displacement, has usurped the leading position."[209]

Whatever may be the etiology of the notion that heresy or sickness or perversion is a partial version of orthodoxy or health or normality, a drawing out of this process may lead to a surprising conclusion: if heresies are produced by dismembering orthodoxy, then could not orthodoxy or truth be reconstituted by putting the heretical pieces back together again? In the words of Santayana, "All the parts of orthodoxy might thus, in isolation, be called heretical, while the sum total and infinite life of heresy would be orthodoxy, or rather would be reality itself."[210]

Transmission of Heresy

Just as orthodox authorities in various traditions devised genealogies of orthodoxy, an "apostolic succession," a "chain of tradition," or a "transmission of the Way" to legitimize their positions, they also invented its perverse mirror image in genealogies of heresy to discredit the opposition. And just as these authorities generally traced the true transmission of orthodoxy back to the founding father of the tradition—Jesus, Muhammad, Moses, or the Confucian sages—so they usually tracked its demonic inverse back to a grand heresiarch. Although the heresiarch might have been originally only a minor historical character, the enormity of the succession of error he spawned required that he be portrayed as a figure of almost Satanic proportions, as discussed in the preceding section.

Even more than the genealogies of orthodoxy outlined above in Chapter Three, these corresponding genealogies of heresy were arbitrarily contrived for polemical purposes. First, these heretical lines of transmission were in most cases invented by orthodox heresiographers, not by their subjects, the alleged heretics. Second, genealogies of heresy, in comparison with most orthodox genealogies, were relatively unstable and imprecise, as well as lacking any institutional basis.[211] The links in the heretical chains of error were seldom joined historically, but usually only in the imaginations of orthodox heresiographers who creatively devised master-disciple relationships between heretical figures who in some cases did not even know of one another's existence.

For all its fearful symmetry, the heresiographical construction of a genealogy of heresy was not contrived simply to form a diabolical complement to the genealogy of orthodoxy. It also gave order and coherence to a very puzzling and diverse set of phenomena by linking them together in a chain of succession. As Bart Ehrman has remarked of early Christian treatments of Gnosticism, "It is hard to engage an opponent who cannot be grasped. Faced with a cacophany of disparate myths, beliefs, and practices, the heresiologists undertook to restore a semblance of coherence to the disparate groups of Gnostics by tracing (or better creating) their various genealogical relationships."[212] The genealogy of heresy having been established, later heresiographers found it both effective and economical to attack later heresies by linking them with already refuted and discredited earlier ones. As Tertullian remarked, "they will be more easily refuted when they are discovered either to have been already in existence at that time [of the apostles] or to have taken their seeds from those which then existed."[213] When the relationship between the earlier and the current heresy seemed remote, heresiographers might creatively draw out the alleged consequences of the former in order to affiliate it ideologically with the latter, a procedure apparently limited only by the imagination of the heresiographer.[214]

In early Christianity, the idea of a genealogy of heresy or of a pseudo-apostolic succession may be traced all the way back to New Testament canonical writings, particularly the Epistle of Jude. According to a recent interpretation of this epistle, its author placed the "false prophets" of his own time "in a long line of 'heretics' beginning with Cain. This suggested that there is a tradition of falsehood and godlessness parallel to the tradition of truth which culminated in the teaching of the apostles."[215] While the apostolic succession transmitted the true teaching, the theology of the heretics was "a deliberate distortion of the truth." Its purpose was to "blaspheme divine truth and lead astray the saints."[216] However, the Epistle of Jude does not link these heretics, including Cain, Balaam, Korah, the Sodomites, and the eschatalogical false prophets of New Testament times, in a strictly genealogical order of succession. Rather, the earlier Old Testament heretics are more like prefigurations of particular types of error that appeared again in the author's own time. A more properly genealogical order, which became the standard line of heretical succession, appears in the work of Justin Martyr (d. 165), who drew the line from Simon Magus to Menander to Marcion. However, even Justin does not specify how heresy was transmitted from one to the other in this line.[217]

Irenaeus, the author of the first extant Christian heresiology, followed this more standard model, tracing heresy from Simon through Menander to the later Gnostics. But he too "does not really provide us with any family tree, or any real demonstrations of connections and relationships."[218] The great church historian, Eusebius, also affirmed this line of heretical succession, which he "put forward as a diabolical counter to the true apostolic succession of the orthodox church."[219] Finally, Epiphanius, the seal of the ancient Christian heresiologists, further extended and universalized this *successio haereticorum*, positing a global genealogy of error "between pre-Christian and Christian heresies, between Hellenic and Christian heresies, [and] between Christian heresies themselves originating from the Samaritans and Simon," albeit with many cases of "forced filiation."[220] In his hands, the idea of an heretical succession became a powerful polemical weapon by which contemporary heretics could be judged guilty by association with earlier, archetypal heresies.

As new heresies arose in later Roman and Byzantine Christianity, orthodox heresiologists continued to link them with earlier ones, further extending the genealogy of error. According to iconophiles in eighth- and ninth-century Byzantium, the heretical iconoclasts were the successors of a number of ancient heretics, including the Manicheans, the Marcionites, the Docetists, and the Samaritans, among others.[221] However, as later heresies were added to earlier ones, it became more difficult to accommodate all of them within a single line of succession. Thus, more complex general schemes made their appearance, such as that by John of Damascus which identified four "parents and archetypes of all heresies."[222]

The idea of a genealogy of heresy by which later heresies were identified as the successors of earlier, archetypal ones, survived the heretical hiatus of the early middle ages in the Latin West to reemerge in the twelfth century when new heresies arose. In describing and categorizing the religious dissenters of their own day, late medieval churchmen drew heavily on ancient heresiological literature. Conditioned by their reading of this literature, these churchmen tended to assume that the dissenters of their own time were spiritual and in some cases even historical descendants of "the heretics of old."[223] But this assumption did not lead them to compare coolly and systematically the new heresies with the old, but rather served primarily to heighten their antiheretical histrionics: "The names of the great heresiarchs of antiquity conjured both the destructive power of heresy to shatter the unity of the church . . . and the majesty and authority of the fathers who had joined and defeated it in battle."[224]

The motif of a genealogy of heresy does not appear so prominently in Sunni Islamic heresiography as in that of early Christianity. This could be a function of the Islamic tendency to trace the origins of heresy more to the influence of other religions than to heresiarchs who might serve more credibly as anchors for heretical lines of succession. Moreover, even such heresiarchs as did appear in Islam were not, so to speak, present at the creation, as were Simon Magus, Cain, or Lao-tzu. Rather, they were generally latter-day figures like Ibn al-Rawandi who were born after the first great sectarian divisions appeared in Islam. Hence, they could hardly be identified as the ultimate progenitors of those sects.

Nevertheless, some Sunni heresiographers did sketch the out-
lines of a genealogical framework. As mentioned in the previous
section of this chapter, a common feature of orthodox Sunni heresiography is the tracing of all later sects to a small number of "mother
sects," usually four or six.[225] The master heresiographer, Shahrastani,
seems to have envisaged "a larger continuum of rebellion throughout
history,"[226] though even he did not symmetrically counterpose a single
genealogy of heresy to that of orthodoxy. Perhaps Sunni heresiographers were more aware than were their Christian counterparts of the
dualist, Manichean, and therefore heretical implications of this sort of
arrangement, and therefore forebore to express it openly. Or perhaps
they feared that sketching a precise genealogy of error might provide a
sort of negative confirmation for Shi'ite imamologies.

Like their counterparts in other traditions, some rabbinic writers
drew a long line of heretical descent from antiquity to their own day.
Haham David Nieto, for example, took "pains to trace the chain of heresy from Zadok and Boethos, via Anan and Saul, through the 'Karaites'
of his own time" (the eighteenth century).[227] More frequently, however,
the rabbis concentrated on simply linking a current heresy to an already
discredited one of former times, often quite unhistorically. This may be
illustrated in rabbinic reactions to the first great medieval heresy, that of
the Karaites.

As Bernard Revel has remarked, "most of the Mediaeval Jewish
scholars seem to agree that Karaism was due to a revival of the Sadducees (Abraham Ibn Daud) or that Sadducean elements are prominent
in it (Saadia, Judah Halevi)."[228] One basis for this identification of the
Karaites with the Sadducees is that both groups apparently rejected the
rabbinic Oral Law.[229] Most Karaites, however, strongly resented this
identification of their sect with the heretical Sadducees, though the
Karaites of nineteenth-century Russia did present themselves as descendants of the Sadducees, and hence as guiltless of the crucifixion of
Jesus.[230]

The debate on the possible link between the Sadducees and the
Karaites did not end with the breakup of rabbinic or normative Judaism toward the end of the eighteenth century, but has continued in
modern scholarship. Indeed, some modern commentators have portrayed this link in grander terms than did medieval rabbinic writers.
One such commentator, Abraham Geiger, put it in the context of "two
distinct, or rather, antagonistic currents [that] were at work shaping
the history of Judaism," thus raising the specter of parallel genealogies
of orthodoxy and heresy.[231] Geiger went so far as to portray the Karaites as "not only . . . the followers and spiritual heirs of the Sadducees,

but their physical descendants" as well.[232] More recent scholars, however, have pointed out that "the Sadducees and Karaites arose in response to different historical circumstances, in different regions, and as a result of different needs."[233]

The Karaite was not the last heretical movement in the history of Judaism to be linked with the Sadducees. In seventeenth- and eighteenth-century Sephardic literature, the term 'Sadducees' was generally applied to "contemporary deniers of the Oral Law."[234] Orthodox rabbis of the eighteenth century condemned the Hasidic *zaddik* in particular as "a sort of reincarnation of the priestly order of ancient days, like the Sadducees."[235]

The great seventeenth-century rabbinic polemicist, Moses Hagiz, associated his primary heretical opponents, the followers of Sabbatai Zvi (1626–1676), with several well-known heresies of the past, including those of the Samaritans, Sadducees, and the Karaites. "Hagiz' goal was to force Sabbatianism into the same byways of Jewish history as other ancient sects."[236] Rabbinic writers of the following century, in turn, linked the new heresy of Hasidism with Sabbatianism as well as earlier Jewish heresies.[237] But as Jacob Katz has pointed out, "The Hasidic movement itself was a new 'historic creation,' whose essential characteristics had not existed previously."[238]

If most Rabbanite versions of the heretical chain of transmission were rather segmented or truncated, some of the alleged heretics themselves forged the links thereof on a grander scale. The Karaites polemically traced their own origins back to the opponents of the biblical King Jeroboam, allegedly the first schismatic in Jewish history and the leader of the sinful majority of his day.[239] From this point, they took biblical allusions to a righteous few or undefiled remnant as referring to their own predecessors.[240] In the middle of the twelfth century, the Karaite apologist Jephet ben Sa'id even compiled a Karaite "'chain of tradition' from Moses to his own day,"[241] albeit a rather skeletal one. Karaite authorities, beginning with Qirqisani in the tenth century, also composed genealogies of rabbinic heterodoxy: "After Jeroboam came the Samaritans, and after them the 'chiefs of the Assembly,' that is the Rabbanites."[242] Thus were the Karaites, like the Shi'ites of Islam, as assiduous in compiling genealogies of both orthodoxy and heresy (from their own point of view) as were their orthodox opponents.

Modern aficionados of Jewish heresies have further developed and even transvalued heretical genealogies. This is particularly evident in the work of Gershom Scholem, perhaps the greatest modern investigator of counterrabbinical Judaism. In his effort "to find a continuity in Jewish esotericism, so as to establish a counter-tradition to the normative," Scholem has linked such diverse sectarian men, movements, and manuscripts as Merkabah mysticism, Jewish Gnosticism, medieval German Hasidism, the *Zohar*, Isaac Luria, Nathan of Gaza and the Sabbatians, Baal Shem Tov and the Hasidim, "with Scholem as philological yet also theological epilogue."[243] In so doing, Scholem apparently transvalued not only heresy, making it one of the "true driving forces in Jewish history,"[244] but also heresiography, which he enlisted in the service of the heretical.

Inasmuch as the orthodox Neo-Confucian "tradition of the Way" did not require direct historical contact for its transmission through the centuries, Neo-Confucian commentators were understandably not so constrained by mere historical or biographical considerations in devising a corresponding tradition of heresy. Even more than their counterparts in other orthodoxies, the Neo-Confucians linked disparate teachers, having little or no historical relationship with one another, in a single heretical tradition. Chu Hsi expressed a simple version of this tradition in positing that "Yang Chu was the disciple of Lao-tzu," and that "the teaching of the Buddha came forth from Yang."[245] Liu Tsung-chou (1578–1646) drew out a more extended line of heresy, starting with Lao-tzu, its great progenitor, with Yang and Mo, the Legalists, Su Shih, and Chang Shih (1133–1180) as later links in the chain.[246] The paramount modern Confucian philosopher, Mou Tsung-san, updated this tradition by placing the modern pragmatist philosopher, Hu Shih, in the same contra-Confucian current as that ancient nemesis of Confucianism, Mo Ti.[247]

Some Ch'eng-Chu scholars of the early Ch'ing era, particularly Lu Shih-i (1611–1672) and Lü Liu-liang (1629–1683), held that all of the great heresies of this tradition were essentially the same, that the links in the heretical chain of transmission simply replicated one another.[248] The seventeenth-century heresiographer, Chang Lieh, even charged the philosopher Wang Yang-ming with the same crimes as those of the infamous first emperor of the Ch'in dynasty: eliminating the boundaries between fields, abolishing feudalism, and burning the *Songs* and *Documents* classics.[249] Other orthodox Ch'ing scholars, however, cast the history of heresy in a more diachronic mold. Fang Tung-shu, for example, portrayed each successive generation of heresiarchs in ancient times, from Lao-tzu, to Chuang-tzu and Lieh-tzu, to Yang and Mo, as departing ever further from the Way.[250] A more obscure Ch'ing scholar, Han T'an (1637–1704), maintained that heresy evolved through the later heretics, such as the Buddhists, having fully and openly expressed what was only implicit in the teachings of the earlier heretics, such as Yang and Mo:

From the traces left by Yang and Mo, [we see that they] definitely had not reached the point of rejecting lord and father. But extrapolating from their sayings, the harm [caused by them] could straightaway [develop to the point of] negating lord and father. Mencius was concerned that the calamity arising from this might be unending. Later, when Buddhist learning entered [China], it straightaway dared to issue forth [this] impropriety [of rejecting lord and father, thus confirming Mencius' fear].[251]

In this schema, there is no question of a direct personal relationship between earlier and later heretics such as might be implied by the word 'genealogy.' The succession, rather, is an intellectual or spiritual one in which the latter-day heretics carry the underlying premises of their predecessors to their logical conclusions. The full implications of an apparently slight departure from orthodoxy thus become manifest over the course of time. In sum, while orthodoxy might be dissipated over the long course of its transmission through the ages from the initial revelation, heresy becomes ever more solidified and salient. Its apotheosis was not in the past, but rather in the present or the not-so-distant future.

Culmination of Heresy

This apotheosis in most traditions was not reached primarily through the development or intensification of any particular heresy but rather through their absorption or amalgamation into one grand composite heresy. In other words, there was a marked tendency in the history of heresiography to identify the most threatening contemporary heresy as a combination of past heresies, a monstrous amalgam that incorporated the worst of all worlds. This rhetorical strategy served to gird the faithful for an imminent armageddon against the most terrible of foes. But it also made the prospect of a decisive triumph more plausible since that foe was now congealed into a single composite adversary. As John Chrysostom (d. 407) put it: "When Goliath fell at the hand of David, the whole army fled. One head was struck and one man died, but the whole army shared in the cowardly rout. So, too, when a single heresy has been struck down and falls, there will be a rout in which all those I mentioned will share."[252]

In early Christian heresiology, the identification of the most threatening current heresy as a summa of past heresies began remarkably early, with the first major heresiologists in the tradition. The author of the earliest extant Christian heresiological treatise, Irenaeus,

declared that the teaching of the Valentinian Gnostics is "the recapitu-
lation of all the heretics."[253] He went on to remark that "Those, then,
who are of the school of Valentinus being overthrown, the whole multitude of heretics are, in fact, also subverted. For all the arguments I
have advanced against their Pleroma . . . will in like manner apply
against those who are of the school of Marcion, and Simon, and
Menander."[254]

The threat of Gnosticism having receded by the fourth century,
the greatest heresiologist of that era, Epiphanius, identified another
heresy, that of the Jewish Christian "Ebionites," as a new epitome of all
error:

> For it was as though a person were to collect a set of jewelry from
> various precious stones, and a garment from clothing of many
> colors, and dress up to be conspicuous. Ebion, in reverse, took
> any item of preaching from every sect if it was dreadful, lethal
> and disgusting, if it was ugly and unconvincing, if it was full of
> contention, and patterned himself after them all. For he has the
> Samaritans' repulsiveness but the Jews' name, the viewpoint of
> the Ossaeans, Nazoraeans and Nasaraeans, the nature of the Cer-
> inthians, and the badness of the Carpocratians.[255]

But in other contexts (or other moods), Epiphanius referred to other
heresies, such as the Carpocratian, as the climax or cumulation of all
earlier ones,[256] indicating, perhaps, that this rhetorical trope was too
valuable to be fully expended on one particular heresy.

In early Byzantium, still other heresies came to the fore to be identified as epitomes of all past error. Cyril of Jerusalem accused Mani and
the Manicheans of "combining all into a single heresy brimful of blas-
phemies and all iniquity," echoing Eusebius's charge that Mani had
stitched together "false and blasphemous doctrines from the innumer-
able long-extinct blasphemous heresies."[257] When Byzantine
theologians first encountered the new religion of Islam, they characterized it as "a syncretic religion," and "a summary of all the heresies that
had arisen within the church."[258] It supposedly combined the Arian
doctrine of God, the Nestorian doctrine of Christ, Manichean and Ori-
genist ideas about demons, and was even influenced by the
Donatists.[259] Byzantine theologians marshalled an even larger number
of heretical contributors to Iconoclasm, which flourished in the eighth
and ninth centuries. At the fifth session of the second council of Nicea
in 781, the Patriarch Tarasius asserted "that the Iconoclasts had imitated
Jews and Saracens, pagans and Samaritans, and above all Manicheans

and Phastasiasts."[260] In various sessions of the same council, the same patriarch added the Marcionites, the Theopaschites, the Docetists, and "those who confused the two natures of Christ" to this list of contributors to Iconoclasm.[261] According to orthodox iconophile authorities, the Iconoclasts were also guilty of combining the evil deeds of the older persecutors of the Church with the evil words of the older heretics to form a more comprehensive amalgam of evil.[262]

In the Latin middle ages, as well, theologians such as Alain de Lille (d. 1202) charged heretics of their own day with having combined all ancient heresies to form a new general heresy.[263] Such an accusation was directed particularly against the Cathars, whose teachings "were connected to those of the Gnostics, the Muslims, the Nestorians, as well as the Monophysites, and the Apollinarists," all quite unhistorically.[264]

The idea that the most threatening current heresy is an amalgam of all former ones has survived in the modern world and is particularly evident in the Catholic Church's response to the "crisis of modernism" in the late nineteenth and early twentieth centuries. To Church authorities, "the modernists came to represent all that was wrong with the modern world."[265] They were, said Pope Pius X in 1907, the "synthesis of all heresies."[266] This group of modernists was neither very unified nor very powerful. But this was beside the polemical point. The modernists were "ideal foes" for the Church, because they could be so easily made to stand for all that the Church opposed. A more mythical version of the summa of all heresies which has survived (and even flourished) in modern times is the figure of the Antichrist. As a recent study of the historical Antichrist remarks, this figure "came to be thought of as possessing a corporate body." He "soon will be fully manifest in that human who will recapitulate every form of sin."[267]

Like their early Christian brethren, Muslim heresiographers tended to portray the most threatening current heresy as a sort of summa or epitome of previous ones. This tendency may be traced back to some of the earliest theological controversies in Islam, those involving the Mu'tazilites. According to Henri Laoust, orthodox heresiographers regarded the Mu'tazilite teaching as a sort of "schismatic syncretism toward which converged some of the main theses of the Qadarites, the Jahmites, and the Kharijites."[268] Early Hanbalite apologists, in particular, presented kalam, the philosophical theology associated with the Mu'tazilites, as the sum and epitome of all religious error.[269] The great Ash'arite heresiographer, al-Baghdadi, in turn accused a Qadarite of having "reconciled four kinds of heresies."[270] And the later Hanbalite polemicist, Ibn Taymiyya, touted the extremist Shi'ites, "whose doctrine combines the philosophy of the Greeks with the religion of the Magians," as syncretic heretics.[271]

With the rise of the Wahhabite fundamentalist movement in eighteenth-century Arabia, Ash'arites and other orthodox Sunni polemicists found a new target that could be charged with syncretizing earlier heresies. In addition to plausibly accusing the Wahhabites of having inherited the legacy of the fideist Hanbalites, they also reproached them "a little self-contradictorily, for being Qarmatians, Zahrite extremists who knew only the letter of the law, and finally Kharijite anarchists incapable of tolerating the least authority."[272]

But the most insidious and perennial heretical *bête noire*, at least from the standpoint of Hanbalite polemicists, was the famous Sufi philosophy of *wahdat al-wujud* ("oneness of being" or "unity of existence"). Ibn Taymiyya, in particular, was disturbed by both the theological and juristic implications of this pantheistic conception, as he interpreted it. Theologically, by erasing distinctions between God and the universe, *wahdat al-wujud* implied that created beings shared God's attributes, a clear commission of the cardinal sin of *shirk*. Juristically, the obliteration of distinctions between God the lawgiver and His subjects, the recipients of God's laws, implied that there could be no *shari'a*.[273] In Taymiyya's view, the harm caused by this antinomian doctrine was more calamitous than the destruction wrought by the Mongol invasions.[274]

Taymiyya not only pilloried *wahdat al-wujud* for the seriousness of its theological errors, but also portrayed it as "the most eclectic of beliefs and a mixture of all errors."[275] So did the seventeenth-century Acheh polemicist, al-Raniri, who accused Sufis of having combined the theological errors of several heterodox groups, including the Zoroastrians, the Metemphychosists, the Incarnationists, and the Brahmins, among others.[276]

It should be apparent that polemical characterizations of *wahdat al-wujud*, as an amalgam of all previous religious errors, were rather fanciful. But it is not so obvious that the category *wahdat al-wujud* itself is in part a heresiographical construction. According to W. C. Chittick, "Ibn Taymiyya probably deserves more credit than anyone else for making the term a center of contention in Islamic history, since . . . it played no important role in the technical vocabulary of [the Sufi philosopher] Ibn al-'Arabi and his direct followers" who were supposedly responsible for the concept.[277] Not only did Taymiyya and his fellow orthodox polemicists highlight this formerly obscure term, but they also modified its meaning to better serve their polemical purposes. The earliest major Sufi philosopher known to have used the term explicitly, Sadr al-Din Qunawi (d. 1274), employed it to mean something strikingly similar to the touchstone Neo-Confucian formula, "principle is one, but its particularizations are diverse." In Qunawi's own words: "Though there is nothing but One *wujud*, It manifests Itself as diverse, multiple, and plural because of the diversity of the realities of the receptacles."[278] Thus, Taymiyya's pantheistic interpretation of *wahdat al-wujud* takes a simplistic and one-sided view of this Sufi conception.

Occasionally, rabbbinic authorities also identified a current heresy as an amalgam of previous ones. In the early centuries A.D., they presented the "two powers in heaven" heresy as a sort of composite that included Samaritan, Christian, and other sectarian elements.[279] However, this "two powers" category came to refer not to any specific heresy but rather to a group of different heresies that compromised monotheism in some way.

The great Karaite heresiographer, al-Qirqisani, presented Christianity, a Jewish heresy by some accounts, as a combination of two more ancient Jewish heresies.[280] A modern historian has, in turn, portrayed Karaism as "a mixture of all the defunct ideologies with which traditional Judaism had come to grips throughout the ages and triumphantly subdued," including "Samaritan theology," "the allegorical method of the Hellenistic school," and even the practices of the "Essene hermits."[281] Finally, later rabbinic polemicists represented the messianic Sabbatian doctrines as "a perversion of all religions," not just those of Judaism.[282]

The tendency to present later heresies as combinations of earlier ones is probably more pronounced in Ch'eng-Chu Neo-Confucianism than in any of the other traditions surveyed here, with the possible exception of the early Christian. However, the heresies that Neo-Confucian polemicists assailed for their compositeness are for the most part limited to Buddhism, particularly the Ch'an sect, and Wang Yang-ming and his followers.

As in other matters heresiographical, Chu Hsi broached this theme in Neo-Confucian heresiography. In a notable anticipation of Chairman Mao's brilliant pronouncement of policy during the Great Leap Forward, Chu stated that the Buddhists of his own time walked on two legs, Yang Chu and Mo Ti.[283] The Ming heresiographer, Feng K'o, specified just how Buddhism had combined these two ancient heresies:

Alas. Mo [taught the doctrine of recognizing] no father. As for the Buddha, he rejected his kin and lived as a hermit, saying [that one should] leave home. Is this not the negation of one's father? Yang [taught the doctrine of recognizing] no lord. As for the Buddha, he abandoned other people and stood alone, saying [that one should] leave the world. Is this not the negation of one's lord? Yang's "negating one's lord" does not necessarily entail negating one's father. And Mo's "negating one's father" does not necessarily entail negating one's lord. Yet the Buddha combined the two negations, thus joining Yang and Mo in one person. If Yang and Mo are like wild beasts, then what of one who unites them?[284]

Later Ch'eng-Chu scholars, particularly Li Kuang-ti (1642–1718), repeated the accusation that the Buddha combined the most objectionable points of Yang and Mo, though Li also charged him with having amalgamated two forms of Taoism.[285]

Among all the forms of Buddhism, Neo-Confucians of the Ch'eng-Chu school singled out Ch'an as the most harmful to the Confucian Tao. The Ming-era heresiographer, Huang Wan (1480–1554), wrote that "of all the heresies, none is greater than Ch'an. Ever since the study of Ch'an has flourished, the Way of the Sages has daily become more chaotic and confused."[286] His close contemporary, Chan Ling, proclaimed that "Ch'an is the heresy of heresies."[287] According to Huang Chen, the reason why Ch'an was the "heresy of heresies" was because of its combinatory character. It incorporated the comic absurdities of the Taoist philosophers, Chuang-tzu and Lieh-tzu, into Buddhism.[288] Ch'an, like Buddhism in general, was a syncretic heresy, only more so.

From the point of view of many late Ming and Ch'ing scholars, the most syncretic, as well as the most threatening heretic of all was a nominal Confucian, Wang Yang-ming. These scholars charged Wang with devising an even more comprehensive summa of heresies than appeared even in Ch'an and other forms of Buddhism. According to Hsiung Tz'u-li, Wang managed to combine the learning of Ch'an with the perverse practice of the hegemonists, classical antagonists of Confucianism, even throwing in the classical philosopher Kao-tzu for good measure:

Wen-ch'eng's [= Wang Yang-ming's] learning was mixed with that of Ch'an. Wen-ch'eng's practical undertakings were purely those of the hegemonists. . . . He strung the two together, [and with his teaching on] human nature's being neither good nor evil, distinctly followed the example set by Kao-tzu.[289]

Like Confucius himself, Wang thus composed a complete concert, albeit of the licentious songs of Cheng rather than the refined music of Shao.

In the same treatise, *A Record of Defending the Way* (Hsien-tao lu), Hsiung also credited (or discredited) Wang with synthesizing another pair of heresies and heretics, those of Kao-tzu and the Northern Sung literatus, Su Shih (= Su Tung-po):

> Kao-tzu only wished to smash Mencius' [teaching on] "goodness"; and Tung-po only wished to smash Master Ch'eng's [teaching on] "reverence." But when Yang-ming's sayings became current, then both "goodness" and "reverence" were shattered together in one fell swoop.[290]

Another orthodox early-Ch'ing scholar, Li Kuang-ti, condemned Confucians of the mid-Ming era in general, not just Wang Yang-ming, for having conflated Confucianism with Mohism, Lao-tzu, and Chuang-tzu.[291]

The latter half of the Ming era was indeed one of the most highly syncretic ages in Chinese intellectual history, as noted above in Chapter Two. It was an age in which the "Unity of the Three Teachings" movement flourished, and in which leading Confucian thinkers sometimes expressed sympathy for Buddhist and Taoist ideas and practices. The heresiographical works composed by orthodox Ch'eng-Chu scholars of the seventeenth century could not help but reflect this legacy. But this does not necessarily mean that these heresiographers' "take" on mid- and late-Ming syncretism was very accurate or perceptive. First, the heresiographers accused late-Ming Confucians of having synthesized the ideas and practices of semilegendary heresiarchs, such as Kao-tzu, Mo-tzu, and Yang Chu, with whom they had little or no filiation, intellectual or otherwise. Second, the orthodox polemic against late-Ming Confucian syncretists followed a negative and reductionist approach, accusing them of having smashed this or that orthodox teaching in favor of its heretical obverse to form a perverse mirror image of orthodoxy. The resulting caricature bore little resemblance to the true face of late Ming syncretism.

Subtlety of Heresy

Although orthodox portrayals of heresy were seldom informed by a very subtle understanding of their subject, they did attribute to heresy itself a nefarious subtlety that made it all the more difficult to detect and combat. As Irenaeus remarked,

Error, indeed, is never set forth in its naked deformity, lest, being thus exposed, it should at once be detected. But it is craftily decked out in an attractive dress, so as, by its outward form, to make it appear to the inexperienced (ridiculous as the expression may seem) more true than the truth itself.[292]

Heresy's subtle seductive powers, moreover, increased with time, as latter-day heresy "learned to state its errors more guardedly, and to defend them more speciously."[293] Thus heresy developed over time not only in the direction of greater comprehensiveness, as later heresies combined earlier ones, but also in the direction of greater subtlety. The closer heresy approached to orthodoxy, or at least the appearance of orthodoxy, the more dangerous it was, because the threat it posed was all the more difficult to detect.

The idea that the most dangerous heresies are those closest to orthodoxy appears not only in premodern religious traditions but in modern ideological ones as well. This theme is particularly prominent in the programs and pronunciamentos of the Third International or Comintern (1919–1943). The program adopted by the Sixth Comintern Congress branded "Socialist reformism" as the "chief enemy of revolutionary Communism." It described "Austro-Marxism" as "a particularly dangerous enemy of the proletariat, more dangerous than the avowed adherents of predatory social imperialism."[294] A Comintern document of 1920 remarks that "In a country like Germany, it is particularly obvious that the opportunist 'leaders,' the reactionary trade union officials, the labour aristocracy and bureaucracy, are incomparably more dangerous to the workers' movement than the avowed white guards of the armed bourgeoisie."[295] For by posing as revolutionaries acting in the workers' interests, the above groups managed to divide, enervate, and mislead the working class much more effectively and efficiently than could the reactionary powers. But so subtle are their machinations and so convincing their protestations that the true character of these bogus social reformers may not be exposed until they have wrought irreparable damage. Their "sugar-coated bullets" are far more devastating than are the real bullets of the avowed enemies of revolution.

In the Christian tradition, the favorite trope for the seductive subtlety of heretics appears in Matthew 7:15 in words attributed to Jesus: "Beware of false prophets who come to you in sheep's clothing, but inwardly are ravening wolves." Several prominent early Christian heresiologists, including Justin Martyr, Tertullian, and Vincent of Lérins, repeated this scriptural warning against the subtlety of heretics, all with appropriate commentary.[296] Vincent, for example, related the biblical admonition to a heresy of his own time, exclaiming that "What a trial do we think that recently was when that wretch Nestorius, suddenly transformed from a sheep into a wolf, began to rend the flock of Christ, while those he was gnawing at still in large part believed him still a sheep and therefore laid themselves open all the more to his sharp teeth?"[297] Cyprian used a different biblical trope, that of the sly and plausible serpent, to signify the subtlety of heresy and the soporific effects it produced:

> It is easy enough to be on one's guard when the danger is obvious; one can stir up one's courage for the fight when the Enemy shows himself in his true colours. There is more need to fear and beware of the Enemy when he creeps up secretly, when he beguiles us by a show of peace and worms himself forward by those hidden approaches which have earned him the name of the "Serpent."[298]

Both Irenaeus and Origen maintained that it was the "ignorant faithful" who were most likely to be seduced by heresy's siren song, because they had not plumbed the depths of orthodox theology.[299] But so subtle was heresy that even some of the most learned and profound theologians of the early Church, including Origen, expressed views later branded as heretical. According to Cardinal Newman, even heresiarchs themselves were unaware of the subtler implications of their heretical stances, which led historically to unintended consequences.[300] The "logic of heresy" may be a particularly baffling form of the cunning of reason.

Besides attributing to heretics an *artful* subtlety designed to disguise their true face and mislead the faithful, orthodox Christian heresiologists also ascribed to them a more *intellectual* subtlety and rhetorical sophistication, inconsonant with the plain truths of the gospel. As Newman remarked, following historians of the early church, "adroitness in debate was the very life and weapon of heresy."[301] Among early Christian heresiologists, Irenaeus was particularly "suspicious of those 'learned' theologians, the Gnostics, with their dangerous science and eloquence."[302] He asserted that it was better and more profitable to "search after no other knowledge except [the knowledge of] Jesus Christ the Son of God, who was crucified for us, than that by subtle questions and hairsplitting expression he should fall into impiety."[303] Irenaeus rhetorically insisted on the rhetorical naivete of his own heresiological work and condemned his heretical opponents for trying to seduce their auditors and readers by using the artifices of rhetoric.[304] A later polemicist, Gregory of Nazianzus (d. 389), went so far as to assert that "The weakness of the argument appears to be part of the mystery, and thus the cleverness of the argument declares the nullification of the cross, as Paul also teaches [1 Cor. 1:17]."[305]

Inasmuch as orthodox Islamic heresiographers often accused their heretical opponents, particularly the extremist Shi'ites, of the gravest theological errors and the most loathsome practices, it was sometimes difficult for them to expound credibly on the subtlety of heresy. However, a noted Sunni heresiographer's list of heresies by the degree of danger they posed to Sunni orthodoxy does indicate that "the movement having the most resemblance to the doctrines of Sunni orthodoxy is the most dangerous, because it is the most difficult to recognize as such."[306] The great Hanbalite polemicist, Ibn Taymiyya, specifically singled out the advocates of the Sufi philosophy of *wahdat al-wujud* as "the greatest danger to Islam in his time" because of "the insidious nature of their errors." Indeed, Taymiyya admitted that he himself had once been impressed by this doctrine until he came to realize its true import.[307]

Like their Christian counterparts, Islamic heresiographers also condemned some of their opponents, particularly the speculative theologians, for their excessive intellectual subtlety and sophistication. Ibn Qudama (d. 1223), for example, criticized "the meddlesome allegorical interpreter . . . affecting cleverness and defying God and his Apostle."[308] And Ibn Taymiyya cautioned that the philosophers' use of human reason to resolve the apparent contradiction between divine power and human free will "can only end in error."[309] The Muslim of today, he said, should follow the example of his pious ancestors who had not concerned themselves with arcane theological speculations.[310]

While the rationalist Mu'tazilites may have been the most intellectually subtle of the heretics, the Isma'ilis were the most artfully so. According to al-Baghdadi, "It is a prerequisite for a missionary of their heresy that he be skillful in dissembling" and that "he be acquainted with the various methods by which parties can be swayed."[311]

Judaism may present an exception to the rule that judged the subtler heresy as the more dangerous, as well as to the "greater proximity—greater hostility" model of religious conflict. Perhaps the precarious political position of postexilic Judaism is in part responsible for rabbinic authorities having generally regarded the subtler heresy as a lesser evil than the obvious one. For the latter might more easily inspire the open apostasy and assimilation of large numbers of Jews, and the decimation of Jewish communities. The righteous remnant was already so small that further shrinkage might well threaten its existence. The subtler heretics, such as the Hasidim, did, after all, belong to the House of Israel and could perhaps be reconciled with normative Judaism. But the greater heresies, such as the Sabbatian, posed a real threat of apostasy, as illustrated when Sabbatai himself converted to Islam under duress.

On the other hand, the noted rabbinic polemicist, Moses Hagiz, held that Sabbatianism posed "the greater threat because it appeared under a legitimate guise." Hagiz characterized the progress of heresies such as Sabbatianism as beginning in subtle minutiae and growing to the point of outright apostasy.[312] Eighteenth-century rabbinic opponents of the Hasidim also expressed the fear that minor deviations might eventually become magnified.[313] Some of these rabbis, such as R. Israel of Zamosc (d. 1772), regarded the Hasidim as an even greater threat to Judaism than were the flagrant heretics and free-thinkers, for "the *hasidim* pretended to be faithful to the tenets of traditional Judaism and therefore posed more of an insidious danger in misleading the youth."[314]

Although they generally refrained from using bestial metaphors of wolfish sheep and plausible serpents to characterize heretics, Neo-Confucian commentators were not slow to attribute to heresy a seductive subtlety and subterfuge that might deceive even the ultra-orthodox. The sixteenth-century Ch'eng-Chu scholar, Lo Ch'in-shun (1465–1547), accused Lu Hsiang-shan of having "outwardly eschewed the name" of Ch'an while he "inwardly employed its substance."[315] Lo's contemporary, Ch'en Chien, regarded Lu as a particularly grave threat to the Way because of his skill in concealing his Ch'an.[316] The orthodox early Ch'ing scholar, Lu Lung-ch'i, saw a larger long-range pattern behind such heretical dissimulations:

> Among Han and T'ang Confucians, those who venerated orthodox scholarship only respected Confucius and Mencius. When the Way of Confucius and Mencius was respected, then the words of the [heterodox] hundred schools of philosophy were obliterated. From T'ang times onward, heretics and crooked scholars, knowing the Confucians' respect for Confucius and Mencius, all relied on Confucius and Mencius to broadcast their own theories. When we talked of Confucius and Mencius, they also talked of Confucius and Mencius. Thus scholars were not able to distinguish the right and wrong of the matter. When Ch'eng and Chu came forth and venerated the orthodox while re-

futing the heterodox, then the Way of Confucius and Mencius was once again glorified, and thus the whole world respected it. But from Sung times onward, heretics and crooked scholars, knowing the Confucians' respect for Ch'eng and Chu, all relied upon Ch'eng and Chu to broadcast their own theories. When we talked of Ch'eng and Chu, they also talked of Ch'eng and Chu. Thus scholars were again not able to distinguish the right and wrong of the matter. As Ch'eng and Chu spoke of "heavenly principle," they also spoke of heavenly principle. Although the name of "heavenly principle" was the same, what it referred to was [as distant] as heaven is from earth.[317]

Lu went on to assert that even staunch adherents of orthodoxy found it difficult if not impossible to detect heresy when it masqueraded as orthodoxy. Small wonder that orthodox heresiographers like Ch'en Chien proclaimed that it was better to be openly heretical, like the Ch'an masters, than to attempt to conceal one's heresy, like Lu Hsiang-shan.[318]

From the point of view of orthodox Ch'eng-Chu scholars, heresy's capacity to disguise its true face increased over time, as heresies became increasingly subtle and difficult to recognize.[319] As Ch'eng Hao remarked, "The reason why the Way is not glorified is that heresy harms it. In the past, this harm was proximate and easy to recognize. But now the harm is deep and difficult to distinguish. In the past, misleading people took advantage of their confusion and ignorance. Now, infiltrating them depends on their cleverness."[320] The progress of Buddhism in China was a case in point:

> In the past there was also a time when Buddhism flourished. But it still only exalted image worship, so the harm it did was very small. But the fashion today is to first speak of human nature, destiny, the Way, and its virtue, which first and foremost stimulates the knowledgeable. Thus the more clever are one's mental faculties, the deeper one sinks.[321]

In the Neo-Confucian tradition, the subtlety of heresy was compounded by the precariousness of orthodoxy, making the Way of the Sages even more delicate and difficult to maintain. In fact, the Neo-Confucians may be credited with having anticipated the "Butterfly Effect—the notion that a butterfly stirring the air today in Peking can transform storm systems next month in New York."[322] One of the most commonly articulated ideas in Neo-Confucian texts, based on a quotation from one of the apocrypha to the *Changes Classic*, is that an infinitesimal error at the beginning will lead to an infinite error by the end. According to Ch'eng I, the heresiographical genius of Mencius lay in his ability to extrapolate the dire end results of the small errors committed by Yang and Mo:

> Yang Chu originally studied rightness and Mo-tzu originally studied co-humanity [both of which were primary Confucian virtues]. But since what they studied was slightly biased, its outcome [eventually] reached the [extreme] point of denying fathers and lords. Mencius wanted to rectify the original source [of this outcome]. Therefore, he extrapolated to that [extreme] point.[323]

A recent scholar has written that "ordinary people, engaging in ordinary behavior, have contributed to extraordinary evil."[324] Ch'eng I (following Mencius) saw the potential for extraordinary evil even in the moral teachings of sages who missed the mark by only a hair's breadth.

EPILOGUE: THE PROVIDENTIALITY OF HERESY

Although they often interpreted heresy as a subtle approximation or partial version of orthodoxy, heresiographers occasionally drew a sharp dichotomy between the two, denying the existence of any middle ground. Ibn Qudama, for example, remarked that "There is nothing outside of Paradise but hell-fire; there is nothing outside of the truth but error; and there is nothing outside of the Sunna but heretical innovation."[1] Along the same line, Fang Tung-shu declared that "the world does not have two Ways. If Mo-tzu is true, then Confucius is false."[2] Cyprian found a scriptural basis for the stark division between orthodoxy and heresy in a statement attributed to Jesus: "He who is not with me is against me; and he who does not gather with me scatters."[3] And rabbinic polemicists of the seventeenth century likewise upheld "an unbridgeable abyss between Sabbatianism and rabbinism."[4] On the other hand, the tendency to draw a sharp divide between saved and damned, or truth and error, with little possibility of social interaction or intellectual mediation, is more characteristic of short-lived sectarian movements than of long-lived major religions. Examples of militantly exclusivist sects that failed, ranging from the Essenes to the Taipings, are abundant enough to illustrate that Manichean universes may not be long for this world.

The polemical position of ancient and medieval heresiographers hardly permitted them to acknowledge the existence of too many shades of gray on the spectrum between orthodoxy and heresy. But some of them did recognize that heresy was not totally "other," and even that it had a part to play in the sacred (or cosmic) economy. Christian heresiologists, and to a lesser extent those in the other traditions surveyed here, pointed out that heretical error might contribute in some way to the establishment of orthodox truth. This insight probably stemmed not so much from the dialectical subtlety of the heresiological imagination as from a fundamental religious belief that even error might perform a positive role in the divine (or cosmic) dispensation, and that even heresy might be of use. If God could use the Devil to good ends, then why not heretics? As St. Paul asserted, "for those who love God all things work together unto good" (Rom. 8:28).

In the Christian tradition, the idea of the providential role of heresy may be traced back to the New Testament writings of Paul, who

remarked in 1 Corinthians 11:19 that "There must be heresies so that
those approved may be manifest among you." Commenting on this
scriptural passage, Cyprian observed that "Thus are the faithful
proved, thus the faithless discovered; thus too even before the day of
judgment, already here below, the souls of the just and unjust are distinguished, and the wheat is separated from the chaff."[5] For Tertullian
also, heresies sifted the faithful, much as did the great persecutions:
"they occur precisely in order to prove faith by testing it."[6] Indeed,
God even arranged the scriptures so as to furnish matter for the heretics, thus giving them "enough rope."[7]

Other early Christian heresiologists credited heresy not only with
testing the faithful, but also with testifying to the status of the Christians as the true people of God. Hegesippus argued that just as the
existence of false prophets in the old Israel attested to the Jews' election
by God, so the presence of heretics among Christian folk established
the latter's claim to be the new Israel: "Just as there were false prophets
beside the holy prophets among you [the Jews], so now with us as well
there are many masters of deceit."[8] Origen also argued that the existence of heretical sects pointed to the richness, if not necessarily the
truth, of Christianity: "Any teaching which has had a serious origin
and is beneficial to life, has caused different sects (*haereseis*)," as exemplified in the numerous Greek medical schools as well as the sects of
the Christian religion.[9]

Third, the assaults of heresy against the faith contributed to the
vigor and vitality of orthodoxy, which might otherwise atrophy for lack
of activity.[10] As Caesarius of Arles put it, "due to the fact that the attack
of objectors besets Catholic doctrine, our faith does not become para-
lyzed through inactivity, but is perfected by much exercise."[11] In his *City
of God*, Augustine goes so far as to deliver a virtual paean to heretics'
capacity to promote the exercise of Christian virtues: "If they have power to do her physical harm, they develop her power to suffer, if they
oppose her intellectually, they bring out her wisdom; since she must
love even her enemies, her loving kindness is made manifest."[12] Some
fifteen hundred years later, Cardinal Newman composed a similar en-
comium, citing heresy's God-given ability "to promote humility—to try
our faith—to rouse the careless to an attentive study, and the religious
to a more earnest realization of the Christian verities—and to subserve
the evolution of these verities in a dogmatic form."[13]

A fourth and final contribution of heresy to the development of
Christian orthodoxy, suggested by the last of Newman's points, is its
having stimulated the clarification and even the constitution of orthodox doctrine. While few if any ancient heresiologists went to the extent

of some modern historians in claiming that orthodoxy was constructed in the first place in response to heretical challenges, Tertullian did express a wish "that the clarification of approved doctrines did not, in a sense, demand the existence of heresies."[14] Augustine similarly remarked that "the refutation of heretics makes the position of the Church, and the sound doctrine it possesses, stand out clearly."[15] Hilary of Poitiers, however, saw such heresy-induced "clarification" of orthodoxy in a less than favorable light. "The guilt of the heretics," he wrote, "compels us to undertake what is unlawful, to scale arduous heights, to speak of the ineffable, and to trespass upon forbidden ground . . . . By the guilt of another we are forced into guilt, so that what should have been restricted to the pious contemplation of our minds is now exposed to the dangers of human speech."[16] Hilary thus lamented the passing of the Church's state of childhood innocence in which the holy mysteries were unsullied by explicit doctrinal formulations.

Islam, like Christianity, has a canonical expression of the providentiality of heresy, or at least of factions, in a commonly cited saying (*hadith*) attributed to the Prophet: "The divergence of opinions in my community is a sign of divine mercy."[17] While this *hadith* might be interpreted as an endorsement of pluralism, it could also be read as a statement that "false views, by presenting a contrast, made possible a more precise formulation of the true doctrines."[18] Islamic heresiographers such as Shahrastani seem to have composed their works in the belief that the exhibition and juxtaposition of the doctrines of the various sects would illuminate the orthodox truth without the need for overt polemics.[19]

According to rabbinic midrash, God himself provided scriptural excuses for heretical error, particularly in Genesis 1:26 ("And God said, Let *us* make man in *our* image, after *our* likeness."). When Moses transcribed this verse from God's dictation, he objected, saying "Sovereign of the Universe, why dost Thou give an opening to the *minim*?" God replied: "Do thou write, and he who wishes to err, let him err."[20] This implies that heretical error, especially that which affirmed the existence of "two powers in heaven," was part of the divine dispensation, though the midrash does not say what its specific role might be. On the other hand, Maimonides did specify that "that which alerted him to the explanation of most of the commandments of the Law was his reading of the texts of the idolaters."[21] In other words, the study of heterodoxy or heresy might lead to the clarification of true doctrine. Liberal nineteenth-century Jewish scholars went on to credit Jewish heresies with having stimulated the refinement and renewal of the Jewish faith, thus preventing the ossification and paralysis of normative Judaism that might have occurred in the absence of heresies.[22] Thus orthodoxy and heresy may interact benignly in rabbinic Judaism, as in the other traditions surveyed.

Finally, even Confucius ascribed an educative value to error, if not to heresy, remarking that "a person's errors are all according to his class. By observing errors one can know [the supreme virtue of] humanity" (Analects 4.7). A scholar of the Ch'ing era, Li Wen-chao, applied the idea of approaching truth through error specifically to characterize the interactions between Confucian orthodoxy and heterodoxy:

> I have often said that unless one investigates the reasons why Buddhism and Taoism are false, then how can one know the reasons why our Confucianism is true; that unless one observes that the various schools of philosophy have purities and impurities among them, then how can one know that we Confucians are the purest of the pure?[23]

Another Ch'ing scholar, Chang Hsüeh-ch'eng, compared the educative role of errors and anomalies in the field of calendrical astronomy with their function in the rectification of moral culture.[24] In both cases, the true Way is originally ineffable and intangible and is revealed only through repeatedly missing the mark.

While Chang Hsüeh-ch'eng's musings on the cosmic significance of error and anomaly may seem to be somewhat pre-scientific, they were in a way prescient of twentieth-century recognitions of the epistemological value and social utility of error. Indeed, modern authorities in various fields have all but celebrated the benefits of error. One such authority, H. Péquignot, observed that "In the past all the people who tried to build a science of the normal without being careful to start from the pathological considered as the immediate given have ended up in often ridiculous failures."[25] An even more authoritative authority, Sigmund Freud, exploited various types of error, the most famous of which is the fabled "Freudian slip," to probe the unconscious. The popular scientific essayist, Lewis Thomas, sees "error" as not just the source of scientific knowledge, but as the driving force in evolution: "The capacity to blunder slightly is the real marvel of DNA. Without this special attribute, we would still be anaerobic bacteria."[26] But the last word on the epistemological and cosmic value of error should by all rights belong to Chairman Mao:

> Communists should not be afraid of making mistakes. Mistakes have a dual character. On the one hand mistakes harm the Party

and the people; on the other they serve as good teachers, giving both the party and the people a good education, and this benefits the revolution.[27]

If error has its educative value, erring groups (or "social deviants") have their social utility. The threat, real or imagined, posed by them strengthens group solidarity and boundary definition, as well as provides a scapegoat to explain reversals suffered by the group without admitting weakness vis a vis an external foe.[28] In fact, so socially useful is the deviant that he might well be regarded as "a natural product of group differentiation," and not as "a bit of debris spun out by faulty social machinery."[29] Nestorius is quoted as having promised an emperor: "Give me, my prince, the earth purged of heretics, and I will give you heaven as a recompense."[30] But a world free of heretics (or any sort of deviants) might be heavenly only for anarchists: "Unless the rhythm of group life is punctuated by occasional moments of deviant behavior, presumably, social organization would be impossible."[31]

On the other hand, it is the heresiographers or their modern analogues, not the heretics or deviants themselves, who transform the raw matter of deviance into something socially useful; they utilize the occasion of heresy to define boundaries, develop solidarity among the ingroup, and even decrease anxieties insofar as a crisis might be made more tractable by reducing it to an internal affair.[32] That they might have been conscious of the importance of some of these functions is suggested by the fact that they sometimes invented heresies (or similar forms of deviance) where and when they became extinct in the state of nature (or culture). Michel Foucault notes such an instance in his well-known account of the demise of leprosy toward the end of the Middle Ages in Europe:

> Leprosy disappeared, the leper vanished, or almost, from memory; these structures remained. Often, in these same places, the formulas of exclusion would be repeated, strangely similar two or three centuries later. Poor vagabonds, criminals, and 'deranged minds' would take the part played by the leper. . . . With an altogether new meaning and in a very different culture, the forms would remain—essentially that major form of a rigorous division which is social exclusion but spiritual reintegration."[33]

But if heresiography serves both orthodoxy and the orthodox, it does quite a disservice to heresy and the heretical. One might suppose that heresiography, by preserving at least a cognitive memory of the heresies it names and criticizes, would facilitate the eventual recovery of their once discredited ideas as well as a restoration of intellectual pluralism. But what heresiography "preserves" is not the essential character of a heresy, but a caricature. Sometimes, this caricature simply reduces heresies to a set of possible ways of denying orthodoxy.[34] Origen, for example, deduced two Christological heresies, Adoptionism and Modalism, from the two principal ways of negating orthodox Christological doctrine. This mode of exposition "deprives each heresy of its individuality, its language, and its problematic," to say nothing of its historical and social existence.[35] Rabbinic heresiographers accomplished a similar feat through their force-fitting of a plethora of historical heresies, ranging from Samaritanism to Sabbatianism, into the procrustean bed of deniers of the Oral Torah. So did the Shi'ite heresiographer, al-Nawbakhti, who classified sects according to their attitude toward 'Ali, despite the fact that the status of 'Ali was not an important issue for some of these sects.[36] Finally, Chu Hsi also cast heresy in the light (or dark) of its alleged negation of an orthodox doctrinal point, remarking that "the learning of the Buddha and Lao-tzu desires 'to advance its knowledge' but does not know that 'the investigation of things' is the means whereby one advances knowledge."[37] Chu thus reduced Buddhist and Taoist heterodoxies to the status of one-sided or incomplete versions of orthodoxy, as expressed in a key doctrinal formula from a classical Confucian text.

By some accounts, heresy, or the idea thereof, has faded into oblivion in the modern world, surviving only in fundamentalist pockets (and ecclesiastical purses). As theologians have agreed to disagree, and as former heresies have become legitimized as churches, both the intellectual and social bases of heresiology seem to have receded, at least in the (post?) Christian West. Indeed, some modern commentators have gone so far as to reverse the traditional evaluations of orthodoxy and heterodoxy, remarking, for example, that narrow orthodoxy "is usually the worst heresy of all," while celebrating heretics of old as heroes who "resemble the saints."[38]

But heretics and heresiographers, like Foucault's lepers and their confiners, may have receded only to reappear in new forms. These new forms vary in different cultures. The eighteenth-century Chinese polymath, Ch'ien Ta-hsin, for example, regarded vernacular novels as a new heterodoxy.[39] But perhaps the most popular candidates for new heresies (and orthodoxies) in the modern world are in the areas of medicine (including psychotherapy) and political ideology.

In both of these areas, there may be historical as well as function-al links between old and new heresiographers. Georges Canguilhem remarks that "From the sociological point of view it can be shown that therapeutics was first a religious, magical activity," while the church historian Jaroslav Pelikan brands Marxism-Leninism as "a kind of Christian heresy."[40] Whatever the case, in the course of the nineteenth century, medical and political orthodoxies came to replace religious ones as the major authorities defining the boundaries between normal and deviant, or approved and condemned. But in the lexicon of thera-peutics, heresy, now transmuted into abnormality, was no longer so much a matter of "choice" as it had been for the ancients. How, then, could it be extirpated? Naturally (or unnaturally), by "hunting for het-erodox genes," through a "genetic inquisition."[41] Political authorities, whose "heretical" nemeses are not quite so congenitally incorrigible, often opt for a more low-tech solution: reeducation.

The notion that mankind has escaped from religious inquisitions only to be confronted by a pair of modern successors, genetic engineer-ing and political reeducation, that may be just as unsparing, does not seem to hold much promise for the ideals of tolerance and pluralism. But if our modern authorities could be persuaded of the social and in-tellectual value of various forms of heresy in contemporary society and culture, we may reasonably hope for a kinder, gentler inquisition.

NOTES

Full citations are given in the notes only for the first appearance in each chapter of those items not included in the bibliography. For an account of the criteria used for selecting works to be included in the bibliography, see the explanatory note to the bibliography.

Introduction

1. Wasserstrom, *Between Muslim and Jew*, p. 154.

2. Watt, *Muslim Intellectual*, p. 118.

3. A contemporary sociologist has noted a similar bias in modern studies of social deviance, remarking that "the emphasis is more on the *sub-culture* and *identity* of the 'deviants' themselves rather than on their oppressors and persecutors." Alexander Liazos, "The Poverty of the Sociology of Deviance: Nuts, Sluts, and Preverts," in *Social Deviance: Readings in Theory and Research*, ed. Henry Pontell (Englewood Cliffs, NJ: Prentice Hall, 1993), p. 168.

4. May, "Marcion in Contemporary Views," p. 134; Sahas, "Art and Non-Art," p. 59.

5. André Suarès, *Péguy*, quoted in *The Great Thoughts*, comp. George Seldes (New York: Ballantine Books, 1985), p. 401.

6. Stephen Jay Gould, *The Panda's Thumb: More Reflections in Natural History* (New York: W. W. Norton, 1980), pp. 40–41.

7. Howard Eilberg-Schwartz, review of *Drudgery Divine: On the Comparison of Early Christianities and the Religions of Late Antiquity*, by Jonathan Z. Smith, in *History of Religions* 32.3 (Feb. 1993): 302.

8. Ibid., p. 303.

9. al-Azmeh, "Orthodoxy and Hanbalite Fideism," p. 253.

10. For a representation of this point of view, see S. Radhakrishnan, *The Hindu View of Life* (New York: Macmillan, 1973), p. 32. A similar viewpoint is expressed in the "mystery religions" of Western antiquity, which "recognized illusions and lower levels of understanding, not morally reprehensible errors."

Randall Collins, *Weberian Sociological Theory* (Cambridge: Cambridge University Press, 1987), p. 217.

11. Rahner, *On Heresy*, p. 7.

12. Brown, *Heresies*, p. 6.

13. A. Abel, "Nature et cause de l'angoisse et du refus dans trois hérésies musulmanes: Le Kharidjisme, la Mu'tazila, le Batinisme," in Le Goff, *Hérésies et sociétés*, p. 67; Laoust, "L'hérésiographie musulmane," p. 158; John Burton, "Quranic Exegesis," in *The Cambridge History of Arabic Literature; Religion, Learning and Science in the Abbasid Period*, eds. M. J. L. Young et al. (Cambridge: Cambridge University Press, 1990), p. 40.

14. Kaufman, *Great Sects and Schisms*, p. 29.

15. Lauterbach, "A Significant Controversy," p. 32.

16. Shmueli, *Seven Jewish Cultures*, p. 10.

17. Carlebach, *Pursuit of Heresy*, p. 277.

18. For a recent expression of this attitude, see Bodde, *Chinese Thought, Society, and Science*, pp. 171–72.

19. As Lionel Jensen has pointed out, the terms 'Confucian' and 'Neo-Confucian' are inventions of Western sinologists, going back to the Jesuit missionaries of the seventeenth century, and have no exact equivalents in classical Chinese. I use them, nonetheless, because the relevant transliterated Chinese terms "have little or no meaning for the many readers who have no scholarly background in Chinese studies," as Anne Birdwhistell has remarked in her recent book, *Li Yong (1627–1705) and Epistemological Dimensions of Confucian Philosophy* (Stanford: Stanford University Press, 1996), p. 2. Perhaps naively, I believe that it is possible to use such terms as 'Confucian' and 'Neo-Confucian' without necessarily endorsing the ideological agenda of those persons who coined them. On the Jesuit "invention" of Confucius, see Lionel Jensen, "The Invention of 'Confucius' and His Chinese Other, 'Kong Fuzi,'" *Positions* 1.2 (Fall 1993): 414–49.

20. Benjamin I. Schwartz, "On the Absence of Reductionism in Chinese Thought," *Journal of Chinese Philosophy* 1.1 (Dec. 1973): 27.

1. Preliminary Overview of Heresy and Heresiography

1. Lewis Thomas, *The Medusa and the Snail: More Notes of a Biology Watcher* (New York: Bantam Books, 1980), p. 31.

2. *The Book of Songs: The Ancient Chinese Classic of Poetry*, trans. Arthur Waley (New York: Grove Press, 1960), p. 210 (Mao #209).

3. Jack Goody, *The Interface between the Written and the Oral* (Cambridge: Cambridge University Press, 1987), p. 67.

4. Ehrman, *Orthodox Corruption of Scripture*, p. 279; Neumark, *Essays in Jewish Philosophy*, p. 102.

5. Erikson, *Wayward Puritans*, p. 21; Nigg, *The Heretics*, p. 122.

6. Lieu, *Manichaeism*, p. 216.

7. Vincent of Lérins, *The Commonitory* 4, p. 40.

8. Lambert, *Medieval Heresy*, p. 3.

9. Gregory of Nyssa, *De filii deitate*, quoted in Frend, *Monophysite Movement*, p. xii.

10. Frend, *Monophysite Movement*, p. xii.

11. W. H. C. Frend, "Popular Religion and Christological Controversy in the Fifth Century," in *Studies in Church History*, vol. 8, eds. G. J. Cuming and D. Baker (Cambridge, 1971), p. 22.

12. Lewis, "Significance of Heresy," p. 44.

13. Coser, *Social Conflict*, p. 112.

14. Ibid., p. 115.

15. Ibid., pp. 68–69.

16. Ehrman, *Orthodox Corruption*, p. 9; Pelikan, *Christian Tradition*, 1:121.

17. Brown, *Heresies*, p. 9.

18. Ibid., p. 42.

19. John Meyendorff, *Byzantine Theology: Historical Trends and Doctrinal Themes* (New York: Fordham University Press, 1974), p. 4.

20. Frend, *Monophysite Movement*, p. 2.

21. Gray, *Defense of Chalcedon*, p. 156.

22. O'Grady, *Heresy*, p. 54; Brown, *Heresies*, p. 24.

23. Richard Haugh, *Photius and the Carolingians: The Trinitarian Controversy* (Belmont, MA: Nordland, 1975), p. 172.

24. Dabashi, *Authority in Islam*, pp. 130–31.

25. Makdisi, "Hanbali School," p. 71; Ormsby, *Theodicy in Islamic Thought*, p. 92.

26. Watt, "Great Community," p. 27. See also Madelung, *Religious Trends*, p. 40; and Allard, *Le problème des attributs divins*, p. 73.

27. al-Ghazali, *Al-Munqidh min al-Dalal* (Deliverance from Error), trans. W. Montgomery Watt, in *Anthology of Islamic Literature from the Rise of Islam to Modern Times*, with an introduction and commentaries by James Kritzeck (New York: New American Library, A Mentor Book, 1975), p. 174.

28. Laoust, "L'hérésiographie musulmane," p. 157.

29. Madelung, *Religious Trends*, passim.

30. al-Ghazali, *Fada'ih al batiniyya wa fada'il al mustazhiriyya*, Dar al qawuniyya li-tiba'ati wa-l nashr (Cairo, 1989), p. 189, quoted in Hogga, *Orthodoxie, subversion et réforme*, p. 47.

31. al-Ghazali, *Al Iqtisad fi-l- i'tiqad*, Dar al amanat (Beirut, 1975), p. 77, quoted in Hogga, *Orthodoxie, subversion, et réforme*, p. 47.

32. Arthur Jeffery, "Introduction," to Jeffery, ed., *A Reader on Islam*, p. 339.

33. Wensinck, *The Muslim Creed*, p. 103.

34. Ibid., pp. 123, 185, and 264.

35. Ibid., p. 103.

36. Schacht, "Theology and Law in Islam," pp. 3–4.

37. Ibid., p. 4.

38. Watt, *Early Islam*, p. 106.

39. George Makdisi, "The Significance of the Sunni Schools of Law in Islamic Religious History," *International Journal of Middle Eastern Studies* 10 (1979): 6–7; Madelung, *Religious Trends*, pp. 28 and 38; Makdisi, *Ibn 'Aqil*, p. 383.

40. Christie-Murray, *A History of Heresy*, p. 9.

41. Biale, *Gershom Scholem*, p. 148.

42. Cohen, "A Virgin Defiled," p. 3; Cohen, "The Significance of Yavneh," p. 42.

43. Segal, *Two Powers in Heaven*, p. 4.

44. For an exchange of views on the existence of orthodoxy in Judaism of the first century A.D., see McEleney, "Orthodoxy in Judaism"; and Aune, "Orthodoxy in First Century Judaism?".

45. Kellner, *Dogma in Medieval Jewish Thought*, p. 3. A similar opinion is expressed by Cohon in his *Jewish Theology*, pp. 102–3.

46. al-Qirqisani, *Jewish Sects*, p. 123.

47. Mishnah Sanhedrin 10:1, in Neusner, trans., *The Mishnah*, p. 604.

48. Hava Tirosh-Rothschild, *Between Worlds: The Life and Thought of Rabbi David ben Judah Messer Leon* (Albany: State University of New York Press, 1991), pp. 142–43 and 149.

49. Kellner, *Maimonides on Judaism*, p. 60.

50. Kellner, *Dogma in Medieval Jewish Thought*, p. 41.

51. Tirosh-Rothschild, *Between Worlds*, p. 144.

52. Maimonides, *Mishneh Torah* 14, "Rebels" 3.1, in *A Maimonides Reader*, ed. and anno. Isadore Twersky (West Orange, NJ: Behrman House, 1972), p. 210.

53. Yizhak Julius Guttmann, *Philosophies of Judaism: The History of Jewish Philosophy from Biblical Times to Franz Rosenzweig*, trans. David W. Silverman (New York: Holt, Rinehart and Winston, 1964), p. 184; Simon, *Jewish Religious Conflicts*, p. 62. The seriousness of the edict of excommunication (*herem*) is indicated by Elijah Schochet's statement that "In its most powerful form, the solemn invocation of a *herem* was, in actuality, a death penalty of sorts—decreeing social and religious death upon the offenders." Schochet, *Hasidic Movement*, p. 11.

54. Cronbach, *Reform Movements in Judaism*, pp. 74–75.

55. Ibid., p. 99; Arthur Mandel, *The Militant Messiah or the Flight from the Ghetto: The Story of Jacob Frank and the Frankist Movement* (Atlantic Highlands, NJ: Humanities Press, 1979), p. 24.

56. See, for example, Brown, *Heresies*, p. 2.

57. See, for example, Paul Unschuld, *Medicine in China: A History of Ideas* (Berkeley: University of California Press, 1985), pp. 57–58; and Richard J. Smith, *Fortune-tellers and Philosophers: Divination in Chinese Society* (Boulder, CO: Westview Press, 1991), p. 51.

58. Alexander Woodside, "State, Scholars, and Orthodoxy: The Ch'ing Academies, 1736–1839," in Liu, ed., *Orthodoxy*, p. 164.

59. Richard J. Smith, "Ritual in Ch'ing Culture," in Liu, ed., *Orthodoxy*, p. 304.

60. de Bary, "Uses of Neo-Confucianism," p. 548.

61. Lu Shih-i, *Ssu-pien lu chi-yao* 29.8a.

62. Yamazaki, *Heki'i*, p. 414.

63. Wang Mao, *Ch'ing-tai che-hsüeh*, p. 76.

64. Schwartz, *World of Thought*, p. 169; see also Ivanhoe, *Ethics*, p. 29.

65. Shu-hsien Liu, "The Problem of Orthodoxy in Chu Hsi's Philosophy," in *Chu Hsi and Neo-Confucianism*, ed. Wing-tsit Chan (Honolulu: University of Hawaii Press, 1986), p. 59.

66. Liu, "Socioethics as Orthodoxy," in Liu, ed., *Orthodoxy*, p. 59.

67. Heinrich von Staden, "Haeresis and Heresy: The Case of the *haireseis iatrikai*," in *Jewish and Christian Self-Definition*, vol. 3, *Self-Definition in the Graeco-Roman World*, eds. Ben F. Meyer and E. P. Sanders (London: SCM, 1982), p. 76.

68. Ibid., p. 76; Simon, "From Greek Haeresis," pp. 104–5.

69. Simon, "From Greek Haeresis," p. 111.

70. Ibid., pp. 106–7 and 112; von Staden, "Haeresis and Heresy," pp. 97–98.

71. Simon, "From Greek Haeresis," p. 111.

72. Ibid., p. 113.

73. Vallée, *Anti-Gnostic Polemics*, p. 81; Young, "Did Epiphanius Know," p. 200.

74. Mlle. C. Thouzellier, "Tradition et résurgence dans l'hérésie médiévale," in Le Goff, *Hérésies et sociétés*, p. 105.

75. Simon, "From Greek Haeresis," p. 109; Le Boulluec, *La notion d'hérésie*, 2:532 and 551.

76. J. De Guibert, "*La notion d'hérésie* chez St. Augustin," *Bulletin de littérature ecclésiastique* 21 (1920): 369. The quotation stating the position of the medieval church on heresy is from Moore, *Origins of European Dissent*, p. ix. For a similar statement by Robert Grosseteste (1175–1253), see Lambert, *Medieval Heresy*, p. 5.

77. This medieval Christian characterization of heresy was anticipated by Augustine. Guibert, "*La notion d'hérésie*," p. 371.

78. Other reasons for generally excluding medieval Christian heresy from this book include: (1) the lack of continuity between ancient and medieval heresy and heresiography, especially in the Latin West, on which see Lambert, *Medieval Heresy*, p. 25; and (2) the focus of medieval Christian heretics on clerical abuses and ecclesiastical pretensions more than on points of doctrine, on which see Jeffrey Burton Russell, *Dissent and Order in the Middle Ages: The Search for Legitimate Authority* (New York: Twayne Publishers, 1992), p. 7.

79. Tertullian, "The Prescriptions against the Heretics" 6, trans. in Simon, "From Greek Haeresis," p. 115.

80. Simon, "From Greek Haeresis," p. 110.

81. Chi-yun Chen, "Orthodoxy as a Mode of Statecraft: The Ancient Concept of *Cheng*," in Liu, ed., *Orthodoxy*, p. 27.

82. W. H. C. Frend, "'And I have other sheep'—John 10:16," in *The Making of Orthodoxy: Essays in Honour of Henry Chadwick*, ed. Rowan Williams (Cambridge: Cambridge University Press, 1989), p. 25.

83. Saint Augustine, *Faith and the Creed*, chap. 10, in *Writings of Saint Augustine*, vol. 15, trans. Charles T. Wilcox et al., in *The Fathers of the Church, A New Translation*, ed. Ludwig Schopp (New York: Fathers of the Church, Inc., 1955), p. 341.

84. S. L. Greenslade, "Heresy and Schism in the Later Roman Empire," in *Schism, Heresy, and Religious Protest*, ed. Derek Baker (Cambridge: At the University Press, 1972), p. 8.

85. Lieu, *Manichaeism*, p. 217.

86. Russell, *Dissent and Order*, p. 3.

87. Lewis, "Significance of Heresy," p. 52.

88. Ibid.

89. J. Robinson, "Bid'a," in *The Encyclopedia of Islam*, new ed., vol. 1, "A–B," eds. H. A. R. Gibb et al. (Leiden: E. J. Brill; London: Luzac and Co., 1960), p. 1199; V. Rispler, "Toward a New Understanding of the Term *bid'a*," *Der Islam* 68 (1991): 320.

90. See, for example, al-Baghdadi, *Moslem Schisms and Sects*, p. 70.

91. Lewis, "Significance of Heresy," p. 56.

92. Ibid.

93. Ibid., p. 58. John Taylor, "An Approach to the Emergence of Heterodoxy in Mediaeval Islam," *Religious Studies* 2 (1967): 198.

94. W. Björkman, "Kafir," in *Encyclopedia of Islam*, new ed., vol. 4, "Iran-Kha," eds. E. van Donzel et al. (Leiden: E. J. Brill, 1978), p. 407.

95. Halm, *Shiism*, p. 2.

96. Fuad I. Khuri, *Imams and Emirs: State, Religion and Sects in Islam* (London: Saqi Books, 1990), p. 27.

97. See, for example, Lewis, "Significance of Heresy," pp. 57–58.

98. Ibid., pp. 51–52.

99. Simon, "From Greek Haeresis," p. 106.

100. Lawrence H. Schiffman, "At the Crossroads: Tannaitic Perspectives on the Jewish Christian Schism," in *Essential Papers on Judaism and Christianity in Conflict from Late Antiquity to the Reformation*, ed. Jeremy Cohen (New York: New York University Press, 1991), p. 444.

101. George Foot Moore, *Judaism in the First Three Centuries of the Christian Era: The Age of the Tannaim*, vol. 3 (Cambridge: Harvard University Press, 1948), p. 68.

102. "Heresy," in *Encyclopedia Judaica*, vol. 8, "He–Ir" (Jerusalem: Keter Publishing House; New York: Macmillan, 1971), p. 359.

103. Gries, "Heresy," p. 341.

104. Allan Lazaroff, *The Theology of Abraham Bibago: A Defense of the Divine Will, Knowledge, and Providence in Fifteenth-Century Spanish Jewish Philosophy* (University, AL: University of Alabama Press, 1981), pp. 19 and 81.

105. Chen, "Orthodoxy as a Mode of Statecraft," pp. 29–30.

106. Kwang-ching Liu, "Introduction," in Liu, ed., *Orthodoxy*, p. 4; *Shuowen chieh-tzu Tuan-chu*, Ssu-pu pei-yao ed., 2B.1a (vol. 1).

107. Chen, "Orthodoxy as a Mode of Statecraft," p. 31.

108. Analects 2.16, trans. in Bodde, *Chinese Thought, Society, and Science*, pp. 40–41.

109. Schwartz, *World of Thought*, p. 130.

110. Bodde, *Chinese Thought, Society, and Science*, p. 40.

111. Horigome Yōzō, *Seitō to itan* (Kyoto, 1964), p. 41; Edward T. Ch'ien, *Chiao Hung and the Restructuring of Neo-Confucianism in the Late Ming* (New York: Columbia University Press, 1986), p. 74.

112. Ch'ien, *Chiao Hung*, p. 75.

113. Ibid., pp. 75–76.

114. *Hsün-tzu* 22.3d, trans. in John Knoblock, *Xunzi: A Translation and Study of the Complete Works*, vol. 3, bks. 17–32 (Stanford: Stanford University Press, 1994), p. 132.

115. Chan, *Chu Hsi: New Studies*, p. 501.

116. de Bary, *Sources of Chinese Tradition*, 1:34; Chen, "Orthodoxy as a Mode of Statecraft," p. 44.

117. A felicitous modern definition of heresy, suggested by one of the anonymous reviewers of this book for SUNY Press, is that heresy is "a claim advanced by one of us, in our name, that some false view is true or that some wrong pattern of action is right." This definition calls to mind the characterization of false teachers in 1 John 2:19: "They went out from us, but they were not of us; for if they had been of us, they would have continued with us."

118. Origen, *Contra Celsum*, p. 3 of "Preface." Cf. Matt. 26:59–63 and Mark 14:55–61.

119. Ehrman, *Orthodox Corruption*, p. 6.

120. Brown, *Heresies*, p. 55. A list of other possible New Testament sources of antiheretical warnings appears in Ehrman, *Orthodox Corruption*, p. 36.

121. Peters, *Heresy and Authority*, p. 14.

122. Tertullian, "The Prescriptions against the Heretics" 33, in Greenslade, ed., *Early Latin Theology*, p. 54.

123. Le Boulluec, *La notion d'hérésie*, 1:110.

124. Johannes Quasten, *Patrology*, vol. 1, *The Beginnings of Patristic Literature* (Westminster, MD: The Newman Press; Utrecht-Brussels: Spectrum, 1950), p. 287.

125. Frend, *Saints and Sinners*, p. 65.

126. Filoramo, *History of Gnosticism*, p. 4.

127. Frank Williams, "Introduction" to Epiphanius, *Panarion*, p. xvi.

128. Filoramo, *History of Gnosticism*, p. 6.

129. Wisse, "Epistle of Jude," p. 133.

130. Judith McClure, "Handbooks against Heresy in the West from the Late Fourth to the Late Sixth Centuries," *Journal of Theological Studies* n.s. 30.1 (April 1979): 187.

131. Ehrman, *Orthodox Corruption*, p. 15.

132. Wisse, "Use of Early Christian Literature," p. 184; Vallée, *Anti-Gnostic Polemics*, p. 75.

133. Vallée, *Anti-Gnostic Polemics*, p. 96; Hilgenfeld, *Ketzergeschichte*, p. 2.

134. Markus, "Problem of Self-Definition," p. 11.

135. Le Boulluec, *La notion d'hérésie*, 2:452.

136. Wilken, *Myth of Christian Beginnings*, p. 84.

137. Ehrman, *Orthodox Corruption*, pp. 9–10; Turner, *Pattern of Christian Truth*, p. 8; Gerhart B. Ladner, "Origin and Significance of the Byzantine Iconoclastic Controversy," *Mediaeval Studies* 2 (1940): 148–49; Pearson, "Anti-Heretical Warnings," p. 193.

138. Wisse, "Use of Early Christian Literature," p. 184.

139. Fyzee, trans., *A Shi'ite Creed*, p. 43.

140. Ormsby, *Theodicy in Islamic Thought*, p. 21.

141. Wensinck, *The Muslim Creed*, p. 88.

142. Keith Lewinstein, "The Azariqa in Islamic Heresiography," *Bulletin of the School of Oriental and African Studies*, University of London 54.2 (1991): 252; Henri Laoust, "La classification des sectes dans le *Farq* d'al-Baghdadi," in Laoust, *Pluralismes dans l'Islam*, p. 137.

143. Ibn 'Asakir, "Exposure of the Calumniator's Lying," p. 159.

144. Lewinstein, "Studies in Islamic Heresiography," p. 19; see also Laoust, "La classification des sectes," p. 170.

145. Watt, *Formative Period*, p. 1.

146. Lewinstein, "Studies in Islamic Heresiography," p. 20.

147. Jean-Claude Vadet, "Présentation de Shahrastani et du Kitab al-Milal," in *Les dissidences de l'Islam*, trans. and ed. Vadet (Paris: Librairie Orientaliste, 1984), pp. ix and 15.

148. Ibid., p. 1.

149. Mashkur, trans., *Les sectes Shiites*, p. 5. Some recent scholars have attributed this work to a contemporary, Sa'd b. 'Abd-Allah al-Qummi. See Watt, *Early Islam*, p. 141.

150. Laoust, *Les schismes dans l'Islam*, p. 459.

151. Jeffrey T. Kenney, "Heterodox Claims on Orthodox Power: An Analysis of an Ibadi Heresiography," in 1990 American Academy of Religion Abstracts, p. 8.

152. Earl Edgar Elder, "Introduction" to al-Taftazani, *Commentary on the Creed of Islam*, pp. xix–xx.

153. al-Ghazali, *Al-Munqidh min al-Dalal*, p. 170.

154. Earl Edgar Elder ("Introduction," p. xix) posits that there were three distinct stages in the development of Islamic creedmaking, the second of which was concerned primarily with the refutation of heresy.

155. Hogga, *Orthodoxie, subversion, et réforme*, p. 45.

156. MacDonald, *Development of Muslim Theology*, p. 196.

157. Ibn Khaldhun, *The Muqaddimah*, 3:54 (6.14).

158. A. Abel, "Nature et cause de l'angoisse et du refus dans trois hérésies musulmanes: Le Kharidjisme, la Mu'tazila, le Batinisme," in Le Goff, *Hérésies et sociétés*, p. 67.

159. Segal, *Two Powers in Heaven*, pp. 147 and 154.

160. Baron, *History of the Jews*, 5:206.

161. Kaufman, *Great Sects and Schisms*, p. 19; Shmueli, *Seven Jewish Cultures*, p. 7.

162. Guttmann, *Philosophies of Judaism*, p. 61; Hartwig Hirschfeld, "Antikäraische Polemik in Sa'adiahs Religionsphilosophie," in *Festschrift zu Hermann Cohens Siebzigstem Geburtstage* (Berlin: Verlag von Bruno Cassiren, 1912), p. 266.

163. Samuel A. Poznanski, "The Karaite Literary Opponents of Sa'adiah Gaon," in *Karaite Studies*, ed. Philip Birnbaum (New York: Hermon Press, 1971), p. 125; Sirat, *History of Jewish Philosophy*, p. 19.

164. Carlebach, *Pursuit of Heresy*, p. 7.

165. Ibid., p. 277.

166. Goldin, trans., *The Fathers* 40, p. 168.

167. Biale, *Gershom Scholem*, pp. 155 passim.

168. Cheng Ju-hsieh, *Lun-yü i-yüan* 1.9b, in *Ching-yüan*, comp. Ch'ien I-chi (Taipei: Ta-t'ung shu-chü, 1970 reprint), 6:2709.

169. Ch'eng I, *Erh-Ch'eng yü-lu*, 1:21.

170. Christoph Harbsmeier, "*Confucius Ridens*: Humor in the Analects," *Harvard Journal of Asiatic Studies* 50.1 (June 1990): 147. The internal quotes are from Analects 15.16.

171. Bodde, *Chinese Thought, Society and Science*, p. 178.

172. Ch'eng Hao, quoted in Chu Hsi, comp., *Reflections on Things at Hand*, p. 299.

173. Chu Hsi, *Ssu-shu chi-chu, Meng-tzu*, p. 91.

174. Chuo Hsiu-yen, "Meng-tzu lun i-tuan," *K'ung-Meng hsüeh-pao* 4 (Sept. 1962): 67.

175. Deuchler, "Reject the False," p. 391.

176. Barrett, *Li Ao*, pp. 139–40. Hsün-tzu's denunciation of six major heterodox thinkers of his time appears in the "Removing Obstructions" (*chieh-pi*) chapter of the *Hsün-tzu*.

177. A similar point is discussed at length and with greater philosophical sophistication in Matthew A. Levey, "Chu Hsi as a 'Neo-Confucian': Chu Hsi's Critique of Heterodoxy, Heresy, and the 'Confucian' Tradition" (Ph.D. diss., University of Chicago, 1991), pp. 37–38, 51, 90 passim.

178. Chu Hsi, "Ta Lü I-tao", from *Chu-tzu ch'üan-shu*, in *Ku-chin t'u-shu chi–ch'eng*, comps. Ch'en Meng-lei et al. (Taipei: Ting-wen shu-chü, 1977 reprint), 59:653.

179. Hsüeh Hsüan, *Tu-shu lu* 3.11a, in Chang Po-hsing, comp., *Cheng-i-t'ang ch'üan-shu*, case 10.

180. Ch'en Chien, *Hsüeh-pu t'ung-pien* 12.161.

181. On the abundance of Chu Hsi's anti-Buddhist writings, see Tokiwa Daijō, *Shina ni okeru Bukkyō to Jukyō Dōkyō* (Tokyo: Tōyōbunko, 1930), p. 351.

182. Tillman, *Confucian Discourse*, p. 41.

183. Ch'en Chien, *Hsüeh-pu t'ung-pien* 12.162.

184. Chan, *Chu Hsi: New Studies*, p. 463; T'ang Chün-i, *Chung-kuo che-hsüeh yüan-lun*, p. 353.

185. Lo Ch'in-shun, *Knowledge Painfully Acquired*, p. 53.

186. Lü Liu-liang, "Ta Chang Chü-jen," in *Lü Wan-ts'un wen-chi* 1.82.

187. Chan, "The *Hsing-li ching-i*," p. 552.

188. Chang, *Neo-Confucian Thought*, 2:334.

189. T'ang Chien, *Ch'ing-hsüeh-an hsiao-chih*, p. 2 of postscript (*pa*).

190. Fang Tung-shu, *Han-hsüeh shang-tui*, p. 6.

191. Conrad Schirokauer, "Neo-Confucians under Attack: The Condemnation of *Wei-hsüeh*," in *Crisis and Prosperity in Sung China*, ed. John Winthrop Haeger (Tucson: University of Arizona Press, 1975), p. 181.

192. Tillman, *Confucian Discourse*, pp. 210–11; Ch'en Chien, *Hsüeh-pu t'ung-pien* 6.71.

2. The Making of Orthodoxies

1. Williams, *Arius*, p. 24.

2. Brown, *Heresies*, p. 113.

3. Dunn, *Unity and Diversity*, p. 380.

4. Jaroslav Pelikan, *The Vindication of Tradition*, The 1983 Jefferson Lectures in the Humanities (New Haven: Yale University Press, 1984), p. 30.

5. Ehrman, *Orthodox Corruption*, p. 7.

6. Georg Strecker, "Foreword to the Second German Edition" of Bauer, *Orthodoxy and Heresy*, p. xi; Gary T. Burke, "Walter Bauer and Celsus: The Shape of Late Second-Century Christianity," *The Second Century* 4.1 (1984): 2.

7. Bauer, *Orthodoxy and Heresy*, pp. 193 and 229 passim; Wisse, "Use of Early Christian Literature," p. 182. For a recent challenge to Bauer's claim, see Robinson, *Bauer Thesis*.

8. Ehrman, *Orthodox Corruption*, p. 7; Robinson, *Bauer Thesis*, pp. 17–18.

9. Dunn, *Unity and Diversity*, p. 292.

10. Ibid., p. 301.

11. Wisse, "Use of Early Christian Literature," pp. 186–87.

12. Pagels, *The Gnostic Gospels*, p. xxii.

13. Filoramo, *A History of Gnosticism*, p. 2; Vallée, *Anti-Gnostic Polemics*, p. 93.

14. Dunn, *Unity and Diversity*, p. 240.

15. The point "that heresy may be a result of poor timing" is also made by Pelikan in his *Christian Tradition*, 1:70.

16. Ehrman, *Orthodox Corruption*, p. 15.

17. Roch Kereszty, "The Unity of the Church in the Theology of Irenaeus," *The Second Century* 4.4 (1984): 205.

18. Some support for this view of theology as the brainchild of heresiography may also be found in the history of New England Puritanism. In his *Wayward Puritans*, Kai Erikson notes that "In the process of defining the nature of deviation, the settlers were also defining the boundaries of their new universe" (p. 23).

19. Robert A. Kraft, "The Development of the Concept of 'Orthodoxy' in Early Christianity," in *Current Issues in Biblical and Patristic Interpretations; Studies in Honor of Merril C. Tenney*, ed. Gerald F. Hawthorne (Grand Rapids: Eerdsmans, 1975), p. 56.

20. Lambert, *Medieval Heresy*, p. 3.

21. Pelikan, *Christian Tradition*, 1:58.

22. Shaw, "African Christianity," p. 12.

23. Karl Baus, "Part One: The Development of the Church of the Empire within the Framework of the Imperial Religious Policy," in Karl Baus et al., *The Imperial Church from Constantine to the Early Middle Ages*, trans. Anselm Biggs, in *The History of the Church*, vol. 2, eds. Hubert Jedin and John Dolan (New York: The Seabury Press, A Crossroad Book, 1980), p. 50.

24. Ibid.

25. Charles E. Raven, *Apollinarianism: An Essay on the Christology of the Early Church* (Cambridge: At the University Press, 1923; New York: AMS reprint, 1978), p. 240.

26. Frend, *Monophysite Movement*, p. 49.

27. Williams, *Arius*, p. 82.

28. Pelikan, *Christian Tradition*, 1:15.

29. Ehrman, *Orthodox Corruption*, p. 8.

30. Ibid., p. 35; Nigg, *The Heretics*, p. 81.

31. O'Grady, *Heresy*, p. 64.

32. Pelikan, "The Two Sees of Peter," pp. 70–71.

33. Georg Strecker, "Appendix 1: On the Problem of Jewish Christianity," in Bauer, *Orthodoxy and Heresy*, p. 284.

34. Baus, "Development of the Church," p. 68.

35. Christie-Murray, *A History of Heresy*, p. 59.

36. Ibid., p. 1.

37. See, for example, the Emperor Constantine's exhortation to the Council of Nicea, as recorded in Socrates, *Church History from A. D. 305–439*, trans. A. C. Zenos, in *A Select Library of Nicene and Post-Nicene Fathers of the Christian Church*, 2d series, eds. Philip Schaff and Henry Ware, vol. 2, *Socrates, Sozomenus, Church Histories* (Grand Rapids: Wm. B. Eerdmans, 1952), p. 9 (1.8).

38. Pelikan, *Christian Tradition*, 2:23.

39. Evans, *Gregory the Great*, p. 141.

40. Brown, *Heresies*, p. 119.

41. Prestige, *Fathers and Heretics*, p. 29.

42. Chi-tsang, "The Profound Meaning of the Three Treatises" (from *San-lun hsüan-i*, in *Taisho daizokyo* 45.1-11), in de Bary et al., *Sources of Chinese Tradition*, 1:303.

43. R. P. C. Hanson, *The Search for the Christian Doctrine of God: The Arian Controversy 318–381* (Edinburgh: T & T Clark, 1988), p. 872.

44. Paul Ricoeur, *Hermeneutics and the Human Sciences: Essays on Language, Action and Interpretation*, trans. and ed. John B. Thompson (Cambridge: Cambridge University Press, 1985), p. 228.

45. Bauer, *Orthodoxy and Heresy*, p. 237.

46. Ehrman, *Orthodox Corruption*, p. 10.

47. Markus, "Problem of Self-Definition," p. 15.

48. Brown, *Heresies*, p. 181.

49. Pseudo-Athanasius, "Synopsis of Sacred Scripture, The Song of Songs 16," in Heine, *Montanist Oracles*, p. 159.

50. O'Grady, *Heresy*, p. 98.

51. Heine, *Montanist Oracles*, p. ix.

52. Jerome, "Epistle 41. To Marcella," in Heine, p. 151.

53. Heine, *Montanist Oracles*, p. ix.

54. Epiphanius, *Panarion* 48, in Heine, p. 29.

55. Joanne McW. Dewart, "The Christology of the Pelagian Controversy," in *Studia Patristica*, vol. 17, ed. Elizabeth A. Livingstone (Oxford: Pergamon Press, 1982), pp. 1222 and 1240.

56. Sahas, "Art and Non-Art," pp. 57–58, 59, and 63.

57. Richard Hanson, "The Achievement of Orthodoxy in the Fourth Century AD," in *The Making of Orthodoxy: Essays in Honour of Henry Chadwick*, ed. Rowan Williams (Cambridge: Cambridge University Press, 1989), p. 153.

58. John Henry Cardinal Newman, "An Essay on the Development of Christian Doctrine," in *Conscience, Consensus, and the Development of Doctrine: Revolutionary Texts by John Henry Cardinal Newman*, ed. and anno. James Gaffney (New York: Doubleday, Image Books, 1992), p. 179.

59. Turner, *Pattern of Christian Truth*, p. 138; George H. Williams, "Preface," to Brown, *Heresies*, pp. xix–xx.

60. Thomas A. Robinson, *The Early Church: An Annotated Bibliography of Literature in English* (Metuchen, NJ, and London: The American Theological Li-

brary Association and The Scarecrow Press, 1993), p. 109; Bauer, *Orthodoxy and Heresy*, p. 236.

61. Watt, *Formative Period*, pp. 5–6; Dabashi, *Authority in Islam*, p. 71; Baldick, *Mystical Islam*, p. 7.

62. Watt, *Formative Period*, pp. 5–6; Baldick, *Mystical Islam*, p. 7.

63. Watt, *Islamic Philosophy and Theology*, p. 19; Baldick, *Mystical Islam*, p. 7.

64. For examples, see Dabashi, *Authority in Islam*, p. 130; and Friedlander, "Heterodoxies of the Shiites," p. 15.

65. Knysh, "Orthodoxy and Heresy," p. 49.

66. Dilip Hiro, *Holy Wars: The Rise of Islamic Fundamentalism* (New York: Routledge, 1989), p. 12.

67. Alfred von Kremer, *Geschichte der Herreschenden Ideen des Islams: Der Gottesbegriff, Die Prophetie und Staatsidee* (Hildesheim: Georg Olms Verlagsbiehhandlung, 1961), p. 34.

68. David Thomas, "Introduction" to *Anti-Christian Polemic in Early Islam: Abu 'Isa al-Warraq's "Against the Trinity"* (Cambridge: Cambridge University Press, 1992); Earl Edgar Elder, "Introduction" to al-Taftazani, *Commentary on the Creed of Islam*, p. xiv; John A. Nawas, "A Reexamination of Three Current Explanations for al-Ma'mun's Introduction of the *Mihna*," *International Journal of Middle East Studies* 26.4 (November 1994): 615.

69. Nagel, "Problem der Orthodoxie," p. 37.

70. G. Hourani, "The Basis of Authority of Consensus in Sunnite Islam," *Studia Islamica* 21 (1964): 13.

71. Watt, *Islamic Creeds*, p. 4.

72. Makdisi, "Hanbali School," p. 71; idem, "Scholasticism and Humanism in Classical Islam and the Christian West," *Journal of the American Oriental Society* 109.2 (1989): 177.

73. al-Baghdadi, *Moslem Schisms and Sects*, pp. 169–70.

74. Watt, *Formative Period*, p. 75; William Thomson, "The Sects and Islam," *Muslim World* 39 (1949): 208. Cf. al-Baghdadi, *Moslem Schisms and Sects*, p. 207.

75. Daftary, *The Isma'ilis*, p. 48; Watt, *Muslim Intellectual*, p. 91.

76. Watt, *Formative Period*, p. 256; Goldziher, *Islamic Theology and Law*, p. 230.

77. For a modern scholar's account of the defining features of Sunnism, see Laoust, *Pluralismes dans l'Islam*, pp. 376–77.

78. Marshall G. S. Hodgson, "How Did the Early Shi'a Become Sectarian," *Journal of the American Oriental Society* 75 (1955): 1.

79. Lewis, "Significance of Heresy," p. 50.

80. Watt, *Formative Period*, p. 251; al-Baghdadi, *Moslem Schisms and Sects*, p. 127.

81. George Makdisi, "Ash'ari and the Ash'arites in Islamic Religious History," *Studia Islamica* 17 (1962): 44–45.

82. Watt, *Islamic Creeds*, p. 3.

83. Watt, *Formative Period*, pp. 167 and 267; Watt, *Islamic Philosophy and Theology*, p. 21.

84. Watt, "Development of the Islamic Sects," p. 90.

85. Watt, *Islamic Philosophy and Theology*, p. 59.

86. Hodgson, "How Did the Early Shi'a Become Sectarian," p. 5.

87. A. S. Tritton, *Islam: Belief and Practices* (London: Hutchinson House, 1954), p. 74.

88. Hodgson, *Order of Assassins*, p. 8.

89. Tritton, *Islam*, p. 72.

90. Hodgson, *Order of Assassins*, pp. 7–8; Watt, *Islamic Philosophy and Theology*, pp. 16–17.

91. Watt, *Formative Period*, p. 38; idem, "Development of the Islamic Sects," p. 86.

92. Watt, *Early Islam*, p. 168.

93. 'Allamah Tabataba'i, "Shi'ism, Zaydism, Isma'ilism, and Shaykhism," in *Shi'ism: Doctrines, Thought, and Spirituality*, eds. Seyyed Hossein Nasr et al. (Albany: State University of New York Press, 1988), p. 85.

94. Peter Berger, *The Heretical Imperative* (Garden City, NY: Anchor Press, 1979), p. 85.

95. Ismaeel, *Difference between the Shii*, p. 17.

96. See, for example, Daftary, *The Isma'ilis*, p. 36.

97. One of the anonymous readers of this book for SUNY Press comments that "It would be well to mention that there are Sufi orders in addition to the classical 'mystical' Sufis that, while still mystical in some senses, are more ve-

hicles for political and social organization than for mystical and theological doctrine."

98. Michel, "Theology of Ibn Taymiyya," p. 29.

99. Laoust, *Les schismes dans l'Islam*, p. 245; idem, "L'hérésiographie musulmane," p. 177.

100. Laoust, *Les schismes dans l'Islam*, pp. 457 and 395.

101. Laoust, "L'hérésiographie musulmane," p. 177.

102. al-Baghdadi, *Moslem Schisms and Sects*, p. 162; Laoust, *Les schismes dans l'Islam*, p. 179.

103. Madelung, *Religious Trends*, p. 47.

104. George Makdisi, "Hanbalite Islam," in *Studies on Islam*, trans. and ed. Merlin L. Swartz (Oxford: Oxford University Press, 1981), p. 248; Laoust, *Les schismes dans l'Islam*, p. 242.

105. Madelung, *Religious Trends*, p. 53; Makdisi, *Ibn 'Aqil*, pp. 376 and 378.

106. al-Shahrastani, *Muslim Sects and Divisions*, p. 78.

107. Henry Corbin, *Histoire de la philosophie islamique*, vol. 1, *Des origines jusquà la mort d'Averroës (1198)* (Paris: Gallimard, 1964), p. 172; Allard, *Le problème des attributs divins*, p. 21.

108. Wensinck, *The Muslim Creed*, p. 58; Jeffery, *A Reader on Islam*, p. 378; von Kremer, *Geschichte der Herrschenden Ideen*, p. 36; Corbin, *Histoire de la philosophie islamique*, p. 170.

109. MacDonald, *Development of Muslim Theology*, pp. 186–87.

110. Elder, "Introduction," p. ix.

111. Allard, *Le problème des attributs divins*, p. 135; Watt, *Islamic Philosophy and Theology*, p. 64; Wilferd Madelung, "The Origins of the Controversy Concerning the Creation of the Koran," *Orientalia Hispanica* 1:513.

112. Elder, "Introduction," p. xv.

113. Allard, *Le problème des attributs divins*, pp. 410–11 and 417.

114. Abraham S. Halkin, "Introduction" to al-Baghdadi, *Moslem Schisms and Sects*, p. iv.

115. Hodgson, *Order of Assassins*, p. 180. As Montgomery Watt has pointed out, the Mu'tazilite position "was not a rationalism in which reason was set above the revealed Scriptures, but one in which reason was assumed to be competent to understand and interpret the main truths contained in the Scriptures,

and with these as basis to fathom the mystery of the Divine nature." See Watt, *Early Islam*, p. 93.

116. Ibn Khaldhun, *The Muqaddimah*, 3:49 (6.14).

117. Allard, *Le problème des attributs divins*, p. 174.

118. Elder, "Introduction," p. xxiii.

119. Coulson, *A History of Islamic Law*, p. 89; Allard, *Le problème des attributs divins*, pp. 87–88; Wensinck, *The Muslim Creed*, p. 91; Ibn Taimiya, *Struggle Against Popular Religion*, p. 86.

120. Allard, *Le problème des attributs divins*, pp. 86 and 287; Laoust, "L'hérésiographie musulmane," p. 165.

121. Wilferd Madelung, "The Spread of Maturidism and the Turks," in idem, *Religious Schools and Sects in Medieval Islam* (London: Variorum Reprints, 1985), II, p. 110.

122. Wensinck, *The Muslim Creed*, p. 94. Eric L. Ormsby makes a similar point in his *Theodicy in Islamic Thought*, p. 28.

123. Hogga, *Orthodoxie, subversion, et réforme*, p. 46.

124. al-Ghazali, *Al-Munqid min Adalal*, p. 85.

125. Madelung, *Religious Trends*, p. 31.

126. Watt, *Islamic Philosophy and Theology*, p. 67. This comparative obscurity may, however, owe more to the geographical isolation of the centers of this school than to its relative insignificance.

127. Madelung, "The Spread of Maturidism," p. 109.

128. Elder, "Introduction," p. xxiii.

129. Ibn 'Asakir, "The Exposure of the Calumniator's Lying," p. 182.

130. Makdisi, "Ash'ari and the Ash'arites," p. 37.

131. Madelung, *Religious Trends*, p. 22.

132. al-Azmeh, "Orthodoxy and Hanbalite Fideism," p. 265.

133. Madelung, "Origins of the Controversy," pp. 515 and 525.

134. Coulson, *A History of Islamic Law*, pp. 101–02.

135. Makdisi, "Ash'ari and the Ash'arites," p. 37.

136. Ibid., pp. 37 and 80.

137. Hourani, "The Basis of Authority," p. 36. The Hanbalites might not only be likened to Protestants, but also characterized as fundamentalists who in some respects "out-fundamentalize" their modern Christian counterparts. See Niels C. Nielsen, *Fundamentalism, Mythos and World Religions* (Albany: State University of New York Press, 1993), p. 90.

138. Knysh, "Orthodoxy and Heresy," p. 66.

139. Watt, *Formative Period*, p. 107.

140. Watt, *Formative Period*, p. 128; Wilferd Madelung, "Early Sunni Doctrine Concerning Faith as Reflected in the *Kitab al-imam* of Abu 'Ubaid al-Qasim b. Sallam (d. 224/839)," in Madelung, *Religious Schools and Sects*, I, pp. 241–42.

141. Ibn Hazm, *Kitab al-fisal fi'l-milal*, trans. in Friedlander, "Heterodoxies of the Shiites," p. 40.

142. Momen, *Introduction to Shi'i Islam*, p. 67.

143. Wilferd Madelung, "Imamism and Mu'tazilite Theology," in idem, *Religious Schools and Sects*, VII, p. 13.

144. al-Ghazali, *Faisal at-Tafriqa bain al-Islam wa'z-Zandaqa*, trans. in Lewis, "Significance of Heresy," p. 58. A recent scholar, Mustapha Hogga, has interpreted Ghazali's "pluralism" as a tactical move designed to undermine the Isma'ilis' pretentions of effecting an authoritarian unification of all Muslims under an infallible imam. Hogga, *Orthodoxie, subversion, et réforme*, p. 59.

145. Neusner, *Formative Judaism*, p. 82.

146. Anthony J. Saldarini, *Pharisees, Scribes, and Sadducees in Palestinian Society: A Sociological Approach* (Wilmington, DE: Michael Glazier, 1988), pp. 220–21.

147. Ibid., p. 221; Samuel S. Cohon, "Pharisaism: A Definition," in *Origins of Judaism*, vol. 2, part 1, *The Pharisees and Other Sects*, ed. Jacob Neusner (New York: Garland, 1990), p. 139.

148. Saldarini, *Pharisees*, p. 221.

149. R. T. Beckwith, "The Pre-history and Relationships of the Pharisees, Sadducees, and Essenes: A Tentative Reconstruction," in *Origins of Judaism*, vol. 2, part 1, p. 85; Ellis Rivkin, *A Hidden Revolution* (Nashville: Abingdon, 1978), p. 256.

150. Rivkin, *Hidden Revolution*, pp. 258, 276, and 239–40.

151. Jacob Neusner, *The Formation of Judaism in Retrospect and Prospect* (Atlanta: Scholars Press, 1990), p. 214.

152. Saldarini, *Pharisees*, p. 214.

153. Salo Wittmayer Baron, *A Social and Religious History of the Jews*, vol. 2, *Ancient Times*, part 2, 2d ed., rev. and enl. (New York: Columbia University Press, 1932), p. 36.

154. Rivkin, *Hidden Revolution*, pp. 145, 156–57, 176, 183–84, 237; Simon, *Jewish Religious Conflicts*, p. 31.

155. Rivkin, *Hidden Revolution*, pp. 247–48; Cohon, "Pharisaism," p. 143.

156. Saldarini, *Pharisees*, p. 231; Cohen, "Significance of Yavneh," p. 37.

157. Cohen, "Significance of Yavneh," p. 45.

158. Neusner, *Formation of Judaism*, pp. 44 and 58.

159. Cohen, "Significance of Yavneh," p. 50.

160. Jacob Neusner, "Pharisaic-Rabbinic Judaism," in *Origins of Judaism*, vol. 2, part 1, p. 442; Neusner, *Formation of Judaism*, p. 44.

161. Goldin, trans., *The Fathers* 4, p. 34.

162. Neusner, "Pharisaic-Rabbinic Judaism," pp. 439 passim.

163. Neusner, *Formation of Judaism*, p. 44.

164. For examples of such condemnations, see Goldin, trans., *The Fathers* 37, p. 153.

165. Cohen, "Significance of Yavneh," p. 41.

166. Guttmann, *Rabbinic Judaism*, p. 174.

167. Ibid., pp. 169 and 171.

168. This is the thesis of E. R. Goodenough's *Jewish Symbols in the Greco-Roman Period*, as reported in Cohen, "A Virgin Defiled," p. 9. On this point, see also Wasserstrom, *Between Muslim and Jew*, p. 46.

169. Shmueli, *Seven Jewish Cultures*, p. 152.

170. Katz, *Tradition and Crisis*, pp. 184–85.

171. Zvi Ankori, *Karaites in Byzantium: The Formative Years, 970–1100* (New York: Columbia University Press, 1959).

172. Mishnah Sanhedrin 10.1, quoted in Cohon, *Jewish Theology*, p. 98.

173. Kellner, *Dogma in Medieval Jewish Thought*, pp. 45 and 48–49.

174. Marc D. Angel, "Authority and Dissent: A Discussion of Boundaries," *Tradition* 25.2 (Winter 1990): 18.

175. Kellner, *Dogma in Medieval Jewish Thought*, p. 19.

176. Kellner, *Maimonides on Judaism*, p. 83.

177. Simon, *Jewish Religious Conflicts*, p. 56.

178. Daniel Jeremy Silver, *Maimonidean Criticism and the Maimonidean Controversy 1180–1240* (Leiden: E. J. Brill, 1965), p. 56.

179. McEleney, "Orthodoxy in Judaism," p. 42.

180. Guttmann, *Rabbinic Judaism*, p. 161.

181. Abravanel, *Principles of Faith*, p. 112.

182. Lauterbach, "A Significant Controversy," pp. 2–3; Simon, *Jewish Religious Conflicts*, p. 17; Kaufman, *Great Sects and Schisms*, p. 25; Guttmann, *Rabbinic Judaism*, p. 127; Rivkin, *Hidden Revolution*, p. 230; Zvi Lampel, *The Dynamics of Dispute: The Makings of Machlokess in Talmudic Times* (New York: Judaica Press, 1992), pp. 242–43; Sirat, *History of Jewish Philosophy*, p. 37; Baron, *History of the Jews*, 5:251; Neusner, *Torah through the Ages*, p. 8.

183. Stuart A. Cohen, *The Three Crowns: Structures of Communal Politics in Early Rabbinic Jewry* (Cambridge: Cambridge University Press, 1990), p. 69.

184. Carlebach, *The Pursuit of Heresy*, p. 273.

185. Ibid., pp. 14 and 255.

186. David of Makow, quoted in Wilensky, "Hasidic-Mitnaggedic Polemics," p. 264; R. Katzenellenbogen, quoted in ibid., p. 263.

187. Jacob Neusner, *Death and Birth of Judaism: The Impact of Christianity, Secularism, and the Holocaust on Jewish Faith* (New York: Basic Books, 1987), p. 4. While not all scholars would agree with Neusner that rabbinic Judaism came to an abrupt end in the late eighteenth century, others also see this era as a major watershed in Jewish history, an era of change unprecedented in scope since the time of Ezra, in which the traditional character of Jewish society was fundamentally changed. See Simon, *Jewish Religious Conflicts*, p. 7; Katz, *Tradition and Crisis*, pp. 184 and 195.

188. Neusner, *Death and Birth*, p. 118.

189. Rodney Taylor, *The Religious Dimensions of Confucianism* (Albany: State University of New York Press, 1990), p. 36.

190. Benjamin A. Elman, *Classicism, Politics, and Kinship: The Ch'ang-chou School of New Text Confucianism in Late Imperial China* (Berkeley: University of California Press, 1990), p. xviii.

191. For an account of some of these terms, see de Bary, "Uses of Neo-Confucianism," p. 544.

192. Wilson, "Genealogy of the Way," p. 2.

193. This definition of orthodoxy by N. J. McEleney appears in Aune, "Orthodoxy in First Century Judaism," p. 1.

194. Wm. Theodore de Bary, "Introduction," in de Bary and the Conference on Seventeenth-Century Chinese Thought, *The Unfolding of Neo-Confucianism* (New York: Columbia University Press, 1975), p. 24. Similar claims, however, might be made for forms of Christianity, Islam, and Judaism as well.

195. Bol, *"This Culture of Ours"*, p. 31.

196. Tillman, *Confucian Discourse*, pp. 7 and 81; John Chaffee, "Chao Ju-yü, Spurious Learning, and Southern Sung Political Culture," *Journal of Sung-Yuan Studies* 22 (1990–92): 36–37.

197. Ch'eng I, quoted in Tillman, p. 45.

198. Tillman, *Confucian Discourse*, pp 28–29; Fang Tung-shu, *Han-hsüeh shang-tui*, p. 36.

199. Chiang I-pin, *Sung-tai ju-shih*, p. 59.

200. James T. C. Liu, "How Did a Neo-Confucian School Become the State Orthodoxy?," *Philosophy East and West* 23.4 (1973): 498.

201. Ching, *To Acquire Wisdom*, p. 17.

202. Wm. Theodore de Bary, *Neo-Confucian Orthodoxy and the Learning of the Mind-and-Heart* (New York: Columbia University Press, 1981), p. 1.

203. Tillman, "A New Direction," p. 464.

204. Ch'en Liang, quoted in Tillman, *Utilitarian Confucianism*, p. 183.

205. de Bary, "Introduction," p. 8.

206. Bol, *"This Culture of Ours"*, p. 329.

207. Shu-hsien Liu, "The Problem of Orthodoxy in Chu Hsi's Philosophy," in *Chu Hsi and Neo-Confucianism*, ed. Wing-tsit Chan (Honolulu: University of Hawaii Press, 1986), pp. 453 and 455.

208. Ibid., p. 455; Gardner, *Learning to Be a Sage*, pp. 74–75.

209. Liu, "Problem of Orthodoxy," p. 455.

210. Liu, "Neo-Confucian School," pp. 503 passim.

211. Ibid., p. 502.

212. Ibid., pp. 502 and 503.

213. Wing-tsit Chan, "The Ch'eng-Chu School of Early Ming," in Wm. Theodore de Bary and the Conference on Ming Thought, *Self and Society in Ming Thought* (New York: Columbia University Press, 1970), p. 43.

214. Benjamin A. Elman, "'Where is King Ch'eng?': Civil Examinations and Confucian Ideology during the Early Ming," *T'oung Pao* 79 (1994): 62.

215. Benjamin A. Elman, "Changes in Confucian Civil Service Examinations from the Ming to the Ch'ing Dynasty," in *Education and Society in Late Imperial China, 1600–1900*, eds. Benjamin A. Elman and Alexander Woodside (Berkeley: University of California Press, 1994), p. 122.

216. Ibid., pp. 111–12.

217. Wilson, *Genealogy of the Way*, pp. 58–59.

218. Chu Wei-cheng, *Coming Out of the Middle Ages: Comparative Reflections on China and the West*, trans. and ed. Ruth Hayhoe (Armonk, NY: M. E. Sharpe, 1990), p. 123. On the role of Confucian Temple ritual in reproducing Ch'eng-Chu orthodoxy, see Thomas A. Wilson, "The Ritual Formation of Confucian Orthodoxy and the Descendants of the Sage," *Journal of Asian Studies* 55.3 (August 1996): 559–84.

219. Wilson, *Genealogy of the Way*, p. 24.

220. Elman, "'Where Is King Ch'eng?'," p. 28.

221. Tillman, *Confucian Discourse*, p. 252.

222. Gardner, *Learning to Be a Sage*, p. 23.

223. Tillman, *Confucian Discourse*, pp. 252–53.

224. Chan, *Chu Hsi: New Studies*, p. 350.

225. Liu, "Neo-Confucian School," p. 504.

226. George Orwell, *The Road to Wigan Pier* (London: V. Gollancz, 1937), p. 177.

227. Irene Bloom, "On the 'Abstraction' of Ming Thought: Some Concrete Evidence from the Philosophy of Lo Ch'in-shun," in *Principle and Practicality: Essays in Neo-Confucianism and Practical Learning*, eds. Wm. Theodore de Bary and Irene Bloom (New York: Columbia University Press, 1979), pp. 75, 86, and 87.

228. Ying-shih Yü, "Foreword" to Tillman, *Confucian Discourse*, p. x. On the subject of Wu Ch'eng's syncretism, see also John W. Dardess, *Confucianism and Autocracy: Professional Elites in the Founding of the Ming Dynasty* (Berkeley: University of California Press, 1983), pp. 78–79.

229. de Bary, *Neo-Confucian Orthodoxy*, pp. 154–56.

230. Wang Yang-ming, *Instructions for Practical Living and Other Neo-Confucian Writings by Wang Yang-ming* 2.176, trans. and anno. Wing-tsit Chan (New York: Columbia University Press, n.d.), p. 163.

231. Ibid. 2.176, p. 164.

232. Shu-hsien Liu, "On Chu Hsi as an Important Source for the Development of the Philosophy of Wang Yang-ming," *Journal of Chinese Philosophy* 11.1 (March 1984): 93, 100, and 104.

233. Ibid., pp. 98–99.

234. Ching, *To Acquire Wisdom*, p. 149.

235. Wang Yang-ming, *Instructions* 1.100, p. 63.

236. Ibid. 2.176, p. 164.

237. Ibid. 1.124, p. 81.

238. Ibid. 1.49, p. 41. See also Wilson, *Genealogy of the Way*, pp. 95–96.

239. Wang Yang-ming, *Instructions* 3.271, p. 220. See Ching, *To Acquire Wisdom*, p. 146, for a brief explanation of the allusion to the *Mencius* in this passage.

240. Kai-wing Chow also notes the strong populist appeal of Wang Yang-ming's definition of heresy in *Rise of Confucian Ritualism*, p. 24.

241. Ch'en Chien, *Hsüeh-pu t'ung-pien* 2.35.

242. Chang Li-hsiang, *Pei-wang lu*, in Yang, comp., *Ch'ing-ju hsüeh-an hsin-pien*, 1:664.

243. T'ung Neng-ling, "Chu-Lu yüan-yüan k'ao," quoted in Kao Ling-yin and Ch'en Ch'i-fang, *Fuchien Chu-tzu hsüeh* (Fuchou: Fuchien jen-min ch'u-pan she, 1986), pp. 426–27.

244. Chu, *Coming*, p. 146; de Bary, *Message of the Mind*, p. 80.

245. Hung-lam Chu, "The Debate Over Recognition of Wang Yang-ming," *Harvard Journal of Asiatic Studies* 48.1 (1988): 48, 69, and 70.

246. Judith A. Berling, *The Syncretic Religion of Lin Chao-en* (New York: Columbia University Press, 1980), p. 3.

247. Berling, *Syncretic Religion*, p. 51.

248. Deuchler, "Reject the False," pp. 400 and 401.

249. Elman, *Classicism, Politics, and Kinship*, p. 88.

250. Lü Liu-liang, "Fu Kao Hui-chan shu," in Morohashi, comp., *Shushi-gaku taikei*, 11:398.

251. Lü Liu-liang, *Lü Wan-ts'un wen-chi, fu-lu*, p. 595; de Bary, *Learning to Be a Sage*, p. 278.

252. Lü, "Yü Shih Yü-shan shu," in *Lü Wan-ts'un wen-chi* 1.48.

253. Lü, *Lü Wan-ts'un wen-chi, fu-lu*, p. 596.

254. de Bary, *Message of the Mind*, p. 134. In general, the early Ch'ing era witnessed a certain popularization and rustication of Ch'eng-Chu philosophy. Wang Mao et al., *Ch'ing-tai che-hsüeh*, p. 34.

255. Lu Lung-ch'i, "Hsüeh-shu-pien, hsia," in idem, *Lu Chia-shu wen-chi* 1.16.

256. Lu Lung-ch'i, "Ta Li Tzu-ch'iao shu," in Hsü Shih-ch'ang, comp., *Ch'ing-ju hsüeh-an* 30.10b.

257. Tu Wei-ming, *Way, Learning, and Politics: Essays on the Confucian Intellectual* (Albany: State University of New York Press, 1993), p. 127. Chang's intellectual career recapitulated the main trend of Confucian intellectual history of the previous hundred years, as he moved from a youthful devotion to Wang Yang-ming, to a mediatory position between Chu and Lu, to a final adherence to Chu Hsi. See Ueda Hiroku, "Chō Yō-en ni okeru Ōgaku hitei," *Chū tetsubun-gaku kaihō*, 2:109–10.

258. Bloom, "Philosophy of Lo Ch'in-shun," p. 111.

259. On the narrowing of orthodoxy in Hinduism, see W. D. O'Flaherty, "The Origin of Heresy in Hindu Mythology," *History of Religions* 10 (1971): 287.

260. See, for example, Hoyt Cleveland Tillman, review of *State and Scholars in T'ang China*, by David McMullen, in *Bulletin of Sung Yuan Studies*, no. 21 (1989), p. 86; Liu, *China Turning Inward*, p. 51; Chaffee, "Chao Ju-yü," p. 37.

261. Tillman, *Confucian Discourse*, pp. 8 and 9.

262. Tillman, "A New Direction," p. 463.

263. Tillman, *Confucian Discourse*, p. 260.

264. Deuchler, "Reject the False," p. 376.

265. On Lu Hsiang-shan, see Huang Wan, *Ming-tao pien*, p. 18.

266. Chang, *Neo-Confucian Thought*, 2:317.

267. Chan, "The *Hsing-li ching-i*," p. 545; T'ang Chün-i, *Chung-kuo che-hsüeh yüan-lun*, p. 692.

268. On-cho Ng, "*Hsing* (Nature) as the Ontological Basis of Practicality in Early Ch'ing Ch'eng-Chu Confucianism: Li Kuang-ti's (1642–1718) Philosophy," *Philosophy East and West* 44.1 (Jan. 1994): 81.

269. Tu, *Way, Learning, and Politics*, p. 138.

270. Here, I have followed the usage of Kai-wing Chow, who employs the word 'purism' to designate "an intellectual impulse that demands the recovery of the 'original' or 'pure' Confucian norms and language. . . . The purism of the Ch'ing scholars was not a clearly defined set of Confucian doctrines; rather, it was an aspiration, or an attitude, that fueled the persistent effort to purge heterodox elements from Confucian Classics and rituals." Chow, *Rise of Confucian Ritualism*, p. 8.

3. The Construction of Orthodoxy

1. R. A. Markus, "The Legacy of Pelagius: Orthodoxy, Heresy and Conciliation," in *The Making of Orthodoxy: Essays in Honour of Henry Chadwick*, ed. Rowan Williams (Cambridge: Cambridge University Press, 1989), p. 214.

2. Eusebius, *History of the Church* 3.32, p. 143.

3. Ibid. 4.22, pp. 181–82. This matter is discussed in Turner, *Pattern of Christian Truth*, p. 3.

4. Glenn F. Chesnut, *The First Christian Histories: Eusebius, Socrates, Sozomen, Theodoret, and Evagrius*, 2d ed., rev. and enl. (Macon, GA: Mercer University Press, 1986), p. 127.

5. Wilken, *Myth of Christian Beginnings*, p. 63.

6. Irenaeus, "Passages from Adversus Haereses to Illustrate Tertullian," in Greenslade, ed., *Early Latin Theology*, p. 70; Firmilian, "Firmilian to Cyprian, His Brother in the Lord, Greeting," in Cyprian, *Letters (1–81)*, p. 298; Hilgenfeld, *Ketzergeschichte*, p. 40; Tertullian, "Prescriptions against Heretics" 35, in *Early Latin Theology*, p. 56; Gregory, *Moralia In Job* 23.4, quoted in Evans, *Gregory the Great*, p. 133.

7. Epiphanius, *The Panarion of St. Epiphanius, Bishop of Salamis; Selected Passages* 1.2, trans. Philip R. Amidon (Oxford: Oxford University Press, 1990), p. 26.

8. Markus, "Problem of Self-Definition," p. 8.

9. Bauer, *Orthodoxy and Heresy*, p. 191.

10. J. Stevenson, ed., *A New Eusebius: Documents Illustrating the History of the Church to A.D. 337*, revised by W. H. C. Frend (London: S.P.C.K., 1987), p. 93.

11. Krumm, *Modern Heresies*, pp. 21–22.

12. Simon, "From Greek Haeresis," p. 114.

13. Lewinstein, "Studies in Islamic Heresiography," p. 4.

14. Watt, "Great Community," p. 25.

15. Ibn Qudama, *Censure of Speculative Theology*, p. 40.

16. Ibn Batta, *La profession de foi*, p. 21.

17. Ibn 'Asakir, "Exposure of the Calumniator's Lying," p. 190.

18. al-Azmeh, "Orthodoxy and Hanbalite Fideism," pp. 258 and 261.

19. Halm, *Shiism*, p. 2.

20. Allard, *Le problème des attributs divins*, p. 79.

21. Cohen, "A Virgin Defiled," pp. 4–5.

22. Guttmann, *Rabbinic Judaism*, p. 130.

23. Hsiung Tz'u-li, *Hsüeh-t'ung* 50.22b, p. 2005. The Japanese Neo-Confucian scholar, Yamazaki Ansai (1618–1682), also posited the primacy of orthodoxy, dating the birth of heresy from the time of Confucius. Yamazaki, *Heki'i*, p. 188.

24. Hsüeh Hsüan, *Hsü tu-shu lu* 4.9, quoted in Jung Chao-tzu, *Ming-tai ssu-hsiang shih* (Taipei: Taiwan K'ai-ming shu-tien, 1969), p. 17.

25. de Bary, *Message of the Mind*, p. 107.

26. Thomas Wilson makes a similar point in his "Genealogy of the Way," p. vi.

27. Hsiao Kung-ch'üan, "Sheng-chiao yü i-tuan," p. 37.

28. Thomas A. Wilson, "Genealogy and History in Neo-Confucian Sectarian Uses of the Confucian Past," *Modern China* 20.1 (Jan. 1994): 9.

29. Barrett, *Li Ao*, pp. 141–43.

30. Han Yü, "Yüan-tao lun," in *Han Ch'ang-li ch'üan-chi* 11.4b (Taipei: Chung-hua shu-chü, 1966). I have followed the translation of this passage given in Wilson, "Genealogy of the Way," p. 31, with a few modifications.

31. Wilson, "Genealogy of the Way," pp. 7–8.

32. Liu, *China Turning Inward*, p. 75.

33. Bol, *"This Culture of Ours"*, p. 302.

34. Yamazaki Michio, "The Tradition of the Way in Japan," in *Chu Hsi and Neo-Confucianism*, ed. Wing-tsit Chan (Honolulu: University of Hawaii Press, 1986), p. 587; Wilson, "Genealogy of the Way," p. 212.

35. Chu Hsi, Preface to *Chung-yung chang-chü*, trans. in Wilson, "Genealogy of the Way," p. 39. This rather cryptic passage from the *Documents Classic* is rendered by Wilson as follows: "The human mind is precarious; the mind of Tao is barely perceptible. Be discerning and single-minded. Hold fast to the mean." See Wilson, *Genealogy of the Way*, p. 86.

36. Wilson, "Genealogy of the Way," pp. 132 passim.

37. Wing-tsit Chan, "Chu Hsi and Yuan Neo-Confucianism," in *Yuan Thought: Chinese Thought and Religion under the Mongols*, eds. Hok-lam Chan and Wm. Theodore de Bary (New York: Columbia University Press, 1982), p. 203.

38. See, for example, Chan, "The *Hsing-li ching-i*," pp. 567–68; Wilson, "Genealogy of the Way," p. 52; Kao P'an-lung, *K'un-hsüeh chi*, in Morohashi, comp., *Shushigaku taikei*, 11:357.

39. de Bary, *Message of the Mind*, p. 228.

40. T'ang Chien, *Ch'ing hsüeh-an hsiao-chih* 2.40; Chang Po-hsing, *K'un-hsüeh lu*, in Hsü Shih-ch'ang, comp., *Ch'ing-ju hsüeh-an* 12.4b; Chang, *Neo-Confucian Thought*, 2:318; Wm. Theodore de Bary, *The Trouble with Confucianism* (Cambridge: Harvard University Press, 1991), pp. 76–77.

41. Lü Liu-liang, "Fu Kao Hui-chan shu," in idem, *Liu Wan-ts'un wen-chi* 1.35; Wm. Theodore de Bary, *Learning for One's Self: Essays on the Individual in Neo-Confucian Thought* (New York: Columbia University Press, 1991), pp. 277 and 345.

42. Wilson, *Genealogy of the Way*, p. 96; Ivanhoe, *Ethics*, p. 111; Ching, *To Acquire Wisdom*, pp. 173–74.

43. Hou Wai-lu, "Preface" to Huang Wan, *Ming-tao p'ien*, p. 11.

44. Chiang Fan, "Preface" to *Sung-hsüeh yüan-yüan chi* (Shanghai: Shanghai shu-tien ch'u-pan she, 1983), p. 2. Just how arbitrary this process of scholastic lineage formation became in Ch'ing times is evidenced by Yü Ying-shih's account of how Chang Hsüeh-ch'eng (1738–1801) force-fitted Huang Tsung-hsi (1610–1695) into the Che-tung lineage in order to achieve balance and symmetry between the Che-tung and Che-hsi lines of transmission. See Yü Ying-shih, *Lun Tai Chen yü Chang Hsüeh-ch'eng—Ch'ing-tai chung-ch'i hsüeh-shu ssu-hsiang-shih yen-chiu* (Taipei: Hua-shih ch'u-pan she, 1977), p. 61.

45. John H. Berthrong, *All Under Heaven: Transforming Paradigms in Confucian-Christian Dialogues* (Albany: State University of New York Press, 1994), pp. 107 and 109. On Mou's updated version of the transmission of the Way, see also Wilson, *Genealogy of the Way*, pp. 194–95.

46. O'Grady, *Heresy,* p. 127.

47. Filoramo, *A History of Gnosticism,* p. 4.

48. Robert M. Grant, *Eusebius as Church Historian* (Oxford: Clarendon Press, 1980), pp. 46 and 59.

49. Mishnah Abot 1.1, in Neusner, trans., *The Mishnah,* p. 672.

50. Jacobs, *Principles of the Jewish Faith,* p. 282.

51. Louis Jacobs, "Historical Thinking in the Post-Talmudic Halakhah," *History and Theory* 27 (1988): 67.

52. Isadore Twersky, *Rabad of Posquières, a Twelfth-Century Talmudist* (Cambridge: Harvard University Press, 1962), p. 101; Jacob S. Minkin, *The World of Moses Maimonides, with Selections from His Writings* (New York: Thomas Yoseloff, 1957), p. 53.

53. Robert Chazan, "Representation of Events in the Middle Ages," *History and Theory* 27 (1988): 42.

54. Cohen, "A Virgin Defiled," p. 8; Le Boulluec, *La notion d'hérésie,* 1:86.

55. Grant, *Eusebius,* p. 46.

56. T. A. M. Fontaine, *In Defence of Judaism: Abraham Ibn Daud; Sources and Structure of ha-Emunah ha-Ramah* (Assen/Maastricht: Van Gorcum, 1990), p. 159.

57. Watt, "Great Community," p. 28.

58. Watt, "Development of the Islamic Sects," p. 82.

59. John D. Barrow, *Theories of Everything: The Quest for Ultimate Explanation* (New York: Fawcett Columbine, 1991), p. 156.

60. Bernard Faure, *The Rhetoric of Immediacy: A Cultural Critique of Chan/Zen Buddhism* (Princeton: Princeton University Press, 1991), p. 19.

61. Le Boulluec, *La notion d'hérésie,* 1:183 and 1:390.

62. Ehrman, *Orthodox Corruption,* p. 6.

63. Robinson, *Bauer Thesis,* p. 6.

64. Irenaeus, *Against Heresies* 1.10, p. 331.

65. Epiphanius, *Panarion* 2.31, trans. Williams, p. 190.

66. Ibid. 2.33, p. 199.

67. Cyprian, *De Ecclesiae Catholicae Unitate* 23, p. 95.

68. Ibid. 7, p. 69.

69. Ehrman, *Orthodox Corruption*, p. 163.

70. Martin Elze, "Häresie und Einheit der Kirche im 2. Jahrhundert," *Zeitschrift für Theologie und Kirche* 71 (1974): 407–8; Prestige, *Fathers and Heretics*, p. 176; Bauer, *Orthodoxy and Heresy*, p. 231.

71. Saint Basil, "To Bishop Epiphanius" (Letter #258), in idem, *Letters, vol. 2 (186–368)*, p. 219, trans. Sister Agnes Clare Way, in *The Fathers of the Church; A New Translation* (New York: Fathers of the Church, Inc., 1955).

72. Lewinstein, "Studies in Islamic Heresiography," p. 5.

73. Wansbrough, *Sectarian Milieu*, pp. 124–25.

74. Watt, "Development of the Islamic Sects," p. 83.

75. Ibn Taymiyya, *Against the Greek Logicians*, p. 153.

76. al-Shahrastani, *Muslim Sects and Divisions*, p. 141.

77. Gries, "Heresy," p. 344.

78. Judah Halevi, *The Kuzari (Kitab al-Khazari): An Argument for the Faith of Israel*, trans. Hartwig Hirschfeld (New York: Schocken Books, 1964), p. 170.

79. al-Qirqisani, *Jewish Sects*, p. 140.

80. *Dipavamsa*, ed. Hermann Oldenberg (New Delhi: Asian Educational Services, 1982), p. 37, in John S. Strong, *The Experience of Buddhism: Sources and Interpretations* (Belmont, CA: Wadsworth Publishing Co., 1995), p. 129.

81. Tang Ch'eng, "Ta Shih Ch'ing-huan shu," in T'ang Chien, *Ch'ing-hsüeh-an hsiao-chih* 6.192.

82. Hsüeh Hsüan, *Tu-shu lu* 3.13a, in Chang Po-hsing, comp., *Cheng-i-t'ang ch'üan-shu,* case 10.

83. Wilson, "Genealogy of the Way," p. 194.

84. Vincent of Lérins, *The Commonitory* 2.2, p. 38.

85. Isidore of Seville, *Etymologies*, bk. 8, "On the Church and the Sects," in Peters, ed., *Heresy and Authority*, p. 48.

86. Tertullian, "The Prescriptions against the Heretics" 26, p. 48.

87. Pelikan, *Christian Tradition*, 1:116.

88. Vallée, *Anti-Gnostic Polemics*, p. 53.

89. Hilary of Poitiers, *The Trinity* 7.3, p. 226.

90. John Henry Cardinal Newman, "Letter 16," *British Magazine* (1837), quoted in Thomas, *Newman and Heresy*, p. 145.

91. Salvador Gomez Nogales, "Sunni Theology," in *The Cambridge History of Arabic Literature; Religion, Learning and Science in the Abbasid Period*, eds. M. J. L. Young et al. (Cambridge: Cambridge University Press, 1990), pp. 7–8.

92. Allard, *Le problème des attributs divins*, p. 427.

93. al-Ghazali, *Faisal at-Tafriqa bain al-Islam wa'z Zandaqa*, quoted in Lewis, "Significance of Heresy," p. 58.

94. Ignaz Goldziher, "Catholic Tendencies and Particularism in Islam," in *Studies on Islam*, trans. and ed. Merlin L. Swartz (Oxford: Oxford University Press, 1981), p. 137.

95. MacDonald, *Development of Muslim Theology*, p. 19. On this point, see also J. Fueck, "The Role of Traditionalism in Islam," in Swartz, *Studies on Islam*, p. 110.

96. Schacht, "Theology and Law in Islam," p. 13.

97. Coulson, *A History of Islamic Law*, p. 86.

98. Ibid., p. 102.

99. Cohen, "Significance of Yavneh," pp. 101 and 103.

100. R. Elazar ben Azaria, quoted in Shmuel Safrai, "Halakha," in *The Literature of the Sages; First Part: Oral Tora, Halakha, Mishna, Tosefta, Talmud, External Tractates*, ed. Shmuel Safrai (Assen/Maastricht: Van Gorcum; Philadelphia: Fortress Press, 1987), p. 173.

101. Neusner, *Formative Judaism*, pp. 6–7; idem, *Torah through the Ages*, p. 62.

102. Isaac E. Barzilay, "Acceptance or Rejection: Manasseh of Ilya's (1767–1831) Ambivalent Attitude toward Hasidism," *The Jewish Quarterly Review* 74.1 (July 1983): 2.

103. Chiang Fen-kung, "Cheng-t'ung," in *Ch'ing-wen hui*, eds. Chu Hsiu-hsia and Yüan Shuai-nan (Taipei: Taiwan shu-tien, 1960), p. 119.

104. Wing-tsit Chan, "Chu Hsi's Completion of Neo-Confucianism," in idem, *Chu Hsi Life and Thought* (Hong Kong: Chinese University Press; New York: St. Martin's Press, 1987), p. 104; idem, "What Is New in Chu Hsi," in ibid., p. 39.

105. Chan, "Chu Hsi's Completion," p. 110.

106. Hu Chü-jen, *Chü-yeh lu* 7.79.

107. Lo Ch'in-shun, *Knowledge Painfully Acquired*, p. 113.

108. Lu Shih-i, *Ssu-pien lu chi-yao* 31.21a; Li Kuang-ti, *Jung-ts'un yü-lu* 20.17b.

109. Rai Shunsui, *Gakutoron*, quoted in Robert L. Backus, "The Motivation of Confucian Orthodoxy in Tokugawa Japan," *Harvard Journal of Asiatic Studies* 39.1 (June 1979): 294. The second quote in the text is a paraphase by Backus, not a direct quotation.

110. de Bary, *Message of the Mind*, pp. 209–10.

111. David Nivison, "Protests Against Conventions and Conventions of Protest," in *The Confucian Persuasion*, ed. Arthur W. Wright (Stanford: Stanford University Press, 1960), p. 179.

112. Coser, *Social Conflict*, p. 91.

113. Vallée, *Anti-Gnostic Polemics*, pp. 100–101; Aloys Grillmeier, S. J., *Christ in Christian Tradition*, vol. 1, *From the Apostolic Age to Chalcedon (451)*, trans. John Bowden (Atlanta: John Knox Press, 1975), p. 7. According to Grillmeier, the orthodox middle incorporated the heretical extremes on the crucial Christological issue:

> [T]he opposed extremes of christological heresy have, in the end, decisively influenced what came to be, in the tension between them, the church's middle road. Chalcedon was to preserve the authentic kernel of what both Monophysitism and Nestorianism wanted to say, and hand it on to the future.

114. Pelikan, *Christian Tradition*, 1:350.

115. Turner, *Pattern of Christian Truth*, p. 132.

116. Daniel J. Sahas, *Icon and Logos: Sources in Eighth-Century Iconoclasm* (Toronto: University of Toronto Press, 1986), p. 51.

117. Gregory of Nyssa, *Catechetical Orations* 3, quoted in Pelikan, *Christian Tradition*, 1:67.

118. Hilary of Poiters, *The Trinity* 5.2, p. 135.

119. St. John of Damascus, "Second Apology of Saint John of Damascus against those who Attack the Divine Images," in idem, *On the Divine Images*, p. 51.

120. Frend, *Monophysite Movement*, p. 125.

121. Epiphanius the Deacon, "Statement of the Sixth Session of the Seventh Ecumenical Council (Nicea, 787)," trans. in Sahas, *Icon and Logos*, p. 87.

122. Nigg, *The Heretics*, p. 74.

123. Brown, *Heresies*, p. 160.

124. Gregory of Nazianzus, Hom. 45, 28, quoted in J. M. Hussey, *The Orthodox Church in the Byzantine Empire* (Oxford: Clarendon Press, 1986), p. 12.

125. Pelikan, *Christian Tradition*, 2:62.

126. Brown, *Heresies*, p. 128.

127. Vincent of Lérins, *The Commonitory* 13, p. 55. On the comparably paradoxical position of orthodoxy in South Indian Hinduism, see David Shulman, "The Enemy Within: Idealism and Dissent in South Indian Hinduism," in *Orthodoxy, Heterodoxy and Dissent in India*, eds. S. N. Eisenstadt et al. (Berlin: Mouton, 1984), pp. 34 and 43.

128. Dunn, *Unity and Diversity*, p. 263.

129. E. Earle Ellis, "Paul and His Opponents: Trends in Research," in *Christianity, Judaism, and Other Greco-Roman Cults*, part 1, *New Testament*, ed. Jacob Neusner (Leiden: E. J. Brill, 1975), p. 282.

130. Brown, *Heresies*, p. 67.

131. O'Grady, *Heresy*, p. 122.

132. Pelikan, *Christian Tradition*, 2:123.

133. For examples of heretical middle ways, those of the Pelagians and of Valentinus, see Frend, *Saints and Sinners*, p. 125; and Elaine Pagels, *The Origin of Satan* (New York: Random House, 1995), p. 166.

134. Ibn Taymiyya, *Struggle Against Popular Religion*, p. 92.

135. al-Tabari, *Commentary on the Qur'an*, trans. in F. E. Peters, *A Reader on Classical Islam* (Princeton: Princeton University Press, 1994), p. 106.

136. Faruqi I. H. Azad, *The Tarjuman al-Qur'an: A Critical Analysis of Maulana Abu'l-Kalam Azad's Approach to the Understanding of the Qur'an* (New Delhi: Vikas, 1982), p. 83.

137. Baldick, *Mystical Islam*, p. 32. Baldick remarks that this picture of Islam "owes much to Louis Massignon's work."

138. Nogales, "Sunni Theology," p. 2.

139. Quoted in Friedlander, "Heterodoxies of the Shiites," p. 1.

140. Lewinstein, "Studies in Islamic Heresiography," p. 18. The *hashwiyya* are those who fill their speeches with quotations from the Qur'an and the Sunna. Knysh, "Orthodoxy and Heresy," p. 56.

141. Laoust, *Les schismes dans l'Islam*, p. 458.

142. Wensinck, *The Muslim Creed*, pp. 105–6.

143. Goldziher, *Islamic Theology and Law*, p. 103; Nogales, "Sunni Theology," p. 8.

144. Ibn 'Asakir, "Exposure of the Calumniator's Lying," p. 171. This summary statement of Ash'ari's position on the divine attributes, however, ignores his early enthusiasm for anthropomorphism, on which see Allard, *Le problème des attributs divins*, p. 92.

145. al-Shahrastani, *Muslim Sects and Divisions*, p. 80.

146. Nafiz Danisman-Tug, "Pourquoi l'Ash'arisme combat-il l'esoterisme et l'idée de la transfusion spirituelle?," *Ilahiyat Fak dergisi* 6 (1957): 154.

147. Nogales, "Sunni Theology," p. 7.

148. Ibn 'Asakir, "Exposure of the Calumniator's Lying," p. 173.

149. Ormsby, *Theodicy in Islamic Thought*, p. 52. See also p. 24.

150. al-Baghdadi, *Moslem Schisms and Sects*, p. 194.

151. al-Ghazali, *Ilya' 'Ulum al-Din* 1.96, quoted in Wensinck, *The Muslim Creed*, p. 100.

152. Ibid.

153. Coulson, *A History of Islamic Law*, p. 104.

154. MacDonald, *Development of Muslim Theology*, p. 27.

155. Laoust, *Les schismes dans l'Islam*, pp. 442–43; Ibn 'Asakir, "Exposure of the Calumniator's Lying," pp. 173–74; Wensinck, *The Muslim Creed*, p. 182.

156. Lewinstein, "Studies in Islamic Heresiography," p. 170.

157. Wensinck, *The Muslim Creed*, p. 85.

158. Michel, "Theology of Ibn Taymiyya," pp. 2 and 394. See also pp. 42 and 45.

159. Ibn Taymiyya, *La profession de foi*, pp. 61–62. In translating this passage from the French, I consulted the paraphrase in Ibn Taimiya, *Struggle Against Popular Religion*, p. 86.

160. Ibn Qudama, *Censure of Speculative Theology*, p. 28.

161. Watt, *Early Islam*, p. 88.

162. Gahiz, *Ar-Risala*, in Nagel, "Problem der Orthodoxie," p. 34. The more usual sense of 'Mu'tazila' is "separatists." It is amazing how creative the ancients (and medievals) were in devising etymologies to support their polemical positions.

163. Ibid., pp. 40–41.

164. Mashkur, trans., *Les sectes Shiites*, p. 17.

165. 'Allamah Tabataba'i, "The Shi'i View of God," in *Shi'ism: Doctrines, Thought, and Spirituality*, eds. Seyyed Hossein Nasr et al. (Albany: State University of New York Press, 1988), p. 116.

166. Murtada Mutahhari, "Shi'i Interpretations of the Qur'an," in *Shi'ism*, p. 32.

167. Baldick, *Mystical Islam*, p. 19.

168. Knysh, "Orthodoxy and Heresy," p. 66.

169. *Yerushalmi Hagigah* 2:1, in *The Talmud of the Land of Israel: A Preliminary Translation and Explanation*, vol. 20, *Hagigah and Moed Qatan*, trans. Jacob Neusner (Chicago: University of Chicago Press, 1986), p. 43.

170. Kellner, *Maimonides on Judaism*, pp. 72–73; Minkin, *World of Maimonides*, p. 359.

171. Dhamari, *Commentary of R. Hoter ben Shelomo*, p. 159.

172. Ralph Marcus, "Pharisees, Essenes, and Gnostics," *Journal of Biblical Literature* 32.3 (1954): 160.

173. Kaufman, *Great Sects and Schisms*, p. 26.

174. Flavius Josephus, *The Antiquities of the Jews* 13.5, in *The Works of Josephus, Complete and Unabridged*, new ed., trans. William Whiston (Peabody, MA: Hendrickson, 1987), p. 346.

175. Kaufman, *Great Sects and Schisms*, p. 48.

176. Ibid., p. 66.

177. Jacobs, *Principles of the Jewish Faith*, p. 292.

178. *Mencius* 7B. 37, p. 202. Compare Analects 13.21.

179. Heiner Roetz, *Confucian Ethics of the Axial Age: A Reconstruction under the Aspect of a Breakthrough toward Postconventional Thinking* (Albany: State University of New York Press, 1993), p. 108.

180. Schwartz, *World of Thought*, p. 259.

181. *Chuang-tzu*, chap. 3 ("Yang-sheng chu"), trans. in de Bary, *Sources of Chinese Tradition*, 1:73.

182. Bodde, *Chinese Thought, Society, and Science*, p. 109.

183. Roetz, *Confucian Ethics*, p. 108.

184. Tillman, "A New Direction," p. 468; idem, *Confucian Discourse*, p. 262.

185. Tiao Pao, "Sung-Lu san-tse," in Yang Hsiang-k'uei, comp., *Ch'ing-ju hsüeh-an hsin-pien*, 2:292.

186. Hsüeh Hsüan, *Tu-shu lu* 3.11a; Lo Ch'in-shun, "Letter to Wang Yang-ming, Summer, 1520," in idem, *Knowledge Painfully Acquired*, p. 178.

187. Chang Li-hsiang," Yü He Shang-yin shu," from *Yang-yüan hsien-sheng ch'üan-chi*, in Yang Hsiang-k'uei, comp., *Ch'ing-ju hsüeh-an hsin-pien*, 1:652.

188. Hsiung Tz'u-li, *Hsien-tao lu*, in Hsü Shih-ch'ang, comp., *Ch'ing-ju hsüeh-an* 38.6b.

189. de Bary, *Message of the Mind*, p. 145.

190. Bol, *"This Culture of Ours"*, p. 274; Tillman, *Utilitarian Confucianism*, p. 140.

191. Liu Feng-lu, *Lun-yü shu-Ho*, in *Huang-Ch'ing ching-chieh*, comps. Juan Yüan et al. (Taipei: Fu-hsin shu-chü, 1972 reprint), 19:14217 (*chüan* 1,298).

192. de Bary, *Message of the Mind*, p. 145.

193. Ch'en Chien, *Hsüeh-pu t'ung-pien* 2.144.

194. *Mencius* 7A. 26, pp. 187–88.

195. Chu Hsi, *Ssu-shu chi-chu*, *Meng-tzu* 7.197.

196. Chiao Hsün, *Tiao-ku chi* (Taipei: Taiwan Shang-wu, n.d.) 9.136.

197. Chiao Hsün, *Lun-yü pu-shu*, in *Huang-Ch'ing ching-chieh* 16:12378 (*chüan* 1,165). Alexander Woodside discusses the significance of Chiao Hsün's redefinition of heresy in his "State, Scholars, and Orthodoxy: The Ch'ing Academies, 1736–1839," in Liu, ed., *Orthodoxy*, pp. 180–81.

4. The Construction of Heresy

1. Wisse, "Use of Early Christian Literature," p. 180.

2. Ehrman, *Orthodox Corruption*, p. 50.

3. Filoramo, *A History of Gnosticism*, p. 2.

4. Epiphanius, *De Fide*, in *The Panarion of Epiphanius*, pp. 641 and 644; Virginia Burrus, "The Heretical Woman as Symbol in Alexander, Epiphanius, and Jerome," *Harvard Theological Review* 84.3 (1991): 240; Young, "Did Epiphanius Know," p. 202.

5. Vallée, *Anti-Gnostic Polemics*, p. 68.

6. Hilary of Poitiers, *The Trinity* 7.6, pp. 229–30.

7. Ibid. 7.7, p. 231.

8. Saint John Chrysostom, *On the Incomprehensible Nature of God*, trans. Paul W. Harkins, in *The Fathers of the Church, A New Translation*, vol. 72 (Washington, DC: The Catholic University of America Press, 1984), p. 274.

9. Gray, *Defense of Chalcedon*, p. 124.

10. Charles Moeller, "Le chalcédonisme et le néo-chalcédonisme en Orient de 451 à la fin du VIe siècle," in *Das Konzil von Chalkedon, Geschichte und Gegenwart*, eds. Aloys Grillmeier and Heinrich Bacht, vol. 1, *Der Glaube von Chalkedon* (Würzburg: Echter-Verlag, 1951), p. 643. See also p. 651.

11. Nina G. Garsoïan, *The Paulician Heresy: A Study of the Origin and Development of Paulicianism in Armenia and the Eastern Provinces of the Byzantine Empire* (The Hague: Mouton and Co., 1967), p. 215.

12. John Cassian, *The Seven Books of John Cassian on the Incarnation of the Lord against Nestorius* 1.2, trans. Edgar C. S. Gibson, in *A Select Library of Nicene and Post-Nicene Fathers of the Christian Church*, 2d ser., eds. Philip Schaff and Henry Wace, vol. 11 (Grand Rapids, MI: Wm. B. Eerdmans, 1955), pp. 551–52.

13. V. I. Lenin, *Left-Wing Communism, an Infantile Disorder: A Popular Essay in Marxian Strategy and Tactics* (New York: International Publishers, 1978), p. 84.

14. Mao Tse-tung, "Some Experiences in Our Party's History," in *Selected Works of Mao Tse-tung*, vol. 5 (Beijing: Foreign Languages Press, 1977), p. 329.

15. Sigmund Freud, "The Sexual Aberrations," in *Three Essays on the Theory of Sexuality by Sigmund Freud* (London: Imago Publishing Co., 1949), p. 38.

16. Ibid., p. 43.

17. Jean Gouillard, "L'hérésie dans l'empire Byzantins des origines au XIIe siècle," *Travaux et Mémoires* 1 (1965): 301.

18. Hippolytus, *The Refutation of All Heresies* 5.5, in *The Ante-Nicene Fathers: Translations of the Writings of the Fathers Down to A.D. 325*, eds. Alexander Roberts and James Donaldson, American Reprint of the Edinburgh Edition, vol. 5, *Hippolytus, Cyprian, Caius, Novatian, Appendix* (Buffalo: The Christian Literature Publishing Co., 1886), p. 58.

19. Firmillian of Caesarea, Epistle 75.7, in Heine, *Montanist Oracles*, p. 101.

20. Vincent of Lérins, *The Commonitory* 24, pp. 73 and 74.

21. Moore, *Origins of European Dissent*, p. 19.

22. Thomas, *Newman and Heresy*, p. 252. According to Rowan Williams, Newman's work is probably more valuable for its "classical exemplification" of heresiographical technique than for its serious scholarship. Williams, *Arius*, p. 6.

23. John Henry Newman, "Annotations on Theological Subjects in the Foregoing Treatises, Alphabetically Arranged," in *Selected Treatises of St. Athanasius in Controversy with the Arians*, trans. and anno. John Henry Newman (London: Longmans, Green, and Co., 1890), 2:143.

24. Ibid., p. 145.

25. For a more recent (though somewhat whimsical) assertion of this idea, see Umberto Eco, *The Name of the Rose*, trans. William Weaver (San Diego: Harcourt Brace and Co., A Harvest Book, 1984), pp. 150–52 passim.

26. Gouillard, "L'hérésie dans l'empire Byzantins," p. 312. One relatively recent instance of this was the Church's constitution of a "modernist" heresy, which actually drove those labelled as heretics to form a movement for their common defense. Lester R. Kurtz, *The Politics of Heresy: The Modernist Crisis in Roman Catholicism* (Berkeley: University of California Press, 1986), pp. 5–6.

27. Rebecca Lyman, "A Topography of Heresy: Mapping the Rhetorical Creation of Arianism," in *Arianism after Arius: Essays on the Development of the Fourth Century Trinitarian Conflicts*, eds. Michel R. Barnes and Daniel H. Williams (Edinburgh: T & T Clark, 1993), p. 47.

28. Kurtz, *Politics of Heresy*, p. 45.

29. Gordon W. Allport, *The Nature of Prejudice*, quoted in Elizabeth Young-Bruehl, *The Anatomy of Prejudices* (Cambridge: Harvard University Press, 1996), p. 17.

30. Elizabeth Young-Bruehl objects that "important differences exist between racism and antisemitism—they are not both 'fascism,' and they are not just prejudice in the singular, an undifferentiated phenomenon." Young-Bruehl, *Anatomy*, p. 4.

31. Peters, *Heresy and Authority*, p. 103.

32. Georg Strecker, "Appendix 1: On the Problem of Jewish Christianity," in Bauer, *Orthodoxy and Heresy*, p. 285.

33. Le Boulluec, *La notion d'hérésie*, 2:509.

34. Frank Kermode, *The Uses of Error* (London: Collins, 1990), p. 7.

35. William J. Collinge, "Introduction," to Saint Augustine, *Four Anti-Pelagian Writings*, trans. John A. Mourant and William J. Collinge, with Introductions and Notes by William J. Collinge (Washington, DC: The Catholic University Press of America, 1992), p. 7.

36. John C. Cavadini, *The Last Christology of the West: Adoptionism in Spain and Gaul, 785–820* (Philadelphia: University of Pennsylvania Press, 1993), p. 1.

37. Cassian, *Seven Books* 5.2, p. 581.

38. Cavadini, *Last Christology*, p. 85.

39. Birger A. Pearson, "Cain and the Cainites," in idem, *Gnosticism, Judaism, and Egyptian Christianity* (Minneapolis: Fortress Press, 1990), p. 105; A. F. J. Klijn and G. J. Reinink, *Patristic Evidence for Jewish-Christian Sects* (Leiden: E. J. Brill, 1970), p. 68.

40. Frank Williams, "Introduction" to Epiphanius, *Panarion*, p. xviii.

41. Watt, *Early Islam*, p. 130.

42. Michael Cook, *Early Muslim Dogma: A Source-Critical Study* (Cambridge: Cambridge University Press, 1981), p. 98.

43. Ibid.

44. Lewinstein, "Studies in Islamic Heresiography," p. 2.

45. Ignaz Goldziher, "Le dénombrement des sectes Mohamétanes," *Revue de l'histoire des religions* 26 (1892): 134.

46. 'Adud al-Din al-Iji, "'Adudiyya," trans. William Montgomery Watt, in idem, *Islamic Creeds*, p. 86.

47. Ibn Batta, *La profession de foi*, p. 16.

48. Friedlander, "Heterodoxies of the Shiites," p. 6; Kate Chambers Seelye, "Introduction" to Ibn Tahir al-Baghdadi, *Moslem Schisms and Sects*, ed. and trans. Seelye (New York: Columbia University Press, 1920; reprint, New York: AMS Press, 1966), pp. 4–5.

49. Watt, "Development of the Islamic Sects," p. 84.

50. Laoust, "L'hérésiographie musulmane," p. 173.

51. Lewinstein, "Studies in Islamic Heresiography," p. 6.

52. Louis Gardet and M. M. Anawati, *Introduction à la théologie musulmane: Essai de théologie comparée*, 3d ed. (Paris: Librairie Philosophique J. Vrin, 1981), p. 148; Roger Arnaldez, *Grammaire et théologie chez Ibn Hazm de Cordoue: Essai*

sur la structure et les conditions de la pensée musulmane (Paris: Librairie Philosophique J. Vrin, 1981), p. 252; Friedlander, "Heterodoxies of the Shi'ites," pp. 31–32.

53. Ibn Hazm, *Kitab al-fisal fi'l-milal,* in Friedlander, "Heterodoxies of the Shi'ites," pp. 31 and 32.

54. Baldick, *Mystical Islam,* p. 64.

55. Lewinstein, "Studies in Islamic Heresiography," pp. 219 and 252.

56. Keith Lewinstein, "Notes on Eastern Hanafite Heresiography," *Journal of the American Oriental Society* 114.4 (1994): 590.

57. Lewinstein, "Studies in Islamic Heresiography," p. 170.

58. al-Shahrastani, *Muslim Sects and Divisions,* p. 16.

59. Ibid., p. 40.

60. Watt, *Formative Period,* p. 4. Watt makes a similar point in his *Islamic Philosophy and Theology,* p. 29.

61. Michel, "Theology of Ibn Taymiyya," p. 44.

62. Watt, "Development of the Islamic Sects," p. 85; Watt, *Formative Period,* p. 148.

63. Lewinstein, "Studies in Islamic Heresiography," p. 131.

64. Ibid., pp. 137 and 152–53.

65. Watt, "Development of the Islamic Sects," p. 86.

66. Watt, *Islamic Philosophy and Theology,* p. 44.

67. al-Shahrastani, *Muslim Sects and Divisions,* p. 98.

68. *Yerushalmi Sanhedrin* 10:5, in *The Talmud of the Land of Israel: A Preliminary Translation and Explanation,* vol. 31, *Sanhedrin and Makkot,* trans. Jacob Neusner (Chicago: University of Chicago Press, 1984), p. 360.

69. Segal, *Two Powers in Heaven,* p. 7.

70. Baron, *History of the Jews,* 5:197.

71. The words within the quotations marks appear in Wansbrough, *Sectarian Milieu,* p. 98.

72. Wilhelm Bacher, "Qirqisani, the Qaraite, and His Work on Jewish Sects," in *Karaite Studies,* ed. Philip Birnbaum (New York: Hermon Press, 1971), p. 280.

73. Kellner, *Dogma in Medieval Jewish Thought*, pp. 22 and 32–33.

74. Segal, *Two Powers in Heaven*, p. 58.

75. Ibid., p. 59.

76. Martin A. Cohen, "'Anan ben David and Karaite Origins," *The Jewish Quarterly Review* 68.3: 130.

77. Carlebach, *Pursuit of Heresy*, p. 10.

78. Ibid., p. 152.

79. Ch'eng I and Ch'eng Hao, *Erh-Ch'eng yü-lu* 16.261. As A. C. Graham has pointed out, twentieth-century scholars have concluded that "egoism was not what Yang Chu taught, but something that Confucians justly or unjustly read into his teaching." A. C. Graham, *Disputers of the Tao: Philosophical Argument in Ancient China* (La Salle, IL: Open Court, 1989), pp. 54–55.

80. Ch'en Chien, *Hsüeh-pu t'ung-pien* 12.160.

81. Yang Ming-shih, in T'ang Chien, *Ch'ing hsüeh-an hsiao-chih* 7.204.

82. Ch'eng Hao, quoted in *Chin-ssu lu*, comp. Chu Hsi, anno. Chiang Yung (Taipei: Kuang-wen shu-chü, 1972 reprint) 13.1.

83. Chu Hsi, *Chu-tzu yü-lei* 126.6b, trans. in Charles Wei-hsün Fu, "Chu Hsi on Buddhism," in *Chu Hsi and Neo-Confucianism*, ed. Wing-tsit Chan (Honolulu: University of Hawaii Press, 1986), p. 396. This passage from Chu Hsi also appears in Ch'en Chien, *Hsüeh-pu t'ung-pien* 7.93.

84. Hu Chü-jen, *Chü-yeh lu* 7.76.

85. Ibid. 7.81.

86. *Mencius* 7B. 26, p. 199.

87. Ch'en Chien, *Hsüeh-pu t'ung-pien* 3.24.

88. Ivanhoe, *Ethics*, p. 9.

89. Chan, *Chu Hsi: New Studies*, p. 452, citing Chu Hsi's *Wen-chi* 54:8a-b; Lu Lung-ch'i, *Wen-hsüeh-lu* (Taipei: Taiwan Shang-wu, 1966) 3.25.

90. de Bary, *Message of the Mind*, p. 3.

91. Ch'en Chien, *Hsüeh-pu t'ung-pien* 6.69.

92. Peter K. Bol, "Chu Hsi's Redefinition of Literati Learning," in *Neo-Confucian Education: The Formative Stage*, eds. Wm. Theodore de Bary and John W. Chaffee (Berkeley: University of California Press, 1989), pp. 161 and 183; Gardner, *Learning to Be a Sage*, pp. 68–69.

93. Fu, "Chu Hsi on Buddhism," p. 396.

94. Chan, *Chu Hsi: New Studies*, p. 469.

95. Huang Tsung-hsi, *Meng-tzu shih-shuo*, p. 1b, in *Li-chou i-chu hui-k'an*, vol. 2 (Taipei: Lung-yan ch'u-pan she, 1969 reprint).

96. Chan, *Chu Hsi: New Studies*, citing *Chu-tzu yü-lei*, chap. 124.

97. Fu, "Chu Hsi on Buddhism," pp. 387 and 390–391.

98. Ch'en Ch'un, *Neo-Confucian Terms Explained (The 'Pei-hsi tzu-i')* by *Ch'en Ch'un 1159–1223*, translated, edited, and with an introduction by Wing-tsit Chan (New York: Columbia University Press, 1986), p. 172; Feng K'o, *Ch'iu-shih pien*, in *Kinsei Kanseki shōkan, shisō sanhen*, comps. Araki Kengo et al. (Tokyo: Chūbun shuppansha), 15:311; Ch'en Chien, *Hsüeh-pu t'ung-pien* 7.90; Lu Lung-ch'i, *Wen-hsüeh lu* 3.25–26; Hsiung Tz'u-li, *Hsüeh-t'ung* 54.16a, p. 2069; Lo Tse-nan, "Tu Meng-tzu cha-chi," in Hsü, *Ch'ing-ju hsüeh-an* 170.4b.

99. Liguori G. Müller, "Introduction" to *The De Haeresibus of Saint Augustine; A Translation with an Introduction and Commentary* (Washington: The Catholic University of America Press, 1956), p. 46.

100. M. Richard, "Le Traité 'De Sectis' et Léonce de Byzance," *Revue d'histoire ecclésiastique* (Louvain) 35 (1939): 701.

101. Hilgenfeld, *Ketzergeschichte*, p. 79; Vallée, *Anti-Gnostic Polemics*, p. 94.

102. Irenaeus, *Against Heresies* 1.23, p. 348.

103. Eusebius, *History of the Church* 2.13, p. 86.

104. Saint Cyril of Jerusalem, *Lenten Lectures (Catecheses)* 6, in *The Works of Saint Cyril of Jerusalem*, trans. Leo P. McCauley, S. J., and Anthony A. Stephenson, 1:156–57 and 158, in *Fathers of the Church*, vol. 61.

105. Vincent of Lérins, *The Commonitory* 24, p. 74.

106. Nigg, *The Heretics*, pp. 20 and 24.

107. Ibid., p. 24.

108. Pearson, "Anti-Heretical Warnings," p. 184.

109. Pagels, *The Gnostic Gospels*, p. 46.

110. R. Mc L. Wilson, "Simon and Gnostic Origins," in *Les actes des apôtres: traditions, rédaction, théologie*, ed. J. Kremer (Leuven: University Press; Gembloux: J. Duculot, 1979), p. 490.

111. Daniel Lawrence O'Keefe, *Stolen Lightning: The Social Theory of Magic* (New York: Continuum, 1982), pp. 139 and 142.

112. Ehrman, *Orthodox Corruption*, p. 185.

113. Nigg, *The Heretics*, p. 58.

114. Hilgenfeld, *Ketzergeschichte*, p. 49.

115. Ibid., p. 64; Vallée, *Anti-Gnostic Polemics*, p. 80; Lieu, *Manichaeism*, p. 128; Burrus, "Heretical Woman," p. 241.

116. Le Boulluec, *La notion d'hérésie*, 2:431; Lieu, *Manichaeism*, p. 129.

117. Hilgenfeld, *Ketzergeschichte*, pp. 32, 34, and 35.

118. Simon, "From Greek Haeresis," p. 103.

119. Hippolytus, *Refutation of All Heresies* 5.1, p. 47.

120. Ibid. prol. 6, 5.1 and 7.2, pp. 74, 47, and 101.

121. Hippolytus, *Refutation of All Heresies* prol. 1, quoted in Simon, "From Greek Haeresis," p. 103.

122. Tertullian, *Adversus Marcionem*, in Peters, *Heresy and Authority*, pp. 30–31.

123. Le Boulluec, *La notion d'hérésie*, 1:123 and 2:455.

124. Quoted in Brown, *Heresies*, p. 3.

125. Krumm, *Modern Heresies*, p. 9.

126. Vallée, *Anti-Gnostic Polemics*, p. 26.

127. Saint Hilary of Poitiers, *The Trinity 7*, in *The Catholic Tradition*, eds. Charles J. Dollen et al., vol. 1, *The Saviour* (Wilmington, NC: McGrath Publishing Co., A Consortium Book, 1979), p. 226.

128. Augustine, *The City of God*, p. 396.

129. William R. Schoedel, "Theological Norms and Social Perspectives in Ignatius of Antioch," in *Jewish and Christian Self-Definition*, vol. 1, *The Shaping of Christianity in the Second and Third Centuries*, ed. E. P. Sanders (London: SCM Press, 1980), p. 46. The internal quotes are from Lewis Coser's *Social Conflict*.

130. Rahner, *On Heresy*, p. 19.

131. M. D. Chenu, "Orthodoxie et hérésie: Le point de vue du théologien," in Le Goff, *Hérésies et sociétés*, p. 11.

132. George Santayana, "Philosophical Heresy," in idem, *Obiter Scripta: Lectures, Essays and Reviews*, eds. Justus Buchler and Benjamin Schwartz (New York: Charles Scribner's Sons, 1936), p. 98.

133. Saint John of Damascus, "First Apology of Saint John of Damascus against those who Attack the Divine Images," in idem, *On the Divine Images*, p. 13.

134. Pelikan, "Two Sees of Peter," p. 66; idem, *Christian Tradition*, 1:112.

135. Tertullian, "The Prescriptions against the Heretics" 17, p. 42.

136. Cyprian, *De Ecclesiae Catholicae* 12, pp. 75–77; Vallée, *Anti-Gnostic Polemics*, p. 84.

137. Prestige, *Fathers and Heretics*, p. 21.

138. Christie-Murray, *A History of Heresy*, p. 92.

139. Brown, *Heresies*, pp. 127 and 99.

140. Newman, "Annotations on Theological Subjects," p. 143.

141. Saint Athanasius, "Three Discourses of Athanasius against the Arians" 1.2, in *Selected Treatises of St. Athanasius*, 1:156.

142. Shaw, "African Christianity," p. 14.

143. Saint Augustine, "Sermon 252" Easter Season, in idem, *Sermons on the Liturgical Seasons*, trans. Sister Mary Sarah Muldowney, R. S. M., in *Writings of Saint Augustine*, 17:328–29, in *The Fathers of the Church* (New York: Fathers of the Church, 1959).

144. Leander of Seville, "Sermon of the Triumph of the Church for the Conversion of the Goths," in *Iberian Fathers*, 1:230, trans. Claude W. Barlow, in *The Fathers of the Church* (Washington, DC: Catholic University of America Press, 1969).

145. al-Shahrastani, *Muslim Sects and Divisions*, pp. 14–15; Laoust, "L'hérésiographie musulmane," p. 171; al-Ghazali, *Al-Munqid min Adalal*, p. 69.

146. Lewis, "Significance of Heresy," p. 43. As Keith Lewinstein has pointed out, Eastern Hanafite heresiographers were less inclined than were their counterparts in the standard heresiographical tradition to connect heretical sects with individual heresiarchs. Lewinstein, "Eastern Hanafite," p. 591.

147. Sarah Stroumsa, "From Muslim Heresy to Jewish-Muslim Polemics: Ibn al-Rawandi's *Kitab al-Damigh*," *Journal of the American Oriental Society* 107.4 (1987): 767. Josef van Ess adds that "He has scandalized pious minds like nobody before or after him in Islam." Josef van Ess, "Ibn ar-Rewandi, or the Making of an Image," *Al-Abhath* 28 (1978–1979): 6.

148. P. Kraus [G. Vagja], "Ibn al-Rawandi," in *The Encyclopedia of Islam*, new ed., vol. 3 (H–Iram), eds. B. Lewis et al. (Leiden: E. J. Brill, 1971): 905.

149. J. L. Kraemer, "Heresy versus the State in Medieval Islam," in *Studies in Judaica, Karaitica and Islamica Presented to Leon Nemoy on His Eightieth Birthday*, ed. Sheldom R. Brunswick (Ramat-Gan, Israel: Bar-Ilan University Press, 1982): 168.

150. al-Taftazani, *Commentary on the Creed of Islam*, p. 8.

151. Elder, "Introduction" to ibid., p. xi.

152. Lewis, "Significance of Heresy," p. 43; al-Baghdadi, *Moslem Schisms and Sects*, p. 130.

153. al-Shahrastani, *Muslim Sects and Divisions*, p. 150; Lewis, "Significance of Heresy," p. 44; Michel, "Theology of Ibn Taymiyya," p. 67; Ismaeel, *Difference between the Shii*, p. 3.

154. Momen, *Introduction to Shi'i Islam*, p. 46; Cf. al-Baghdadi, *Moslem Schisms and Sects*, p. 44.

155. Wasserstrom, *Between Muslim and Jew*, p. 157.

156. S. M. Stern, "Abu'l-Qasim al-Busti and His Refutation of Isma'ilism," in idem, *Studies in Early Isma'ilism* (Leiden: E. J. Brill, 1983), pp. 305–6.

157. S. M. Stern, "The 'Book of the Highest Initiation' and Other Anti-Isma'ili Travesties," in *Studies in Early Isma'ilism*, p. 63.

158. Madelung, *Religious Trends*, p. 95.

159. Daftary, *The Isma'ilis*, p. 87.

160. al-Baghdadi, *Moslem Schisms and Sects*, p. 107.

161. al-Ghazali, quoted in Ignaz Goldziher, *Streitschrift des Gazali gegen die Batinijja-Sekte* (Leiden: E. J. Brill, 1956 reprint), p. 110.

162. Hodgson, *Order of Assassins*, p. 131.

163. Abu Ja'far, quoted in Fyzee, *A Shi'ite Creed*, pp. 100–101.

164. Matti Moosa, *Extremist Shiites: The Ghulat Sects* (Syracuse: Syracuse University Press, 1988), p. 414.

165. Ibn Taymiyya, *Struggle Against Popular Religion*, pp. 95–96.

166. Laoust, *Les schismes dans l'Islam*, p. 454.

167. Menasseh was also the name of the evil king in the Old Testament who arrested Isaiah.

168. Jacobs, *Principles of the Jewish Faith*, p. 216.

169. Maimonides, "The Text of Maimonides' Thirteen Principles," in Kellner, *Dogma in Medieval Jewish Thought*, p. 15.

170. *Yerushalmi Sanhedrin* 10:1, p. 319.

171. Segal, *Two Powers in Heaven*, p. 9.

172. Ibid., p. 62.

173. I. Gruenwald, "The Problem of Anti-Gnostic Polemic in Rabbinic Literature," in *Studies in Gnosticism and Hellenistic Religions*, eds. R. van den Brock and M. J. Vermaseren (Leiden: E. J. Brill, 1981), p. 179.

174. Ithamar Gruenwald, "Aspects of the Jewish-Gnostic Controversy," in *The Rediscovery of Gnosticism*, vol. 2, *Sethian Gnosticism*, ed. Bentley Layton (Leiden: E. J. Brill, 1980), pp. 720–21. Alternative accounts of the etiology of Elisha's heresy appear in Moses Gaster, *The Exempla of the Rabbis: Being a Collection of Exempla, Apologues and Tales Culled from Hebrew Manuscripts and Rare Hebrew Books* (New York: KTAV Publishing House, 1968), p. 86.

175. Abravanel, *Principles of Faith*, p. 113.

176. Gehaliahu G. Stroumsa, "Aher: A Gnostic," in Layton, ed., *Rediscovery of Gnosticism*, 2:818.

177. Gruenwald, "Anti-Gnostic Polemic," p. 81; S. E. Isenberg, "An Anti-Sadducee Polemic in the Palestinian Targum Traditions," *Harvard Theological Review* 63 (1970): 442.

178. Yosef Hayim Yerushalmi, *From Spanish Court to Italian Ghetto; Isaac Cardoso: A Study in Seventeenth-Century Marranism and Jewish Apologetics* (New York: Columbia University Press, 1971), p. 255.

179. Ya'qub al-Qirqisani, "History of Jewish Sects," in *Karaite Anthology: Excerpts from the Early Literature*, trans. and anno. Leon Nemoy (New Haven: Yale University Press, 1952), p. 45.

180. For a rabbinic presentation of Jeroboam as a heresiarch, see *Yerushalmi Sanhedrin* 10:2, pp. 326–27.

181. Yerushalmi, *From Spanish Court*, p. 339.

182. Maimonides, *Commentary on M. Berakhot* 8.8, quoted in Baron, *History of the Jews*, 5:172.

183. Ya'qub al-Qirqisani, trans. in Leon Nemoy, "Al-Qirqisani's Account of the Jewish Sects and Christianity," *Hebrew Union College Annual* 7: 358.

184. Saadiah Gaon, Ms. Vatican 266f. 73b., quoted in Gershom G. Scholem, *Major Trends in Jewish Mysticism* (New York: Schocken Books, 1961), p. 97.

185. Gries, "Heresy," p. 344.

186. Louis Jacobs, *Theology in the Responsa* (London: Routledge and Kegan Paul, 1975), pp. 45 and 46.

187. *Mencius* 3B. 9; Huang Tsung-hsi, *Meng-tzu shih-shuo* 3.5a; Lu Shih-i, *Ssu-pien lu chi-yao* 32.3b.

188. Chu Hsi, in Chang Chiu-shao, *Li-hsüeh lei-pien* 8.8a, in *Ssu-k'u ch'üan-shu chen-pen, liu chi*, comp. Wang Yun-wu (Taipei: Taiwan Shang-wu, n.d.), vol. 186.

189. Hsiung Tz'u-li, *Hsüeh-t'ung* 50.23a, p. 2007.

190. de Bary, *Message of the Mind*, p. 102.

191. Feng K'o, *Ch'iu-shih pien*, p. 312; de Bary, *Message of the Mind*, p. 149.

192. Lu Lung-ch'i, *San-yü-t'ang jih-chi* (Taipei: Taiwan Shang-wu, 1965), p. 101.

193. See, for example, Tillman, *Utilitarian Confucianism*, p. 211.

194. *Hsün-tzu chi-chieh* 15.261–262; John Knoblock, *Xunzi: A Translation and Study of the Complete Works*, vol. 1, *Books 1–6* (Stanford: Stanford University Press, 1988), p. 214.

195. *Chuang-tzu*, chap. 33, trans. in Bodde, *Chinese Thought, Society and Science*, p. 181.

196. Wilson, *Genealogy of the Way*, pp. 117–18.

197. Peter N. Gregory, *Tsung-mi and the Sinification of Buddhism* (Princeton: Princeton University Press, 1991), p. 23.

198. Ch'eng, *Erh-Ch'eng yü-lu* 5.61.

199. Chu Hsi, "Su Huang-men Lao-tzu chieh," in "Tsa-hsüeh pien," in *Chu-tzu ta-ch'üan* (Taipei: Chung-hua shu-chü, 1965), *wen-chi* 72.24b (vol. 9); Chu Hsi, quoted in Ch'en Chien, *Hsüeh-pu t'ung-pien* 4.52.

200. Li Kuang-ti, *Tu Meng-tzu cha-chi* B.23b, in *Ssu-k'u ch'üan-shu chen-pen, chiu chi*, comp. Wang Yun-wu (Taipei: Taiwan Shang-wu, 1979), vol. 65.

201. Shih Te-ts'ao, *Meng-tzu fa-t'i*, in *Tseng-pu Sung-Yüan hsüeh-an*, comps. Huang Tsung-hsi and Ch'üan Tsu-wang (Taipei: Chung-hua shu-chü, 1970) 40.11b (vol. 3).

202. Hsü Ch'ien, *Tu Meng-tzu ts'ung-shuo*, p. 13b, in idem, *Ssu-shu ts'ung-shuo*, in *Ching-yüan*, comp. Ch'ien I-chi (Taipei: Ta-t'ung shu-chü, 1970 reprint), 6:2946.

203. Chang Li-hsiang, "Yü Ho Shang-yin shu," from *Yang-yüan hsien-sheng ch'üan-chi*, in Yang Hsiang-k'uei, comp., *Ch'ing-ju hsüeh-an hsin-pien*, 1:652–53.

204. Chang Li-hsiang, "Yü Shen Yin-t'ung shu," in T'ang Chien, *Ch'ing-hsüeh-an hsiao-chih* 1.15.

205. Tiao Pao, *Ch'ien-shih cha-chi* (Shanghai: Shang-wu, 1936) A.6.

206. Wilhelm Halbfass, *Tradition and Reflection: Explorations in Indian Thought* (Albany: State University of New York Press, 1991), p. 61.

207. Lenin, *Left-Wing Communism*, p. 82. Franz Borkenau calls this tract "perhaps the most powerful thing Lenin has ever written," comparing it "for force of argument, realism, directness and convincing power, with Machiavelli's *Il Principe*." Franz Borkenau, *World Communism: A History of the Communist International* (Ann Arbor: The University of Michigan Press, 1962), p. 191.

208. Claude Bernard, "Lectures on Animal Heat" 8.391, quoted in Canguilhem, *The Normal and the Pathological*, p. 71.

209. Freud, "The Sexual Aberrations," p. 36.

210. Santayana, "Philosophical Heresy," p. 104.

211. Le Boulluec, *La notion d'hérésie*, 1:108.

212. Ehrman, *Orthodox Corruption*, p. 120. Le Boulluec makes a similar point in *La notion d'hérésie*, 1:169.

213. Tertullian, "The Prescriptions against the Heretics" 33, pp. 53–54.

214. This is the gist of Cardinal Newman's heresiographical method. Thomas, *Newman and Heresy*, p. 105.

215. Wisse, "Epistle of Jude," p. 143.

216. Ibid.

217. May, "Marcion in Contemporary Views," p. 138; Le Boulluec, *La notion d'hérésie*, 1:87; Hilgenfeld, *Ketzergeschichte*, pp. 26 passim.

218. Irenaeus, *Against Heresies*, prol. 3 and 3.3, pp. 414 and 416; Filoramo, *A History of Gnosticism*, p. 3; Wilson, "Simon and Gnostic Origins," p. 485.

219. Birgir A. Pearson, "Eusebius and Gnosticism," in *Eusebius, Christianity, and Judaism*, eds. Harold W. Attridge and Gohei Hatta (Detroit: Wayne State University Press, 1990), p. 298.

220. Vallée, *Anti-Gnostic Polemics*, p. 70.

221. Ambrosios Giakalis, *Images of the Divine: The Theology of Icons at the Seventh Ecumenical Council* (Leiden: E. J. Brill, 1994), pp. 49–50.

222. Saint John of Damascus, *On Heresies*, in *Saint John of Damascus, Writings*, trans. Frederic H. Chase, Jr., in *Fathers of the Church*, 37:111.

223. Peters, *Heresy and Authority*, pp. 5–6.

224. Moore, *Origins of European Dissent*, p. 244.

225. Laoust, "L'hérésiographie musulmane," p. 175; Lewinstein, "Studies in Islamic Heresiography," p. 138.

226. Jeffrey T. Kenney, "The Emergence of the Khawarij: Religion and the Social Order in Early Islam," JUSUR 5 (1989): 5.

227. Jakob J. Petuchowski, *The Theology of Haham David Nieto: An Eighteenth-Century Defense of the Jewish Tradition*, rev. ed. (New York: KTAV Publishing House, 1970), p. 7.

228. Bernard Revel, "The Karaite Halakah and Its Relation to Sadducean, Samaritan, and Philonian Halakah," in *Karaite Studies*, p. 6.

229. Yoram Erder, "The Karaites' Sadducee Dilemma," *Israel Oriental Studies* 14: *Concepts of the Other in Near Eastern Religions*, eds. Ilai Alon et al. (Leiden: E. J. Brill, 1994): 216.

230. Daniel J. Lasker, "Rabbanism and Karaism: The Contest for Supremacy," in *Great Schisms and Sects in Jewish History*, eds. Raphael Jospe and Stanley M. Wagner (New York: KTAV Publishing House, 1981), p. 58; Philip E. Miller, *Karaite Separatism in Nineteenth-Century Russia: Joseph Solomon Lutski's Epistle of Israel's Deliverance* (Cincinnati: Hebrew Union College Press, 1993), pp. 5–6.

231. Revel, "Karaite Halakah," p. 9.

232. Ibid., p. 13.

233. Cohen, "'Anan ben David," p. 140.

234. Yerushalmi, *From Spanish Court*, p. 259.

235. Kaufman, *Great Sects and Schisms*, p. 62.

236. Carlebach, *Pursuit of Heresy*, p. 10.

237. Wilensky, "Hasidic-Mitnaggedic Polemics," p. 260; Simon Dubnow, *Geschichte des Chassidismus*, trans. from the Hebrew by A. Steinberg (Berlin: Jüdischen Verlag, 1931; reprint 1982), 2:186.

238. Katz, *Tradition and Crisis*, p. 197.

239. Shmueli, *Seven Jewish Cultures*, p. 154.

240. Cronbach, *Reform Movements in Judaism*, p. 73.

241. Baron, *History of the Jews*, 5:256.

242. Ibid., 5:254.

243. Harold Bloom, *The Strong Light of the Canonical: Kafka, Freud and Scholem as Revisionists of Jewish Culture and Thought* (New York: The City College, 1987), p. 63.

244. Biale, *Gershom Scholem*, p. 154.

245. Chu Hsi, *Chu-tzu yü-lei*, comp. Chang Po-hsing (Taipei: Taiwan Shang-wu, 1973) 7.229.

246. Liu Tsung-chou, *Lun-yü hsüeh-an*, in *Liu Chi-shan Huang Li-chou ho-chi*, comp. Su Te-yung (Taipei: Cheng-chung shu-chü, 1970), p. 79.

247. Mou Tsung-san, "Shih-tai yü kan-shou," in idem, *Mou Tsung-san chi*, comps. Huang K'e-chien and Lin Shao-min (Peiching: Ch'ün-yen ch'u-pan she, 1993), pp. 605–6.

248. Lu Shih-i, *Ssu-pien lu* 32.8b-9a; Lü Liu-liang, "Ta Wu Ch'ing-yen shu," in idem, *Lü Wan-ts'un wen-chi* 1.65–66.

249. Chang Lieh, *Tu-shih chih-i*, in T'ang Chien, *Ch'ing hsüeh-an hsiao-chih* 3.85.

250. Fang Tung-shu, *Han-hsüeh shang-tui*, p. 4.

251. Han T'an, "Yang Mo," in Hsü Shih-ch'ang, comp., *Ch'ing-ju hsüeh-an* 51.42b.

252. Saint John Chrysostom, "Homily XI," in idem, *On the Incomprehensible Nature*, pp. 273–74.

253. Irenaeus, *Against Heresies*, prol. 4., p. 462.

254. Ibid. 2.31, pp. 406–7.

255. Epiphanius, *Panarion* 2.30, p. 120.

256. Vallée, *Anti-Gnostic Polemics*, p. 88.

257. Cyril, *Catecheses* 6, p. 160; Eusebius, *History of the Church* 7.31, p. 320.

258. Pelikan, *Christian Tradition*, 2:230.

259. Ibid.; Daniel J. Sahas, *John of Damascus on Islam, the "Heresy of the Ishmaelites"* (Leiden: E. J. Brill, 1972), p. 73.

260. Tarasius, quoted in Garsoïan, *The Paulician Heresy*, p. 200.

261. Daniel J. Sahas, "Introduction" to *Icon and Logos: Sources in Eighth-Century Iconoclasm* (Toronto: University of Toronto Press, 1986), p. 21.

262. Pelikan, *Christian Tradition*, 2:118.

263. Thouzellier, "Tradition et résurgence," p. 109.

264. Jaroslav Pelikan, *The Christian Tradition: A History of the Development of Doctrine*, vol. 3, *The Growth of Medieval Theology (600–1300)* (Chicago: University of Chicago Press, 1978), pp. 238–39.

265. Kurtz, *Politics of Heresy*, pp. 9–10.

266. Ibid., p. 7.

267. Bernard McGinn, *Antichrist: Two Thousand Years of the Human Fascination with Evil* (San Francisco: Harper, 1994), p. 78.

268. Laoust, *Les schismes dans l'Islam*, p. 52.

269. Allard, *Le problème des attributs divins*, p. 112.

270. al-Baghdadi, *Moslem Schisms and Sects*, p. 94.

271. Ibn Taymiyya, *Against the Greek Logicians*, p. 104.

272. Laoust, *Les schismes dans l'Islam*, p. 331.

273. Wael B. Hallaq, "Introduction" to Ibn Taymiyya, *Against the Greek Logicians*, p. xxvi.

274. Ibid., pp. xii and xxvii.

275. Michel, "Theology of Ibn Taymiyya," p. 14.

276. Muhammad Naguib Syed al-Attas, *Raniri and the Wujudiyyah of Seventeenth-Century Acheh* (Singapore: Printed for the MBRAS by Malaysia Printers, 1966), p. 18.

277. W. C. Chittick, "Wahdat al-wujud in Islamic Thought," *Bulletin of the Henry Martyn Institute of Islamic Studies* 10.1 (1991): 21.

278. Qunawi, quoted in ibid., p. 14.

279. Segal, *Two Powers in Heaven*, p. 153.

280. Nemoy, trans., "Al-Qirqisani's Account," p. 377.

281. Kaufman, *Great Sects and Schisms*, p. 39.

282. Carlebach, *Pursuit of Heresy*, p. 147.

283. Chu Hsi, *Chu-tzu yü-lei*, quoted in Chiang I-pin, *Sung-tai ju shih*, p. 7.

284. Feng K'o, *Ch'iu-shih pien*, pp. 49–50.

285. Li Kuang-ti, *Jung-ts'un yü-lu* 20.10b and 20.22a.

286. Huang Wan, *Ming-tao pien* 1.2.

287. Chan Ling, *I-tuan pien-cheng*, pp. 9–10, in *Kinsei Kanseki shōkan, shisō zokuhen*, comps. Araki Kengo et al. (Tokyo: Chūbun shuppansha), vol. 5.

288. Huang Chen, *Tung-fa chiang-i*, in *Sung-Yüan hsüeh-an* 86.3a.

289. Hsiung Tz'u-li, *Hsien-tao lu*, in Hsü Shih-ch'ang, comp., *Ch'ing-ju hsüeh-an* 38.14a.

290. Ibid. 38.8b.

291. Li Kuang-ti, quoted in T'ang Chien, *Ch'ing-hsüeh-an hsiao-chih* 6.172.

292. Irenaeus, *Against Heresies*, prol. 1, p. 315. Le Boulluec makes a similar point, remarking that according to the heresiologists, "all the heretics' powers of seduction rest on the art of simulation, on the way in which they disguise their doctrines beneath the most fashionable ornaments" (*La notion d'hérésie*, 1:126).

293. John Henry Newman, *Monophysitism* (Shorter MS), p. 6, quoted in Thomas, *Newman and Heresy*, p. 217.

294. Milroad M. Drachkovitch and Branko Lazitch, "The Third International," in *The Revolutionary Internationals, 1864–1943*, ed. Drachkovitch (Stanford: Stanford University Press, 1966), p. 185.

295. "Extracts from an ECCI Letter to All Left-Wing Members of the USPD, To the KPD and the KAPD," November 1920, in *The Communist International, 1919–1943; Documents*, ed. Jane Degras (London: Oxford University Press, 1956–65), pp. 202–3.

296. Saint Justin Martyr, *Dialogue with Trypho*, in *Writings of Saint Justin Martyr*, trans. Thomas B. Falls (Washington, DC: Catholic University of America Press, 1965), p. 200, in *Fathers of the Church*, vol. 6; Peters, *Heresy and Authority*, p. 29; Vincent of Lérins, *The Commonitory* 25, p. 75.

297. Vincent of Lérins, *The Commonitory* 9, p. 50.

298. Cyprian, *De Ecclesiae Catholicae* 1, p. 57.

299. Le Boulluec, *La notion d'hérésie*, 2:481.

300. Thomas, *Newman and Heresy*, p. 20.

301. John Henry Newman, *The Arians of the Fourth Century*, p. 31, quoted in Thomas, *Newman and Heresy*, p. 38.

302. Gérard Vallée, "Irenaeus's Refutation of the Gnostics," in Sanders, ed., *Jewish and Christian Self-Definition*, 1:181.

303. Irenaeus, *Against Heresies* 2.26, p. 397.

304. Le Boulluec, *La notion d'hérésie*, 1:153.

305. Gregory of Nazianzus, "Gregory of Nazianaus's Third Theological Oration Concerning the Son," in *The Trinitarian Controversy*, trans. and ed. William G. Rusch (Philadelphia: Fortress Press, 1980), p. 146.

306. Makdisi, *Ibn 'Aqil*, p. 341.

307. Michel, "Theology of Ibn Taymiyya," p. 13.

308. Ibn Qudama, *Censure of Speculative Theology*, p. 23.

309. Michel, "Theology of Ibn Taymiyya," p. 55.

310. J. Fueck, "The Role of Traditionalism in Islam," in *Studies on Islam*, trans. and ed. Merlin L. Swartz (Oxford: Oxford University Press, 1981), p. 119.

311. al-Baghdadi, *Moslem Schisms and Sects*, pp. 138–39.

312. Carlebach, *Pursuit of Heresy*, pp. 157–58 and 258.

313. Schochet, *Hasidic Movement*, p. 75.

314. Ibid., p. 29.

315. Lo Ch'in-shun, *Knowledge Painfully Acquired* 2.41, p. 140.

316. Ch'en Chien, *Hsüeh-pu t'ung-pien* 9.122.

317. Lu Lung-ch'i, "Hsüeh-shu pien, shang," in idem, *Lu Chia-shu wen-chi* 1.10.

318. Ch'en Chien, *Hsüeh-pu t'ung-pien* 5.91.

319. de Bary makes a similar point in his *Message of the Mind*, p. 116.

320. Ch'eng Hao, in Chang Chiu-shao, *Li-hsüeh lei-pien* 8.2a.

321. Ch'eng I and Ch'eng Hao, *Erh-Ch'eng yü-lu* 1.19.

322. James Gleick, *Chaos: Making a New Science* (New York: Penguin Books, 1987), p. 8. The more technical name for this phenomenon is "sensitive dependence on initial conditions" (ibid).

323. Ch'eng I, *Erh-Ch'eng yü-lu* 11.172. Also translated in Ivanhoe, *Ethics*, p. 23.

324. Fred E. Katz, *Ordinary People and Extraordinary Evil* (Albany: State University of New York Press, 1993), p. 1.

Epilogue

1. Ibn Qudama, *Censure of Speculative Theology*, p. 42.

2. Fang Tung-shu, *Han-hsüeh shang-tui*, p. 60.

3. Cyprian, "Letter #69: Cyprian to Magnus, His Son, Greeting," in idem, *Letters (1–81)*, p. 244.

4. Carlebach, *Pursuit of Heresy*, p. 16.

5. Cyprian, *De Ecclesiae Catholicae* 10, p. 73.

6. Tertullian, "Prescriptions against the Heretics" 1, p. 31. See also p. 33.

7. Ibid. 39, p. 60; Peter Iver Kaufman, "Tertullian on Heresy, History and the Reappropriation of Revelation," *Church History* 60.2 (June 1991): 167.

8. Hegesippus, quoted in Le Boulluec, *La notion d'hérésie*, 1:69–70.

9. Origen, *Contra Celsum* 3.12, p. 135.

10. Le Boulluec, *La notion d'hérésie*, 2:462, citing Origen.

11. Saint Caesarius of Arles, "St. Jerome on the Censers of Core and Dathan," in idem, *Sermons*, vol. 2 (81–186), pp. 144–45, trans. Sister Mary Magdeleine Mueller, O. S. F., in *The Fathers of the Church: A New Translation*, vol. 47 (Washington, DC: The Catholic University of America Press, 1964).

12. Augustine, *City of God* 17, p. 172.

13. John Henry Newman, note to Newman's translation of *The Ecclesiastical History of M. L'Abbé Fleury*, 3:272, quoted in Thomas, *Newman and Heresy*, p. 232.

14. Tertullian, *On the Soul*, trans. Edwin A Quain, S. J., in *Tertullian; Apologetic Works*, p. 185, in *Fathers of the Church*, vol. 10.

15. Saint Augustine, *Confessions* 7.19, trans. Vernon J. Bourke, in *Writings of Saint Augustine*, 5:190, in *Fathers of the Church*.

16. Hilary of Poitiers, *The Trinity* 2.2, p. 36.

17. Laoust, *Les schismes dans l'Islam*, pp. 459–60.

18. Watt, *Formative Period*, pp. 2–3.

19. al-Shahrastani, *Muslim Sects and Divisions*, p. 12.

20. Quoted in Simon, *Jewish Religious Conflicts*, p. 44.

21. Dhamari, *Commentary of R. Hoter ben Shelomo*, p. 119.

22. Shmueli, *Seven Jewish Cultures*, p. 195.

23. Li Wen-chao, quoted in T'ang Chien, *Ch'ing-hsüeh-an hsiao-chih* 7.216.

24. Chang Hsüeh-ch'eng, *Wen-shih t'ung-i* 3.41–42 ("T'ien-yü" chap.) (Taipei: Kuang-wen shu-chü, 1967).

25. H. Péquignot, *Initiation à la médicine*, p. 26, quoted in Canguilhem, *The Normal and the Pathological*, p. 285.

26. Lewis Thomas, "The Wonderful Mistake," in idem, *The Medusa and the Snail: More Notes of a Biology Watcher* (New York: Bantam Books, 1980), p. 24.

27. Mao Tse-tung, "Some Experiences in Our Party's History," in *Selected Works of Mao Tse-tung*, vol. 5 (Beijing: Foreign Languages Press, 1977), p. 329.

28. Coser, *Social Conflict*, pp. 71 and 106–7.

29. Erikson, *Wayward Puritans*, p. 19.

30. Nestorius, quoted in Socrates, *The Ecclesiastical History of Socrates Scholasticus* 7.29, rev. and anno. A. C. Zenos, in *A Select Library of Nicene and Post-Nicene Fathers of the Christian Church*, 2d. ser., eds. Philip Schaff and Henry Wace, vol. 2, *Socrates, Sozomenus: Church Histories* (Grand Rapids: Wm. B. Eerdmans, 1952), p. 169.

31. Erikson, *Wayward Puritans*, p. 4.

32. On the last point, see Thomas M. Lessl, "Heresy, Orthodoxy, and the Politics of Science," *Quarterly Journal of Speech* 74 (1988): 24. Thanks are due to my LSU colleague, Kenneth Zagacki, for pointing out this article to me.

33. Michel Foucault, *Madness and Civilization: A History of Insanity in the Age of Reason*, trans. Richard Howard (New York: New American Library, A Mentor Book, 1967), p. 18.

34. Compare a recent characterization of "postmodern thought" as "that thought which refuses to turn the Other into the Same." Simon During, "Postmodernism or Post-colonialism Today," in *Postmodernism: A Reader*, ed. Thomas Docherty (New York: Columbia University Press, 1993), p. 449.

35. Le Boulluec, *La notion d'hérésie*, 2:538–39; see also pp. 530–31, 536, and 544.

36. Watt, *Early Islam*, p. 155.

37. Chu Hsi, "Ta Chiang Te-kung," in Wang Mou-hung, "Chu-tzu lun-hsüeh chieh-yao yü," in Wang, *Chu-tzu nien-p'u* (Taipei: Taiwan Shang-wu, 1971), p. 350.

38. Dunn, *Unity and Diversity*, p. 377; Krumm, *Modern Heresies*, p. 3; Nigg, *The Heretics*, p. 13.

39. Chow, *Rise of Confucian Ritualism*, p. 6.

40. Canguilhem, *The Normal and the Pathological*, p. 127; Jaroslav Pelikan, *The Vindication of Tradition*, The 1983 Jefferson Lectures in the Humanities (New Haven: Yale University Press, 1984), p. 13.

41. Canguilhem, *The Normal and the Pathological*, p. 280.

GLOSSARY OF CHINESE TERMS
IN THE TEXT

Ch'an 禪
cheng 正
cheng-tao 正道
Cheng-Chu 程朱
chi ta-ch'eng 集大成
ch'i 氣
ch'ü 曲
chung 中
chung hsing-che 中行者
hsieh 邪
Huang-Lao 黃老
i-tuan 異端
jen-hsing 人性
li (benefit) 利
li (moral principle) 理
li-hsüeh 理學
li-i fen-shu 理一分殊
Lu-Wang 陸王
p'ien 偏
pu-cheng 不正
pu-tuan 不端
ssu-tuan 四端
ta-chung 大中
T'ai-chou 泰州
Tao 道
Tao-hsüeh 道學
Tao-t'ung 道統
tsa-hsüeh 雜學
Tung-lin 東林
wei-hsüeh 偽學
yin 淫

SELECTED BIBLIOGRAPHY

This bibliography includes only those items that are cited in the notes to more than one chapter. Full bibliographical information for those items cited in only one chapter is given in the first citation in the chapter in which they appear.

Abravanel, Isaac. *Principles of Faith (Rosh Amanah)*. Translated with an Introduction and Notes by Menachem Marc Kellner. Rutherford, NJ: Fairleigh Dickinson University Press; London: Associated Universities Press, 1982.

Allard, Michel. *Le problème des attributs divins dans la doctrine d'al-As'ari et de ses premiers grands disciples*. Beirut: Imprimerie Catholique, 1965.

Augustine, Saint. *The City of God*. Bks. 17–22. Translated by Gerald G. Walsh and Daniel J. Honan. In *Writings of Saint Augustine*. Vol. 8. In *The Fathers of the Church, A New Translation*. Vol. 24. Washington, DC: The Catholic University of America Press, 1964.

Aune, David E. "Orthodoxy in First Century Judaism? A Response to N. J. McEleney." *Journal for the Study of Judaism in the Persian, Hellenistic, and Roman Periods* 7 (1976): 1–10.

al-Azmeh, Aziz. "Orthodoxy and Hanbalite Fideism." *Arabica* 35 (1988): 253–66.

al-Baghdadi, Abu-Mansur 'Abd-al-Kahir ibn Tahir. *Moslem Schisms and Sects (al Fark bain al-firak)*. Part 2. Translated by Abraham S. Halkin. Tel Aviv: Palestine Publishing Co., 1935.

Baldick, Julian. *Mystical Islam: An Introduction to Sufism*. New York: New York University Press, 1989.

Baron, Salo Wittmayer. *Social and Religious History of the Jews*. 2d ed., rev. and enl. Vol. 5, *Religious Controls and Dissensions*. New York: Columbia University Press, 1957.

Barrett, T. H. *Li Ao: Buddhist, Taoist, or Neo-Confucian?* Oxford: Oxford University Press, 1992.

Bauer, Walter. *Orthodoxy and Heresy in Earliest Christianity*. 2d German ed. With added appendices by George Strecker. Translated by a team from the Philadelphia Seminar on Christian Origins. Edited by Robert A. Kraft and Gerhard Krodel. Philadelphia: Fortress Press, 1971.

Biale, David. *Gershom Scholem: Kabbalah and Counter-History.* Cambridge: Harvard University Press, 1979.

Bodde, Derk. *Chinese Thought, Society and Science: The Intellectual and Social Background of Science and Technology in Pre-modern China.* Honolulu: University of Hawaii Press, 1991.

Bol, Peter K. *"This Culture of Ours": Intellectual Transitions in T'ang and Sung China.* Stanford: Stanford University Press, 1992.

Brown, Harold O. J. *Heresies: The Image of Christ in the Mirror of Heresy and Orthodoxy from the Apostles to the Present.* Garden City, NJ: Doubleday, 1984.

Canguilhem, Georges. *The Normal and the Pathological.* Translated by Carolyn R. Fawcett. New York: Zone Books, 1991.

Carlebach, Elisheva. *The Pursuit of Heresy: Rabbi Moses Hagiz and the Sabbatian Controversies.* New York: Columbia University Press, 1990.

Chan, Wing-tsit. *Chu Hsi: New Studies.* Honolulu: University of Hawaii Press, 1989.

————. *"The Hsing-li ching-i* and the Ch'eng-Chu School of the Seventeenth Century." In Wm. Theodore de Bary and the Conference on Seventeenth-Century Chinese Thought. *The Unfolding of Neo-Confucianism.* New York: Columbia University Press, 1975, pp. 543–79.

Chang, Carsun. *The Development of Neo-Confucian Thought.* Vol. 2. New York: Bookman Associates, 1962.

Chang Po-hsing, comp. *Cheng-i-t'ang ch'üan-shu* (Collected Works from the Hall of Justice and Rightness). Taipei: I-wen yin-shu-kuan, 1968 reprint.

Ch'en Chien. *Hsüeh-pu t'ung-pien* (Comprehensive Critique of Scholarly Obscurations). Taipei: Taiwan Shang-wu, 1966.

Ch'eng I and Ch'eng Hao. *Erh-Ch'eng yü-lu* (Recorded Conversations of the Two Ch'engs). Compiled by Chu Hsi. Taipei: Taiwan Shang-wu, 1966.

Chiang I-pin. *Sung-tai ju-shih t'iao-ho-lun chi p'ai-fo-lun chih yen-chiu—Wang An-shih chih jung-t'ung Ju-shih chi Ch'eng-Chu hsüeh-p'ai chih p'ai-fo fan-Wang* (A Study of the Harmonization of Confucianism and Buddhism and of the Rejection of Buddhism in the Sung Era—Wang An Shih's Synthesis of Confucianism and Buddhism and the Ch'eng-Chu School's Rejection of Buddhism and Opposition to Wang). Taipei: Taiwan Shang-wu, 1988.

Ching, Julia. *To Acquire Wisdom: The Way of Wang Yang-ming.* New York: Columbia University Press, 1976.

Chow, Kai-wing. *The Rise of Confucian Ritualism in Late Imperial China: Ethics, Classics, and Lineage Discourse.* Stanford: Stanford University Press, 1994.

Christie-Murray, David. *A History of Heresy.* Oxford: Oxford University Press, 1990.

Chu Hsi and Lü Tsu-ch'ien. *Reflections on Things at Hand: The Neo-Confucian Anthology Compiled by Chu Hsi and Lü Tsu-ch'ien.* Translated with Notes by Wing-tsit Chan. New York: Columbia University Press, 1967.

Chu Hsi. *Ssu-shu chi-chu* (Collected Commentaries on the Four Books). Taipei: Hsüeh-hai ch'u-pan she, 1974.

Cohen, Shaye J. D. "The Significance of Yavneh: Pharisees, Rabbis, and the End of Jewish Sectarianism." In *Origins of Judaism.* Vol. 2, Part 1, *The Pharisees and Other Sects.* Edited by Jacob Neusner. New York: Garland, 1990.

———. "A Virgin Defiled: Some Rabbinic and Christian Views on the Origins of Heresy." *Union Theological Seminary Quarterly Review* 36.1 (Fall 1980): 1–11.

Cohon, Samuel S. *Jewish Theology: A Historical and Systematic Interpretation of Judaism and Its Foundations.* Assen: Royal VanGorcum, 1971.

Coser, Lewis. *The Functions of Social Conflict.* Glencoe, IL: Free Press, 1956.

Coulson, N. J. *A History of Islamic Law.* Edinburgh: At the University Press, 1964.

Cronbach, Abraham. *Reform Movements in Judaism.* New York: Bookman Associates, 1963.

Cyprian. *De Ecclesiae Catholicae Unitate.* In Cyprian. *De Lapsis and De Ecclesiae Catholicae.* Text and Translation by Maurice Bévenot. Oxford: At the Clarendon Press, 1971.

———. *Letters (1–81).* Translated by Sister Rose Bernard Donna. In *The Fathers of the Church, A New Translation.* Vol. 51. Washington DC: The Catholic University of America Press, 1964.

Dabashi, Hamid. *Authority in Islam: From the Rise of Muhammad to the Establishment of the Umayyads.* New Brunswick, NJ: Transaction Publishers, 1989.

Daftary, Farhad. *The Isma'ilis: Their History and Doctrines.* Cambridge: Cambridge University Press, 1990.

de Bary, Wm. Theodore. *The Message of the Mind in Neo-Confucianism.* New York: Columbia University Press, 1989.

———. "The Uses of Neo-Confucianism: A Response to Professor Tillman." *Philosophy East and West* 43.3 (July 1993): 541–55.

de Bary, Wm. Theodore, Wing-tsit Chan, and Burton Watson, comps. *Sources of Chinese Tradition.* Vol. 1. New York: Columbia University Press, 1960.

Deuchler, Martina. "Reject the False and Uphold the Straight: Attitudes toward Heterodox Thought in Early Yi Korea." In *The Rise of Neo-Confucianism in Korea.* Edited by Wm. Theodore de Bary and JaHyun Kim Haboush. New York: Columbia University Press, 1985, pp. 375–410.

Dhamari, Mansur Suleiman. *The Commentary of R. Hoter ben Shelomo to the Thirteen Principles of Maimonides.* Translated, Edited, and Annotated by David R. Blumenthal. Leiden: E. J. Brill, 1974.

Dunn, James D. G. *Unity and Diversity in the New Testament: An Inquiry into the Character of Earliest Christianity.* Philadelphia: The Westminster Press, 1977.

Ehrmann, Bart D. *The Orthodox Corruption of Scripture: The Effect of Early Christological Controversies on the Text of the New Testament.* New York: Oxford University Press, 1993.

Epiphanius of Salamis. *The Panarion of Epiphanius of Salamis.* Bk. 1 (Sections 1–46). Translated by Frank Williams. Leiden: E. J. Brill, 1987.

Erikson, Kai T. *Wayward Puritans: A Study in the Sociology of Deviance.* New York: John Wiley and Sons, 1966.

Eusebius. *The History of the Church from Christ to Constantine.* Translated with an Introduction by G. A. Williamson. New York: Penguin Books, 1984.

Evans, G. R. *The Thought of Gregory the Great.* Cambridge: Cambridge University Press, 1986.

Fang Tung-shu. *Han-hsüeh shang-tui* (Exchanges of Views on Han Learning). Taipei: Taiwan Shang-wu, 1968.

Filoramo, Giovanni. *A History of Gnosticism.* Translated by Anthony Alcock. London: Basil Blackwell, 1991.

Frend, W. H. C. *The Rise of the Monophysite Movement: Chapters in the History of the Church in the Fifth and Sixth Centuries.* Cambridge: At the University Press, 1972.

———. *Saints and Sinners in the Early Church: Differing and Conflicting Traditions in the First Six Centuries.* Wilmington, DE: Michael Glazier, 1985.

Friedlander, Israel. "The Heterodoxies of the Shiites in the Presentation of Ibn Hazm." *Journal of the American Oriental Society* 28 (1907): 1–80.

Fyzee, Asaf A. A. *A Shi'ite Creed: A Translation of "Risalatu'l-I'tiqadat" of Muhammad b. 'Ali Ibn Babawayhi al-Qummi Known as Shaykh Saduq.* London: Oxford University Press, 1940.

Gardner, Daniel K. *Learning to Be a Sage: Selections from the "Conversations of Master Chu, Arranged Topically," by Chu Hsi.* Translated with a Commentary by Daniel K. Gardner. Berkeley: University of California Press, 1990.

al-Ghazali. *Al-Munqid min Adalal (Erreur et Délivrance)*. Translated with an Introduction and Notes by Farid Jabre. Beirut: Commission internationale pour la traduction des chefs-d'oeuvre, 1959.

Goldin, Judah, trans. *The Fathers According to Rabbi Nathan*. New Haven: Yale University Press, 1955.

Goldziher, Ignaz. *Introduction to Islamic Theology and Law*. Translated by Andras and Ruth Hamori. Princeton: Princeton University Press, 1981.

Gray, Patrick T. R. *The Defense of Chalcedon in the East (451–553)*. Leiden: E. J. Brill, 1979.

Greenslade, S. L., trans. and ed. *Early Latin Theology: Selections from Tertullian, Cyprian, Ambrose, and Jerome*. Philadelphia: Westminster Press, 1956.

Gries, Ze'ev. "Heresy." In *Contemporary Jewish Religious Thought: Original Essays on Critical Concepts, Movements, and Beliefs*. Edited by Arthur A. Cohen and Paul Mendes-Flohr. New York: Charles Scribner's Sons, 1987, pp. 339–52.

Guttmann, Alexander. *Rabbinic Judaism in the Making: A Chapter in the History of the Halakhah from Ezra to Judah I*. Detroit: Wayne State University Press, 1970.

Halm, Heinz. *Shiism*. Translated by Janet Watson. Edinburgh: Edinburgh University Press, 1991.

Heine, Ronald E. *The Montanist Oracles and Testimonia*. Macon, GA: Mercer University Press, 1989.

Hilary of Poitiers, Saint. *The Trinity*. Translated by Stephen McKenna. In *The Fathers of the Church, A New Translation*. New York: Fathers of the Church, Inc., 1954.

Hilgenfeld, Adolf. *Die Ketzergeschichte des Urchristentums*. Leipzig, 1884. Reprint, Hildesheim: Georg Olms Verlagshuchhandlung, 1963.

Hodgson, Marshall G. S. *The Order of Assassins: The Struggle of the Early Nizari Isma'ilis against the Islamic World*. The Hague: Mouton, 1955.

Hogga, Mustapha. *Orthodoxie, subversion, et réforme en Islam, suivi de textes politique de Gazali*. Paris: Librairie Philosophique J. Vrin, 1993.

Hsiao Kung-ch'üan. "Sheng-chiao yü i-tuan" (The Sagely Teaching and Heresy). In *Hsiao Kung-ch'üan hsien-sheng ch'üan-chi* (Collected Works of Mr. Hsiao Kung-ch'üan). Vol. 9. Taipei: Lien-ching ch'u-pan shih-yeh kung-ssu, 1983, pp. 36–55.

Hsiung Tz'u-li. *Hsüeh-t'ung* (Orthodox Tradition of Learning). Vol. 2. Edited by the Editorial Department of the Complete Works of Confucian Culture. Chinan: Shantung Friendship Press, 1990.

Hsü Shih-ch'ang, comp. *Ch'ing-ju hsüeh-an* (Cases on Ch'ing Confucian Learning). Taipei: Shih-chieh shu-chü, 1979 reprint.

Hsün-tzu chi-chieh (*Hsün-tzu* with Collected Explications). Annotated by Wang Hsien-ch'ien. Taipei: Shih-chieh shu-chü, 1974.

Hu Chü-jen. *Chü-yeh lu* (Records of [Hu] Chü-yeh). Taipei: Taiwan Shang-wu, 1966.

Huang Wan. *Ming-tao pien* (An Elucidation of the Way). Peiching: Chung-hua shu-chü, 1983.

Ibn 'Asakir, Abu'l-Qasim 'Ali b. al-Hasan b. Hibatallah Thiqataddin. "The Exposure of the Calumniator's Lying Concerning What Has Been Imputed to the Imam Abu 'l-Hasan al-Ash'ari." In *The Theology of al-Ash'ari*. Translated and Edited by Richard J. McCarthy. Beirut: Imprimerie Catholique, 1953.

Ibn Batta al-'Ukbari. *La profession de foi d'Ibn Batta*. Translated and Edited by Henri Laoust. Damascus: Institut Français de Damas, 1958.

Ibn Khaldhun. *The Muqaddimah: An Introduction to History.* Translated by Franz Rosenthal. London: Routledge and Kegan Paul, 1958.

Ibn Qudama, Muwaffaq al-Din 'Abd Allah ibn Ahmad. *Ibn Qudama's Censure of Speculative Theology: An Edition and Translation of Ibn Qudama's "Tahrim al-nazar fi kutub ahl al-kalam," with Introduction and Notes*. Translated and Edited by George Makdisi. London: Luzac, 1962.

Ibn Taymiyya, Ahmad ibn 'Abd al-Halim. *Ibn Taymiyya Against the Greek Logicians*. Translated with an Introduction and Notes by Wael B. Hallaq. Oxford: Clarendon Press, 1993.

————. *Ibn Taimiya's Struggle Against Popular Religion: With an Annotated Translation of his "Kitab iqtida' as-sirat al-mustaqim mukhalafat ashab al-jahim."* Translated and Edited by Muhammad Umar Memon. The Hague: Mouton, 1976.

————. *La profession de foi d'Ibn Taymiyya: texte, traduction et commentaire de la "Wasitiyyah."* Translated and Edited by Henri Laoust. Paris: Librairie Orientaliste Paul Geuthner, 1986.

Irenaeus. *Against Heresies.* In *The Ante-Nicene Fathers: Translations of the Writings of the Fathers down to A.D. 325*. Edited by Alexander Roberts and James Donaldson. American Reprint of the Edinburgh Edition. Vol. 1, *The Apostolic Fathers—Justin Martyr—Irenaeus*. Buffalo: The Christian Literature Publishing Co., 1885.

Ismaeel, Saeed. *The Difference between the Shii and the Majority of Muslim Scholars*. Carbondale, IL: A Muslim Group, n.d.

Ivanhoe, Philip J. *Ethics in the Confucian Tradition: The Thought of Mencius and Wang Yang-ming*. Atlanta: Scholars Press, 1990.

Jacobs, Louis. *Principles of the Jewish Faith: An Analytical Study*. New York: Basic Books, 1964.

Jeffery, Arthur, ed. *A Reader on Islam*. The Hague: Mouton, 1962.

John of Damascus, Saint. *On the Divine Images: Three Apologies Against Those Who Attack the Divine Images*. Translated by David Anderson. Crestwood, NY: St. Vladimir's Seminary Press, 1980.

Katz, Jacob. *Tradition and Crisis: Jewish Society at the End of the Middle Ages*. Translated by Bernard Dov. Cooperman, NY: New York University Press, 1993.

Kaufman, Reuben. *Great Sects and Schisms in Judaism*. New York: Jonathan David, 1967.

Kellner, Menachem. *Dogma in Medieval Jewish Thought: From Maimonides to Abravanel*. Oxford: Oxford University Press, 1986.

———. *Maimonides on Judaism and the Jewish People*. Albany: State University of New York Press, 1991.

Knysh, Alexander. "Orthodoxy and Heresy in Medieval Islam: An Essay in Reassessment." *Muslim World* 83.1 (January, 1993): 48–67.

Krumm, John M. *Modern Heresies*. Greenwich, CT: The Seabury Press, 1961.

Lambert, Malcolm. *Medieval Heresy: Popular Movements from the Gregorian Reform to the Reformation*. 2d ed. Oxford: Blackwell, 1992.

Laoust, Henri. "L'hérésiographie musulmane sous les Abbassides." *Cahiers de civilisation médiévale* 10.2 (April–June 1967): 157–78.

———. *Pluralismes dans l'Islam*. Paris: Librairie Orientaliste Paul Geuthner, 1983.

———. *Les schismes dans l'Islam: Introduction à une étude de la religion musulmane*. Paris: Éditions Payot, 1965.

Lauterbach, Jacob Z. "A Significant Controversy between the Sadducees and the Pharisees." In *Origins of Judaism*. Vol. 2, Part 2, *The Pharisees and Other Sects*. Edited by Jacob Neusner. New York: Garland, 1990, pp. 1–33.

Le Boulluec, Alain. *La notion d'hérésie dans la littérature grecque IIe–IIIe siècles*. Vol. 1, *De Justin à Irénée*. Paris: Études Augustiniennes, 1985.

———. *La notion d'hérésie dans la littérature grecque IIe–IIIe siècles*. Vol. 2, *Clément d'Alexandrie et Origène*. Paris: Études Augustiniennes, 1985.

Le Goff, Jacques et al. *Hérésies et sociétés dans l'Europe pré-industrielle 11e–18e siècles: Communications et debats du Colloque de Royaumont présentés par Jacques Le Goff*. Paris: Mouton, 1968.

Lewinstein, Keith. "Studies in Islamic ʿHeresiography: The Khawarij in Two *Firaq* Traditions." Ph.D. diss., Princeton University, 1989.

Lewis, Bernard. "Some Observations on the Significance of Heresy in the History of Islam." *Studia Islamica* 1 (1953): 43–63.

Li Kuang-ti. *Jung-ts'un yü-lu* (Recorded Conversations of [Li] Jung-ts'un). In *Ying-yin ssu-k'u ch'üan-shu chen-pen, chiu-chi* (Reprints of Rare Editions from the *Complete Library in Four Treasuries*, ninth series). Vol. 198. Compiled by Wang Yun-wu. Taipei: Taiwan Shang-wu, 1979 reprint.

Lieu, Samuel N. C. *Manichaeism in the Later Roman Empire and Medieval China*. 2d ed. Tübingen: J. C. B. Mohr (Paul Siebeck), 1992.

Liu, James T. C. *China Turning Inward: Intellectual-Political Changes in the Early Twelfth Century*. Cambridge: Council on East Asian Studies, Harvard University, 1988.

Liu, Kwang-ching, ed. *Orthodoxy in Late Imperial China*. Berkeley: University of California Press, 1990.

Lo Ch'in-shun. *Knowledge Painfully Acquired: The "K'un-chih chi" by Lo Ch'in-shun*. Translated, Edited, and with an Introduction by Irene Bloom. New York: Columbia University Press, 1987.

Lu Lung-ch'i. *Lu Chia-shu hsien-sheng wen-chi* (Prose Works of Mr. Lu Chia-shu). Taipei: Taiwan Shang-wu, 1965.

Lu Shih-i. *Ssu-pien lu chi-yao* (An Epitome of the *Record of Thinking and Sifting*). In *Ying-yin ssu-k'u ch'üan-shu chen-pen, ssu-chi* (Reprints of Rare Editions from the *Complete Library in Four Treasuries*, fourth series). Vols. 130–32. Compiled by Wang Yun-wu. Taipei: Taiwan Shang-wu, 1974 reprint.

Lü Liu-liang. *Lü Wan-ts'un hsien-sheng wen-chi* (Prose Works of Mr. Lü Wan-ts'un). Taipei: Wei-hsin shu-chü, 1968 reprint.

MacDonald, Duncan B. *Development of Muslim Theology, Jurisprudence, and Constitutional Theory*. New York: Russell and Russell, 1965.

Madelung, Wilferd. *Religious Trends in Early Islamic Iran*. Columbia Lectures on Iranian Studies, 4. Albany: The Persian Heritage Foundation under the imprint of Bibliotheca Persia, 1988.

Makdisi, George. "The Hanbali School and Sufism." *Humaniora Islamica* 2 (1974): 61–72.

———. *Ibn 'Aqil et la résurgence de l'Islam traditionaliste au Ve/XIe siècle*. Damascus: Institut Français de Damas, 1963.

Markus, R. A. "The Problem of Self-Definition: From Sect to Church." In *Jewish and Christian Self-Definition*. Vol. 1, *The Shaping of Christianity in the Second and Third Centuries*. Edited by E. P. Sanders. London: SCM Press, 1980, pp. 1–15.

Mashkur, M. J., trans. *Les sectes Shiites* (a translation of al-Nawbakhti's *Firaq al-Shi'a*). 2d ed. Tehran, 1980.

May, Gerhard. "Marcion in Contemporary Views: Results and Open Questions." *The Second Century* 6.3 (Fall 1987–1988): 129–51.

McEleney, N. J. "Orthodoxy in Judaism of the First Christian Century." *Journal for the Study of Judaism in the Persian, Hellenistic, and Roman Periods* 4 (1973): 19–42.

Mencius. Translated with an Introduction by D. C. Lau. Harmondsworth, Eng.: Penguin Books, 1970.

Michel, Thomas F. "The Theology of Ibn Taymiyya and His Critique of Christianity." In *A Muslim Theologian's Response to Christianity: Ibn Taymiyya's "Al-Jawab Al-Sahih."* Edited and Translated by Thomas F. Michel. Delmar, NY: Caravan Books, 1984, pp. 1–135.

Momen, Moojan. *An Introduction to Shi'i Islam: The History and Doctrines of Twelver Shi'ism*. New Haven: Yale University Press, 1985.

Moore, R. I. *The Origins of European Dissent*. New York: St. Martin's Press, 1977.

Morohashi Tetsuji et al., comps. *Shushigaku taikei* (Outline of Chu Hsi Studies). Vol. 11, *Shushi no kōkei (jō)* (Chu Hsi's Successors). Tokyo: Meitoku shuppansha, 1978.

Nagel, T. "Das Problem der Orthodoxie im frühen Islam." In *Studien zum Minderheitenproblem im Islam* 1. Bonn: Selbstverlag des Orientalischen Seminars der Universität Bonn, 1973.

Neumark, David. *Essays in Jewish Philosophy*. Edited by Samuel S. Cohon. Amsterdam: Philo Press, 1971.

Neusner, Jacob. *Formative Judaism; Second Series: Religious, Historical, and Literary Studies*. Chico, CA: Scholars Press, 1983.

———. *Torah through the Ages: A Short History of Judaism*. London: SCM Press; Philadelphia: Trinity Press International, 1990.

———, trans. *The Mishnah: A New Translation*. New Haven: Yale University Press, 1988.

Nigg, Walter. *The Heretics*. Translated by Richard and Clara Winston. New York: Alfred A. Knopf, 1962.

O'Grady, Joan. *Heresy: Heretical Truth or Orthodox Error: A Study of Early Christian Heresies.* Longmead, Eng.: Element Books, 1985.

Origen. *Contra Celsum.* Translated with an Introduction and Notes by Henry Chadwick. Cambridge: At the University Press, 1953.

Ormsby, Eric L. *Theodicy in Islamic Thought: The Dispute over al-Ghazali's "Best of All Possible Worlds."* Princeton: Princeton University Press, 1984.

Pagels, Elaine. *The Gnostic Gospels.* New York: Random House, 1979.

Pearson, Birger A. "Anti-Heretical Warnings in Codex IX from Nag Hammadi." In idem. *Gnosticism, Judaism, and Egyptian Christianity.* Minneapolis: Fortress Press, 1990.

Pelikan, Jaroslav. *The Christian Tradition: A History of the Development of Doctrine.* Vol. 1, *The Emergence of the Catholic Tradition (100–600).* Chicago: University of Chicago Press, 1973.

———. *The Christian Tradition: A History of the Development of Doctrine.* Vol. 2, *The Spirit of Eastern Christendom (600–1700).* Chicago: University of Chicago Press, 1974.

———. "The Two Sees of Peter: Reflections on the Pace of Normative Self-Definition East and West." In *Jewish and Christian Self-Definition.* Vol. 1, *The Shaping of Christianity in the Second and Third Centuries.* Edited by E. P. Sanders. London: SCM Press, 1980, pp. 57–73.

Peters, Edward, ed. *Heresy and Authority in Medieval Europe: Documents in Translation.* Philadelphia: University of Pennsylvania Press, 1980.

al-Qirqisani, Ya'qub. *Ya'qub al-Qirqisani on Jewish Sects and Christianity: A Translation of "Kitab al-Anwar, Book 1," with Two Introductory Essays.* Translated by Wilfrid Lockwood. Frankfurt am Main: Verlag Peter Lang, 1984.

Rahner, Karl. *On Heresy.* Translated by W. J. O'Hara. Freiburg: Herder, 1964; London: Burns and Oates.

Robinson, Thomas A. *The Bauer Thesis Examined: The Geography of Heresy in the Early Christian Church.* Lewiston/Queenston: The Edwin Mellen Press, 1988.

Sahas, Daniel J. "The Art and Non-Art of Byzantine Polemics: Patterns of Refutation in Byzantine Anti-Islamic Literature." In *Conversion and Continuity: Indigenous Christian Communities in Islamic Lands, Eighth to Eighteenth Centuries.* Edited by Michael Gervers and Ramzi Jibran Bikhazi. Toronto: Pontifical Institute of Mediaeval Studies, 1990, pp. 55–73.

Schacht, Joseph. "Theology and Law in Islam." In *Theology and Law in Islam.* Edited by G. E. von Grunebaum. Wiesbaden: Otto Harrassowitz, 1971, pp. 3–23.

Schochet, Elijah Judah. *The Hasidic Movement and the Gaon of Vilna.* Northvale, NJ: Jason Aronson, 1994.

Schwartz, Benjamin I. *The World of Thought in Ancient China.* Cambridge: The Belknap Press of Harvard University Press, 1985.

Segal, Alan F. *Two Powers in Heaven: Early Rabbinic Reports about Christianity and Gnosticism.* Leiden: E. J. Brill, 1977.

al-Shahrastani, Muhammad ibn 'Abd al-Karim. *Muslim Sects and Divisions: The Section on Muslim Sects in "Kitab al-milal wa 'l-nihal."* Translated by A. K. Kazi and J. G. Flynn. London: Kegan Paul International, 1984.

Shaw, Brent D. "African Christianity: Disputes, Definitions, and Donatists." In *Orthodoxy and Heresy in Religious Movements: Discipline and Dissent.* Edited by Malcolm R. Greenshields and Thomas A. Robinson. Lewiston: The Edwin Mellen Press, 1992, pp. 5–34.

Shmueli, Efraim. *Seven Jewish Cultures: A Reinterpretation of Jewish History and Thought.* Translated by Gila Shmueli. Cambridge: Cambridge University Press, 1990.

Simon, Marcel. "From Greek Haeresis to Christian Heresy." In *Early Christian Literature and the Classical Intellectual Tradition: In Honorem Robert M. Grant.* Edited by William R. Schoedel and Robert L. Wilken. Paris: Éditions Beauchesne, 1979, pp. 101–16.

Simon, Maurice. *Jewish Religious Conflicts.* London: Hutchinson House, 1950.

Sirat, Colette. *A History of Jewish Philosophy in the Middle Ages.* Cambridge: Cambridge University Press, 1985.

al-Taftazani, Mas'ud ibn 'Umar. *A Commentary on the Creed of Islam; Sa'd al-Din al-Taftazani on the Creed of Najm al-Din al-Nasafi.* Translated with Introduction and Notes by Earl Edgar Elder. New York: Columbia University Press, 1950.

T'ang Chien. *Ch'ing-hsüeh-an hsiao-chih* (Brief Account of Cases in Ch'ing Learning). Taipei: Taiwan Shang-wu, 1969.

T'ang Chün-i. *Chung-kuo che-hsüeh yüan-lun; yüan chiao p'ien* (A Fundamental Exposition of Chinese Philosophy; On Teaching). Hong Kong: Hsin-ya yen-chiu-suo, 1975.

Tertullian. "The Prescriptions against the Heretics." In *Early Latin Theology: Selections from Tertullian, Cyprian, Ambrose, and Jerome.* Translated and Edited by S. L. Greenslade. Philadelphia: Westminster Press, 1956, pp. 25–64.

Thomas, Stephen. *Newman and Heresy: The Anglican Years.* Cambridge: Cambridge University Press, 1991.

Tillman, Hoyt Cleveland. *Confucian Discourse and Chu Hsi's Ascendancy.* Honolulu: University of Hawaii Press, 1992.

———. "A New Direction in Confucian Scholarship: Approaches to Examining the Differences between Neo-Confucianism and *Tao-hsüeh.*" *Philosophy East and West* 42.3 (July 1992): 455–74.

———. *Utilitarian Confucianism: Ch'en Liang's Challenge to Chu Hsi.* Cambridge: Harvard University Press, 1982.

Turner, H. E. W. *The Pattern of Christian Truth: A Study in the Relations between Orthodoxy and Heresy in the Early Church.* Bampton Lectures for 1954. London: A. R. Mombray, 1954.

Vallée, Gérard. *A Study in Anti-Gnostic Polemics: Irenaeus, Hippolytus, and Epiphanius.* Waterloo, Ont.: Wilfrid Laurier University Press, 1981.

Vincent of Lérins. *The Commonitory.* In *Early Medieval Theology.* Translated and Edited by George E. McCracken and Allen Cabaniss. Philadelphia: Westminster Press, 1957.

Wang Mao et al. *Ch'ing-tai che-hsüeh* (Philosophy in the Ch'ing Era). Anhwei jen-min ch'u-pan she, 1992.

Wansbrough, J. *The Sectarian Milieu: Content and Composition in Islamic Salvation History.* Oxford: Oxford University Press, 1978.

Wasserstrom, Steven M. *Between Muslim and Jew: The Problem of Symbiosis under Early Islam.* Princeton: Princeton University Press, 1995.

Watt, W. Montgomery. *Early Islam: Collected Articles.* Edinburgh: Edinburgh University Press, 1990.

———. *The Formative Period of Islamic Thought.* Edinburgh: At the University Press, 1973.

———. "The Great Community and the Sects." In *Theology and Law in Islam.* Edited by G. E. von Grunebaum. Wiesbaden: Otto Harrassowitz, 1971, pp. 25–36.

———. *Islamic Creeds: A Selection.* Edinburgh: Edinburgh University Press, 1994.

———. *Islamic Philosophy and Theology: An Extended Survey.* Edinburgh: At the University Press, 1985.

———. *Muslim Intellectual: A Study of al-Ghazali.* Edinburgh: At the University Press, 1963.

———. "The Study of the Development of the Islamic Sects." In *Acta Orientala Neerlandica: Proceedings of the Congress of the Dutch Oriental Society Held in*

Leiden on the Occasion of Its 50th Anniversary. Edited by P. W. Pestman. Leiden: E. J. Brill, 1971, pp. 82–91.

Wensinck, A. J. *The Muslim Creed.* Cambridge: Cambridge University Press, 1932.

Wilensky, Mordecai L. "Hasidic-Mitnaggedic Polemics in the Jewish Communities of Eastern Europe: The Hostile Phase." In *Essential Papers on Hasidism, Origins to Present.* Edited by Gershon David Hundert. New York: New York University Press, 1991, pp. 244–71.

Wilken, Robert L. *The Myth of Christian Beginnings.* Notre Dame, IN: University of Notre Dame Press, 1971.

Williams, Rowan. *Arius: Heresy and Tradition.* London: Darton, Longman and Todd, 1987.

Wilson, Thomas A. *Genealogy of the Way: The Construction and Uses of the Confucian Tradition in Late Imperial China.* Stanford: Stanford University Press, 1995.

———. "Genealogy of the Way: Representing the Confucian Tradition in Neo-Confucian Philosophical Anthologies." Ph.D. diss., University of Chicago, 1988.

Wisse, Frederik. "The Epistle of Jude in the History of Heresiology." In *Essays on the Nag Hammadi Texts in Honour of Alexander Böhlig.* Edited by Martin Krause. Leiden: E. J. Brill, 1972, pp. 133–43.

———. "The Use of Early Christian Literature as Evidence for Inner Diversity and Conflict." In *Nag Hammadi, Gnosticism, and Early Christianity.* Edited by Charles W. Hedrick and Robert Hodgson. Peabody, MA: Hendrickson, 1986, pp. 177–90.

Yamazaki Ansai. *Heki'i* (Heresies Refuted). In *Shushigaku taikei* (Outline of Chu Hsi Studies). Vol. 12, *Chōsen no Shushigaku; Nihon no Shushigaku* (Korean Chu Hsi Studies; Japanese Chu Hsi Studies). Compiled by Morohashi Tetsuji et al. Tokyo: Meitoku shuppansha, 1977.

Yang Hsiang-k'uei, comp. *Ch'ing-ju hsüeh-an hsin-pien* (A New Compilation of Cases on Ch'ing Confucian Learning). Chinan: Ch'i-Lu shu-she, 1988.

Young, F. M. "Did Epiphanius Know What He Meant by 'Heresy'?" In *Studia Patristica* 17.1. Edited by Elizabeth A. Livingstone. Oxford: Pergamon Press, 1982.

INDEX

Aaron, 145
Abbasid caliphate, 50, 55
Abel, 61, 146
Abravanel, Isaac, 67, 145
Abu Ja'far, 143
Adam, 145
adoptionism, 104, 124, 140, 176. *See also* Christological issue
Against All Heresies (Irenaeus), 9, 25, 42
Akhabaris, 112
Alain de Lille, 159
Alcuin, 124
'Ali, 53, 107, 109–10, 111, 126, 176
Allah, 11, 109. *See also* God
allegorism, 109
Allport, Gordon, 123
Analects of Confucius, 22, 32, 101, 115
Anan, 154
anthropomorphism, 29, 110, 111, 127, 129, 213 n. 144. *See also* God, anthropomorphic ideas of
Antichrist, 135, 136, 138, 143, 147, 159
Apollinarists, 159
apostasy, 23, 68, 166, 167
apostates, 18
Apostle's Creed, 10
apostolic succession, 92–93, 94, 136, 151, 152. *See also* orthodoxy, transmission of
Arian controversies, 47, 48
Arianism, 8, 43–44, 122–23, 158
Arians, 26, 120, 141
Aristotle, 113, 137
Arius, 46, 49, 120, 134, 137, 141
Artemon, 86
al-Ash'ari: on attributes of God, 108, 213 n. 144; as conciliator, 99, 108; as founder of school, 55–57, 58; as her-

esiographer, 28; as innovator, 88; not an Ash'arite, 56–57
Ash'arism: development of, 57; as middle way, 28, 107, 108–10, 112, 127; as orthodoxy, 28, 55–56, 57, 58, 59, 88, 107, 112, 125; theology of, 99
Ash'arites: as conciliatory, 99; as extremists, 110, 127; and Hanbalites, 29, 57, 58, 111; as heresiographers, 28, 29; and Sufis, 55; and Wahhabites, 160
Athanasius, 26, 140–41
Augustine, Saint, 1, 17, 18–19; as heresiologist, 26; on heretics, 43, 138, 141, 172, 173; on Manicheanism, 19; on Pelagianism, 48, 124; on source of heresy, 134; on the Trinity, 105
Au'idiya, 111
Azad, Maulana, 106

Baal Shem Tov, 156
al-Baghdadi: on the Batinis, 143, 144; on free agency, 109; as heresiographer, 28, 125; on *ijma'*, 51; on the Isma'ilis, 143, 166; on the Kharijites, 10; on the middle way, 107; on orthodox unity, 96; on the Qadarites, 159; on the Sufis, 55
Balaam, 152
Baldick, Julian, 106–7
Bardesan, 143
Basil of Caesarea, 18, 96
Basilidites, 124, 137
Batinis, 112, 143, 144
Bauer, Walter, 40–41, 43, 44, 49, 96
Berthrong, John, 92
Bibago, Abraham, 21

Shih Te-ts'ao, 149
Shi'ism: development of, 53–54;
   imamology, 53–54; as middle way,
   112; as orthodox, 51, 54; primacy
   of, 88; survival of, 54
Shi'ites, 99, 146, 155; as extreme, 127;
   extremists, 19, 54, 55 60, 109, 142,
   143, 158–59, 166 (see also *ghulat*; Isma'ilis); self-perception, 53; standard of orthodoxy, 52, 53, 94, 126;
   and Sunnis, 60, 100; Twelver, 54,
   60, 143
shirk (polytheism), 19, 54, 160
Shu-ching. See *Documents Classic*
sifat (unity and attributes of God), 56.
   See also God, attributes of
Sifatiya, 127
Silas, 47
Simon Magus, 158; as heresiarch, 26,
   135–36, 137, 144, 145, 152, 153; and
   Saint Peter, 45
Simon, Marcel, 18
sixteen-character transmission, 91,
   102, 114
Smith, Richard, 15
social deviance, 2, 175, 179 n. 3
Sodomites, 152
Songs Classic, 7, 156
Ssu-ma Kuang, 71
Stalin, Joseph, 136
Stoics, 138
Su Shih, 72, 116, 134, 149, 156; as here-
   tic, 35, 133, 163
Suarès, André, 2
Sufis, 20, 54–55, 112, 160
Sufism, 54–55, 195–96 n. 97
Sufrites, 128
Sun Ch'i-feng, 80
Sung Learning, 70. *See also* Ch'eng-
   Chu school; *Li-hsüeh*; Neo-Confu-
   cianism; Tao Learning
Sung Lien, 77
Sung-Yüan hsüeh-an (Huang Tsung-hsi), 36
sunna (standard practice), 94, 96, 110,
   212 n. 140; as standard of ortho-
   doxy, 52, 53

Sunnism: chain of tradition, 94; development of, 52–53; heresiographers
   in, 96; as middle way, 107, 109, 127;
   primacy of, 87, 88, 128; schools of
   12, 57, 100
Sunnites: as conciliatory, 99–100, 101;
   condemn innovations, 87–88; as orthodox, 52, 54, 57, 58, 128; and
   Shi'ites, 53
Symmachian heresy, 125
syncreticm (Confucian), 76–77, 79–80,
   81–82, 84, 101, 163, 202 n. 228
Syntagma (Justin Martyr), 25

al-Tabari, 106
al-Taftazani, 29, 142
T'ai-chou school, 80
Taipings, 171
takyif (spirit of inquiry), 57
Talmud, 4, 62, 65, 145; disparagement
   of, 68–69, 93; on the middle way,
   112; and *Mishneh Torah*, 67; Tractate
   Kuthim, 30; Tractate Sanhedrin,
   129. *See also* Oral Torah
Tang Ch'eng, 97
T'ang Chien, 36, 91–92
Tao Learning, 73; criticism of, 36–37,
   72; as orthodoxy, 69, 71, 73, 74, 76,
   83; primacy of, 89; revival of 73, 81;
   self- definition, 91; strong points
   of, 75–76; unification of, 98. *See also*
   Ch'eng-Chu school; *Li-hsüeh*; Sung
   Learning; Neo-Confucianism
Taoism, 3, 16, 162; as extreme, 115,
   131; as heterodox, 22, 71, 84, 133,
   148, 173; as Neo-Confucian heresy,
   23, 24; novelty of, 89; partiality of,
   101, 150; reconciliation with Confucianism, 78, 80; transmission of,
   90
Tao-t'ung (orthodox line of transmission), 71, 73, 91, 151, 156
Tarasius, Patriarch, 158–59
Teng Hsiao-p'ing, 73
Tertullian, 164; on heresy, 18, 138, 139,